MORE THAN A WOMAN

ALSO BY CAITLIN MORAN

NONFICTION
How to Be a Woman
Moranthology
Moranifesto

FICTION
How to Build a Girl
How to Be Famous

MORE THAN A WOMAN

CAITLIN MORAN

HARPER  PERENNIAL

NEW YORK • LONDON • TORONTO • SYDNEY • NEW DELHI • AUCKLAND

HARPER ● PERENNIAL

Also published in Great Britain in 2020 by Ebury Press,
an imprint of Random House Group Company.

HarperCollins books may be purchased for educational,
business, or sales promotional use. For information, please email
the Special Markets Department at SPsales@harpercollins.com.

FIRST U.S. EDITION

Designed by Jamie Lynn Kerner

Library of Congress Cataloging-in-Publication Data has been applied for.

ISBN 978-0-06-289371-0 (pbk.)
ISBN 978-0-06-303749-6 (library edition)

20 21 22 23 24 LSC 10 9 8 7 6 5 4 3 2

*For Sal, Loz, and Nadia—Team Tits. The wind beneath
my bingo wings. Except bingo wings don't exist.
See chapter 5.*

CONTENTS

CONTENTS

MORE THAN A WOMAN

September 2010

I AM IN THE SPARE ROOM, WHICH DOUBLES AS MY OFFICE, AND I HAVE just finished my day's work. Typing the last full stop with a flourish, I light a cigarette, and lean back in my chair. Today is the day I finished writing *How to Be a Woman*, and I am exhausted—but jubilant. Like a salmon that's just spawned a super-chunky hardback through its mental vent.

I have tried to put every conceivable female wisdom into a single, 220-page volume—spanning the entirety of a straight, white, working-class woman's experience in a mere 89,000 words. I have thoroughly chronicled the most difficult years of a woman's life: thirteen to thirty. The painful years of constructing yourself. The messy, panicky, scared, brave years, where you have to invent—and then reinvent—yourself, over and over, until you finally find peace in the bones you're in.

Those are the *dark* decades, I muse. Thank God that once a woman gets to thirty, she knows the worst bit is over! She is strong in herself, and ready to enjoy the next epoch. *I* am ready to enjoy the next epoch! This is the beginning of my *true*, real, great life—right *now!*

By way of celebration, I try to blow a smoke ring. I fail. Oh well—plenty of time to practice in the coming, empty weeks! Now I've achieved perfection! I'm going to have time for all *kinds* of amazing hobbies!

There is a small commotion behind me.

"Oh my GOD—*press save!* You're making me *anxious.* Why would you finish a document and not press save? Do you not remember how much work you've lost over the years?"

I turn around—and there, sitting on the bed, is what I would describe as an "elderly" woman in a leopard-print coat, with messy hair, regarding me with a sigh. I stare.

"Nanna?" I say, eventually.

For it appears to be—my nan. But wearing Doc Martens boots. *My* Doc Martens boots. *Why is my dead grandmother here, dressed like an aging indie kid? Is her ghost having a breakdown in Heaven? Whoever she is, she seems preternaturally peeved by my reaction.*

"Nanna?" "Nanna?" You cheeky cow—it's *me. You.* I'm *you.* From the future. "Nanna?" Jesus Christ, I'm only forty-fucking-four.

I look again. Oh God—it *is* me. Me—but much more grays Future Me is looking at me like she's expecting me to freak out—but, obviously, I'm not going to give her the satisfaction. We've all seen *all* the *Back to the Future*s. We all know how this stuff works. I'm going to act cool.

"Oh, yeah," I shrug. "You *are* me. From the future. Sweet. Fag?"

I offer her a cigarette, politely.

"No," she says, primly. "I've given up. It's so bad for you, and it really starts *hurting* once you get to thirty-eight. It's a disgusting habit."

"Suit yourself."

I drag on my fag. She hesitates for a minute—and then reaches over for the packet.

"I still have the odd one here or there, though. At parties. They don't count."

She lights it up. We both exhale together.

"So," I say, looking at her. Yeah—it does look like me. Her hair's shorter. She's got *two* gray streaks in it. Her adult acne, I note, is still present—suggesting the new serum I bought only the other week is a fucking liar. And her nose—her nose seems bigger than my nose. How has that happened?

"It keeps growing all your life," we say, in synchronization. And then, still in sync: *"Like Granddad's."*

We both sigh.

"So, I presume you're here because of some cataclysmic future event, which you've come to warn me of?" I say, casually, pressing save, in case losing this document *is* the future cataclysmic event. If it is, this is the worst *Terminator*-inspired plot ever. It's all backed up on my external hard drive, for a start.

"No, not really," she says. "I'm here for a laugh."

"What?"

"Well, things are a bit . . . *lively*, in 2020, and I could do with a lighthearted giggle, so I've come to bask in a more . . . *innocent* me."

She reclines on the bed. There's an odd cracking sound.

"That's my back," she says, still prone. "Well, my back *and* my pelvis. You won't *believe* what happens to them as you get into your forties."

"What have you done to my back?!" I ask. "I *need* that!"

"Oh, the back's *nothing*," she says, sitting up again with a series of *ooof* sounds. "Look at *this*."

She points to her neck. There's something hanging off it.

"A wattle. *Our* wattle. Touch it."

I tentatively wobble the stalactite of loose skin, like a turkey's neck, with my finger. It keeps swaying for a good ten seconds after I finish. I wince. She tuts at me.

"I've grown to kind of love it, to be honest," she says. "I wobble it on difficult days. It's like an enjoyable stress toy."

Now I'm near her, I look at her more closely. Yes, she has a wattle, and seems programmed to endlessly complain—but she still looks pretty fresh and cheerful. *Why?*

"Botox, mate," she says, reclining again. "Sorry—I'm just going to stay here for a bit. I am *knackered*."

"*Botox!* You have Botox! But—you *can't!* It's not feminist! I've just written a whole chapter on why it's a betrayal of every value I have!"

I gesture to my laptop.

"Yeah," she says, dragging on her fag. "That's one of the reasons I've come back for a laugh. It's really *funny*," she says, beginning to giggle. "It's really *funny* how you think you've got everything figured out. You think"—and here, she becomes hysterical—"you think you've done the hard bit, don't you? You're thirty-four, with two small kids and you think—HAAAAA!—that you know *everything*."

By now, she's coughing and wheezing. I can see why she's tried to cut down on the fags—her lungs sound like bagpipes.

"Well, I kind of think I *do*," I say, briskly. "Let me remind you—I have just gone through adolescence and my twenties, beset by bullshit on all sides, which I have nobly battled, and eventually triumphed over. Periods, pubic hair, masturbation, losing my virginity, battling an eating disorder, discovering feminism, living through an abusive relationship, shunning an expensive wedding, taking Ecstasy, having an *incredibly* painful first birth, and a perfect second one. I've had an abortion, I've been to a sex club with Lady Gaga, discovered what true love is, confronted sexism, worked out my position on pornography, raised my children into strong and capable people, and, finally, found some jeans that fit—Whistles Barrel Leg, fifty-nine pounds. I'm thirty-four, and I *know* that all the statistics say that *this*—*this* is about to be the best period *of my life*. Not an actual *period* period. No. An *era*. I'm about to enter the Era of Supremacy, because I am a grown-ass feminist woman who's worked out *all* my shit and is mere *weeks* away from my *proper* life beginning: one where I will be confident and elegant—like Gillian Anderson in everything—at the height of my attractiveness, with a capsule wardrobe, and probably going on walking holidays where I do emotional oil paintings of the best fells I've scaled."

She stares at me.

"I've done all the hard stuff," I reiterate. "*I know how to be a woman*. This is where it all gets *good*."

There's a pause—and then she comes over and hugs me.

"Mate," she says, with impossible tenderness. "Mate, mate, *mate*."

"What?" I say, face muffled in her bosom. She's wearing a cashmere jumper. "Things can't be *that* bad in the future! Cashmere is a luxury fabric! In the future, am I—am I a *millionaire*?"

"No. Thirty-nine pounds ninety-nine, Uniqlo," she says, still crushing my face into her tits. "Look. It's great you're optimistic. I *love* that energy. Keep it coming! It's just—it's just that, 'being a woman' isn't enough for the next part of your life."

"What? What do you mean?"

"Well, you're just about to enter middle age, bab. Your previous problems were all problems with *yourself.* Young woman problems. But when you enter middle age, you'll know you're middle aged, because all your problems are . . . *other people's* problems."

"I don't get you."

"A sorted, middle-aged woman isn't just a woman, anymore. You have to become—*more* than 'a woman.'"

She squats down in front of me and takes my hands in hers. She makes another *oooof* sound.

"Just stretching my glutes," she explains. "Look, obviously I can't be specific, because, like, *time will explode,* but your thirties, forties, and fifties—that's when you start dealing with real Big Woman Shit. That's when all your friends start divorcing. It's when you and your partner's careers clash with each other. It's when sex becomes almost impossible. It's when your parents suddenly get old and need caring for. It's when, God help you, your kids become teenagers."

"But surely that's the *easy* bit! I can't wait! They can make their own breakfast! I'm going to be *free!*"

"Haven't you just written 20,000 words on how fucking awful your teenage years were?"

I nod.

"Imagine being your parents."

My heart stops for a minute. Oh.

"Mate, you're just about to become the Fourth Emergency Service," she continues. "Your life's about to become a call center for people who are *exploding.*"

She mimes being the operator on a switchboard: "Hello? Caller One? You're my mom, you live two hundred miles away, and you've fallen down some stairs? Oh my God, I'm so sorry! Hang on—I'm go-ing to have to put you on hold; I've got another call coming through. Caller Two—how can I help you? You're my best friend, and you've just seen your husband getting off with the babysitter in Starbucks? Get in a cab and come straight over here—I'm quickly going to talk to Caller Three. Caller Three—CALM DOWN! You're my teenage daughter, and you've just realized you're not beautiful, and your life is meaningless? OH GOD."

She mimes putting the phone down again.

"You know your husband?"

My heart leaps.

"IN THE FUTURE, IS IT MARK RUFFALO? OH MY GOD—I KNEW IT!!!"

She puts her hand up, to cancel my spiraling hope: "No. No—it's still the same one."

We look at each other.

"Ah. Well, I *suppose* that's . . . good."

"You know how when you're trying to get someone in customer service to e.g., mend your telly, for example, and they keep fobbing you off with some arse called Simon or Dev, who just fucks it up even more? And your husband always says—"

"He always says, 'You need to keep asking to be transferred until you get put through to a middle-aged Scottish woman called Janet—because she's *always* the one who goes, Ach, what a pickle. I'll sort this out in two minutes.' And—she does!"

"Yes. *The Janet Theory.*"

"*The Janet Theory.*"

"Yes. Well."

She points at me.

"*You're* Janet, now. You're the Janet in everyone's lives. If any-thing's going to get sorted out, *you're* the one who's going to have to do it. No more messy nights out, or voyages of self-discovery. You are about to be required to hold the fabric of society together. For no pay. That's what being a middle-aged woman is."

We fall into a silence. There's a lot to digest.

"So—no fell-walking holidays or oil paintings, then?" I ask, sadly.

"No."

I can't deny it—it's a bit of a downer. I've met my future self, and she's Captain Buzzkill. I instinctively massage my neck, to relieve my stress. Ah, yes—I can see where that wattle will form. It's already starting to *yield*. I can see how it will be a comfort, in the years to come.

"Still," I say, brightening. "The good news is you're now doubtless about to give me some manner of enchanted amulet, or crucial spell—the one that got you through those hard times."

For the first time, Future Me looks shifty.

"Er, no."

"Well—how *did* you get through those hard times?"

Future Me looks even more shifty. I feel the first stirrings of panic.

"Hang on—you *have* got through this bad bit, haven't you? You've come back to see me now because you succeeded in your quest, and everything's okay again?"

Future Me stands up.

"Well, I must be going—the time machine portal thingy is running out. Just remember, Caitlin—*follow your heart!*"

She disappears. Now I'm just *furious*. *She* knows that *I* know the answer is *never* to "follow your heart." Your heart's a fucking *idiot*—it just wants to sit on the sofa and watch *Say Yes to the Dress*. The true answer is always make a fucking brilliant plan, and then endure with it beyond all normal parameters of exhaustion, until you eventually triumph.

Why is Me lying to me? What should I prepare for? I have so many questions!

There's another commotion, and Future Me reappears.

"Oh, thank God!" I say. "You're back! I knew me wouldn't let me down! Quick! Tell me things! What stocks should I invest in? Should I do neck exercises? Did you even *try* to marry Mark Ruffalo? TELL ME WHAT I NEED TO PREPARE FOR!!!!!!"

Future Me looks at me, stricken.

"I just came back for these," she said, taking my fags. "And—and—"

I stare at her. Just one wisdom. *Just one.*

"And . . . drink as much as you can now—because once you get to forty, you can't drink anymore. All your enzymes give up, and the hangovers kill you."

"I CAN'T EVEN DRINK????"

"Bye. And—good luck. I love you. You're a good kid."

She fist-bumps me and disappears.

"More than a woman?" I say, disconsolately. "I have to become '*more* than a woman?' What—*two* women?"

I hear a voice, calling through the ether: "That would be useful. Because *it gets so much fucking worse.*"

A human being should be able to change a diaper, plan an invasion, butcher a hog, conn a ship, design a building, write a sonnet, balance accounts, build a wall, set a bone, comfort the dying, take orders, give orders, cooperate, act alone, solve equations, analyze a new problem, pitch manure, program a computer, cook a tasty meal, fight efficiently, die gallantly.

—ROBERT A. HEINLEIN, DESCRIBING THE AVERAGE DAY OF A MIDDLE-AGED WOMAN

Providence has its appointed hour for everything. We cannot command results—we can only strive.

—MAHATMA GANDHI, DESCRIBING IN GREATER AND MORE EFFICIENT DETAIL THE AVERAGE DAY OF A MIDDLE-AGED WOMAN

CHAPTER ONE

The Hour of "The List"

❧

7:00 A.M.

Some Years Later

THE ALARM CLOCK GOES OFF. I WAKE.

I am a modern woman, and I do modern things, so I have set the alarm to go off five minutes before the kids' do. This is so I can spend the first five minutes of every day Being Thankful.

I learned about Being Thankful a couple of years ago, from some experts—a conversation on Facebook—and now I do it every day; like in the way you're supposed to do yoga every day, but I don't, because the idea of yoga, perversely, makes me tense.

By way of contrast, Being Thankful is quite relaxing. You simply make sure you're comfortable—and then mentally list all the things in your life that make you happy. I like lists, and I like being happy, and I'm extremely good at lying down, so it immediately appealed to me. I now do it every day. It's very satisfying.

Today's list runs as follows:

1. I'm not homeless.
2. I'm not ill.
3. My family isn't ill.
4. My husband is a pleasant and amusing man.

5. I still haven't been fired.

6. Time for coffee!

I get out of bed. I have started to feel a bit stiff in the mornings—but nothing that heartily saying "oooof!" out loud won't cure.

"Oooof!" I say, tottering over to the toilet. I have a satisfying wee, check the loo roll to see if I've started my period—for a woman, toilet paper is by way of a printout, or receipt, of all your internal doings—note that I haven't, and then pick up my phone; Being Thankful that I have a phone. I want to see what the weather's going to be today, so I can work out if I need a jumper or not, and then Be Thankful for the invention of "layering." But, when I look at the screen, I see the last thing I looked at last night: "The List."

I instantly de-relax. The List is the one constant in my life. In many ways, The List *is* my life. The List is the eternal note I keep open on my phone—the running totalizer of all the jobs that need doing, but which I haven't got round to yet. Some of the items have been on there since I got pregnant. My youngest child is now seven. The List is the shadow self of Being Thankful. Being Thankful is about rejoicing in what you *are*. The List is, essentially, a running apology for what you are *not*, yet. All middle-aged women have a list like this:

- Blinds for bedroom
- Kids' passports
- Cut cats' claws
- Clean gutters
- Tax return
- START RUNNING
- Stick tarpaulin on broken windowsill
- Buy coat hooks
- Moth repellent
- Light bulbs: bathroom, hall, bedroom
- Lino basement
- Caz birthday present

- MEDITATE???
- BOOK HOLIDAY
- PELVIC FLOOR EXERCISES
- Doctor allergies Nancy?
- Pension
- Replace IUD
- Leaky toilet fix
- Broken sink—replace
- Read Das Kapital
- Fleas
- Secondary schools Lizzie?
- Driving lessons
- Yoga????? STRETCHING???? New leggings?????
- INVOICES!
- Order new fucking online banking dongle that actually works
- Cervical smear

THAT'S ONLY THE first page. There are five.

These are all the things that stand between me and a perfect life.

I choose to view this list with what I call "spirited determination"—it is the twenty-first century, so I am grateful this list does not include "agitate for women's votes," or "discover radiation, then, ironically, die of it." I am a grafter who believes in hard work. I know that, unless you are a spirited and beautiful heiress, life is, essentially, a to-do list, which begins with "escape this vagina," and ends with "escape this Earth"—and so there's no point in moaning about it. However onerous The List might seem, it will, eventually, set me free—for I am one five-page list away from becoming a happy, accomplished woman with a perfect house, exemplary accounts, excellent capsule wardrobe, well-brought-up family, fabulous job, and a pelvic floor so redoubtable, every trampoline will fear me.

I decide to give a moment of thankfulness for The List. I refuse to see the list as a burden. No. The List is my *guide to life*. All I need to do is carefully apportion each hour of the day to a specific task, in order to maximize my productivity—and then I reckon I will have ticked *everything* off it by, say, 2020. I'll have *definitely* done it by 2020. And then my *real* life can, finally, begin. I can buy a trampoline!

I PUT ON my bathrobe—which has never been washed. It has face-mask crust on the neck. I must wash this bathrobe! I put "wash bath-robe" on The List—and go downstairs.

Because I am married to a good and amusing man who is also an early riser, Pete is downstairs, getting the kids ready.

The kitchen is very bright. Very bright. This is because I have a hangover, which I haven't mentioned so far, as it's entirely my fault, and I am being brave and noble.

"How was last night?" Pete asks, cheerfully, putting cereal on the table for the kids. Because they are now nine and seven, we don't need to put plastic sheeting on the floor anymore. That's one job off The List!

"Oh, very good. We got a lot of important work done," I say, discreetly palming two Berocca tablets into a glass, and filling it with water.

The "important work" was me and three siblings sitting on my patio until 4 a.m., discussing the impending divorce of our parents. Things are escalatingly grim between them, and it can only end one way. This conversation was deemed to be "gin work." For reasons I can't quite remember now, it involved, around 11 p.m., me standing on a chair and crying as I sang "Everything's Alright" from *Jesus Christ Superstar*. However much I tried, no one else would join in with me.

"Yeah—I saw you 'working' on Twitter," Pete says.

I don't remember posting anything on Twitter. I look on my phone and scroll down my timeline.

Oh. That's interesting. At midnight, I appear to have posted a picture of my bare feet, with a Jacob's Cream Cracker wedged be-tween each toe. I see this ostensibly lighthearted piece of drunken tomfoolery has gathered, so far, two rape threats and someone call-ing my feet "unfuckable." My *feet*.

Whilst buttering toast for the kids—in order to establish, through a selfless action, that I am not drunk now, and am a good person, underneath it all—I ring my sister, Caz.

"Hey hey. Dude, why did you let me go on Twitter and post a picture of my bare feet with a Jacob's Cream Cracker between each toe?" I ask her.

"We spent half an hour trying to stop you," she replies. "You were obdurate. Then you fell over. You feeling that this morning?"

I touch the bump on the back of my head. Ah, yes. I remember now. That cupboard took a hell of a wallop on the way down. I look out onto the patio. It's covered in empty glasses and bottles. In the center of the table is Nancy's special Little Mermaid plate. It is heaped with cigarette butts. I close the blinds, so she won't see it.

"Mom! How do you clean shoes?"

Lizzie has put her sneakers on the table. They used to be white—but they are now caked in mud. The laces look like oomska filth-snakes. I stare at them. Christ—they look how the inside of my head feels.

"I'll do them later, bab. Wear something else today."

"I don't have anything else! My feet have grown! You *said* you'd get me new shoes!"

Ah, yes. Yesterday's shoe-buying expedition that got canceled, when we had to flea bomb the house. It all seemed to be going so well until the cat—who sneaked back into the house through an open window—inhaled the flea bomb, went "all weird," and started acting like a Vietnam veteran who'd taken too much acid. We had to take her to the vet—they put her in a cage overnight, to "come down." That was £100. Jesus. We could have bought six new cats for that. *Better* ones. Betty very much views my herb garden as a luxuriously scented litter box.

I start cleaning the shoes. Then I realize the sponge I'm cleaning them with is covered in lamb fat and is making the issue much, much worse. I get the shoe cleaning tin out of the cupboard, and google "cleaning white sneakers."

"So, Cate—you remember what the final conclusion of last night's meeting was?" Caz asks, tentatively, still on the phone.

Following the instructions of a man on YouTube, I start scrubbing the sneakers with my special shoe brush. *Why* are the most popular shoes for children and young adults white sneakers? *Why* would we invent a system of clothing whereby the item that comes *constantly into contact with the ground* is generally made of white fabric? It's entirely impractical—the worst possible outcome, footwear-wise. This is a con by capitalism to make us buy new white sneakers every four months.

"Last night," Caz says, on the phone, slightly more urgently. "You do remember what you said last night? It was a brave conclusion, man—but we're all behind you."

There are few things more terrifying than someone praising you for being "brave." Caz once called a haircut of mine—where I'd tried to get a black bob, like one of the Corrs—"brave." I simply wore a hat for the next three months.

"*What* did I say?" I ask.

Pete is pointing at the kitchen clock. It's time for the kids to go. I hand Lizzie her half-scrubbed, damp sneakers.

"Sit near a radiator," I say, kindly, as she puts them on, and squelches off to the bus. Nancy follows her. I wave goodbye, distractedly.

"We talked it over," Caz continues, "and we all agreed that, while the parents are divorcing, Andrew can't live with them. It's disrupting his A-Level revision. So, you said he'd move in with you."

"*I* said that?" I ask, faintly.

"'I'm already parent to two children—a third will be easy!' you said," Caz recalls. "'It will be cool to have a brother in the house! The more Morans, the merrier!'"

"I said that to *you*?" I ask, sitting down. Pete is looking at me, mouthing, *What's happening?*

"No—you said that to *him*. You rang Andrew and *told* him he has to move in with you. 'Fuck the parents' bullshit,' you said. 'You have a haven of peace in our house. Come live in our spare room.' Then you fell over."

"We don't have a spare room!" I cry.

"I think you meant the loft," Caz says.

The loft! The one perfect thing in my life? The room with all my Ordnance Survey maps of Wales pinned on the wall, and the complete works of Sue Townsend on the shelves, and where—most importantly—I can lock the door, and smoke out of the VELUX window?

"Andrew was *super* happy," Caz says. "He said, 'Finally—I can get my nieces into *Red Dwarf*. It's going to be smegging *awesome!*'"

I sit, staring at the table. I notice Nancy has left her packed lunch. I'll have to go and drop it off. I strongly dislike going to the kids' school. As a working mother, I rarely go, and people can be so judgmental. There's always one mom at the gates, beaming, "Oh! We haven't seen *you* here for a while! Is everything *okay*?"

Last time one of them said that, I replied, "They've let me out on electronic tag!" but her humor was very weak, and she didn't appreciate it. She never spoke to me again. So, in a way—result!

I stare at the bloody lunch box. *Oh, God. My teenage brother Andrew, living with us. I haven't even asked Pete! Or the girls! We really should have had a family meeting about this—one without gin.*

I start quietly singing "Everything's Alright" from *Jesus Christ Superstar*, for comfort.

"Ah. You're remembering now," Caz says, then hangs up.

The phone rings again. It's Andrew.

"Hey, *roommate*," he says. "You're a pal. I'm all packed. I'll be over around lunchtime?"

A second call is coming through. I see it's from the vet. *Fuck! We forgot to pick up the cat! Two nights now!* Another *one hundred pounds. I hate that cat.*

Enraged, I do my pelvic floor exercises. Then I realize I'm just clenching my bum, give in, have a fag, and order some moth repellent online.

I *will* tick something off The List today! I *will* be triumphant! I WILL END TODAY THANKFUL. THESE ARE THE BEST YEARS OF MY LIFE.

CHAPTER TWO

The Hour of Married Sex

⤳

8:00 A.M.

PETE STANDS BY THE WINDOW.

"Wait for it; *wait for it*," he says, watching the kids at the bus stop.

I hover tensely in the doorway.

"Aaaaaaand—they're on the bus!" he says. Still watching the departing bus, he takes his trousers off. It's *on*.

With the children gone, it's time to start the day with a vital part of our to-do list: the Maintenance Shag.

My friend Sali came up with the concept of the Maintenance Shag—it's the shag middle-aged people have to schedule because they're so busy, and have such small children, that if it wasn't written on the calendar using a special, childproof code (ours is "wocka wocka wocka!" in tribute to Fozzie Bear), it might not happen for months, possibly years. One is still free, of course, to have spontaneous, carefree sex as and when one wishes, but the Maintenance Shag is there just to keep the wheels of commerce oiled, as it were. I think every person in a long-term relationship knows the feeling when it's been so long since you've done it that the whole concept seems like some madly improbable dream you once had—like being Barack Obama, or suddenly flying, or being Barack Obama and flying.

As we're both freelancers, we can schedule the Maintenance Shag for Fridays at 8 a.m.—as soon as the kids have left for school. We have learned to wait until we have visual confirmation that they're actually on the bus after the Incident of 2009, wherein someone returning for their net ball kit heard the screamed injunction, "DON'T COME IN THE KITCHEN—WE'RE TRYING TO CATCH A RAT!," and possibly had their sex education put back five years.

I run upstairs, to "prepare" myself. In the early days of our courtship, my "preparation" would have included washing, leg shaving, toothbrushing, flossing, the application of hold-up stockings, and the lighting of mood-enhancing candles. We might start with an hour of fruity chat, and then gradually slide into a long, languorous sheet-tangling hump lasting many, many hours—with seconds, and then pudding for all.

Fifteen years later, and my preparation entails swilling a blob of Colgate around my mouth, then spitting it out, taking off my pajamas, and fluffing up my pubes so they look a bit less like an old coir doormat, and a bit more like, well, a *new* coir doormat. I then shout, "COME ON, SEXY—LET'S DO IT! BEFORE THE WINDOW CLEANER COMES!"

Pete runs up the stairs, trouserless, taking off his T-shirt, and stands by the bed.

"So—the delicate dance of seduction begins," he says.

IN A MARRIAGE, it's vital to keep the sexual spark going. Every source agrees on this—from *Good Housekeeping* to an overly frank Uber driver I had once. It acts as a memory bridge to why you got together in the first place—two giddy, young people who once fell in love. For, in almost every respect, those two people will have now disappeared, and what was once forged by the power of your white-hot sexual attraction, now continues on the basis of your ability to remind each other to do vital tasks ("Have you swabbed the cat's stitches?") in the least accusatory way possible.

Segueing into this problem is the way female sexuality works. Although there will always be notable exceptions (e.g., The Legendary Spontaneous Pret A Manger Toilet Shag of 2007) by and large, women take a bit longer to get in the mood for sex than men. We have to establish a bit of a *vibe,* get some kind of *scenario* going—which is difficult to weave into the everyday schedule of bullshit.

There are ways to do it, of course. Sending each other erotic texts, DMs, or emails during the day is highly recommended by sex therapists. "Spend all day turning up the *heat* on your *libido,* until you *can't wait to rip each other's clothes off,*" they say.

That's because sex therapists love recommending absolutely insane balls—for who of us, in the modern age, does not have a text or email account that duplicates itself to another, forgotten, device? Sending a saucy mid-afternoon belfie can all too easily lead to a *Dora the Explorer*–seeking child picking up an iPad, asking, "Mommy—why did you send Daddy a picture of two hams pressed together?"

And if photos are difficult, words are harder. *So* much harder. I am a *professional* writer who discusses the en-rude-inating aspects of life more than most; but, time and time again, when writing—whether in the pages of *The Times,* or in a quick pre-pumping text to my husband—I find that when I try to describe something I am thinking, feeling, or wanting, sexually, that I tumble into a void. A silence. I reach out for the word, or phrase—and there is nothing there. Female sexuality has a stunted, almost empty, lexicon.

Let us take, for instance, sexual arousal. *Enhornening.* The key aspects of female sexual arousal are (1) swelling of the vulva and (2) the production of lubrication. The mirroring aspects in male sexual arousal are (1) the swelling of the penis and (2) ejaculation. OH MY GOD LOOK AT HOW MANY RUDE WORDS THERE ARE IN THOSE TWO SENTENCES.

Consider, for a moment, the ripe lexicon that exists for these male phenomena—a stroll through the vibrant linguistic joy of human inventiveness. Boner, lob-on, schwing, "Kong has awoken," tumescence, morning glory, hard-on, bonk-on.

Words for ejaculate, meanwhile, triumphantly splatter all over the face of language: spunk, baby gravy, man custard, cum, spaff.

You could spend all day recalling synonyms for all the stiffies, and the jizz.

By way of contrast, let us turn to the ladies. How do *we* talk about getting sexually aroused? What words or phrases do *we* have? There's "wide-on"—"Looking at this picture of the young Beastie Boys is giving me a wide-on"—but I'm not sure I'm down with a synonym that makes me sound like I've got a massive, gaping fanny. I don't want something that conjures images of a double garage door swinging open, revealing an admirable storage facility. It doesn't sound like something to take pride in—the way "raging hard-on" does. Vaginal capaciousness is only a boasting matter if you're in a room full of women all in the final stages of birth, and you can shout out "Guys, turns out, my vadge is *so roomy*! I don't want to boast, but I think I've got the biggest vadge here! Fuck you all! This kid's barely touching the *sides*! This is gonna be a *cinch*! I'm gonna *sneeze* it out!" And they all jealously applaud you.

But in every other situation, we're supposed to pretend our fannies are so sprightly and tight that we regularly cut off the circulation in our gynecologist's hands. It's supposed to be like a mousetrap down there. A clenched fist of sex-joy. "I can't get the lid off this jam jar! Hang on—let me stick it up my wedge. *Plenty* of traction up there. It's *grippy*!"

So, "wide-on"—no. I don't feel like that's empowering me. It doesn't make me swagger. Wide-on . . . doesn't give me a wide-on. I don't feel like I'm conjuring up an unrefusable offer if I text "I am so WIDE right now" to my beloved.

What else do we have? I've got a friend who says, "He makes my fanny fizzy"—which vividly describes the disruption in one's pants one can experience when, e.g., watching the bit in *Blade Runner* when Harrison Ford puts his finger in his mouth. "Fanny flutters" is another—the phrase coined in 2019's *Love Island* by the unashamedly vadge-touting contestant Maura Higgins, and which so delightfully describes that multistarburst explosion a lady experiences when watching Mark Ruffalo e.g., put on a cardigan, whilst looking delightfully rumpled.

"That butters my crumpet" has a pleasing air—one imagines this is the term Miss Marple would use, if she ever met a retired colonel with a twinkle in his eye. And I have a fondness for "lady boner"— why *not* borrow the words of men? We borrow their shirts and socks. I'm happy to borrow a couple of their sexy words, too.

But it's not a long-term solution. We need to have dozens of words of our own—invented by us, used by us, to describe us.

Over the years, I've had to go off-road in relaying my lady horniness to either (a) friends, during a conversation about someone hot, or (b) to my lovers, so they might know they need to turn off a BBC4 documentary on Talking Heads *right now*, as they are needed in my basement.

"Call coming through on line *Phwoaaaargh*," has been useful; as has, for lovers of the right generation, "Bagpuss is waking up." I also like "Come into my secret volcano base (by which I mean my vagina)."

Sometimes, I just cut to the chase—I point to my genitals, scream, and say, "Something's happening! Quick! Help me! *With sex!*"

But it continues to be a difficult area. Linguistically, I mean. My actual "area" is very straight-forward. It operates on a strict "one in, one out" policy, and its opening times are 7 a.m. to 10 p.m. After that, it ignores all rings on the doorbell, relaxes with a slim volume of improving poetry, lights off by 11 p.m.

However, the lexicon of female arousal is *bountiful* compared to the dictionary of female lubrication. Because there are no other words for vaginal lubrication save "vaginal lubrication"—which is simply half a sentence describing it, rather than a handy word we could all use. I am willing to bet no woman on Earth has ever said, erotically, "Feel my bounteous vaginal lubrication," whilst swanning around in a negligee, feeling ace. I just don't think that's ever happened. It couldn't. It's scientifically impossible.

"I'm *so wet*," is the nearest we get—but it does carry with it the faint inference you might simply have sat on something damp; or, indeed, done a little wee. Also, whilst men saying "I am so hard" is a powerful, positive thing—outside the bedroom, "He's a hard man" is said admiringly—when someone outside the bedroom is described as "wet," we are usually referring to *either* Ross from *Friends* in "Pathetic Mode" or a Conservative MP from the 1980s, opposed to Margaret Thatcher's more radical policies. If your vadge has just become dry as a desert whilst reading that last sentence, you are not alone. "Wet" makes me *sandy*.

As for "moist"—well, in 2017, it was voted *the most hated word in the world*. There are just two colloquial descriptors for vaginal lubrication, and half of them have been voted *the most hated word in the world*. That is a massive kick in the vadge—but, also, understandable, as "moist" just isn't a sexy word. If I think of a "moist vulva"—and I am obviously biting down on a wooden spoon in mortification at this phrase—it conjures up an image of, frankly, mildew. Mildew on a shower curtain. Or else, a vadge that's just a bit *sweaty*—like a ham, in Saran wrap, in the fridge. Consequently, a coital event in which *either* participant uses the word "moist" is a guaranteed disaster. "Moist" is a boner-killing, vadge-closing spell. Within just ten minutes of it being uttered, a couple will find themselves sitting on the edge of the bed, half-dressed, fuckless, and resignedly ordering an Uber. The word *moist* is a borderline hate crime against the be-vulva'd. "Moist" is the end of all joy.

So, with "wet" and "moist" both out of play, yet again, the horny modern woman has had to embrace the same DIY philosophy as the punk movement, and simply create what she needs, using attitude and, if necessary, spit. If you, or your lover, were raised as Catholics, referring to the moistures of lasciviousness as "The Virgin Mary's Guilty Tears" might lend a forbidden frisson. Or, if one of you is into mechanics, you could call it your "saucy WD-40." Fans of *The Great British Bake Off* could lob in a "This is really greasing my muffin tin," and if you're of *either* a meteorological bent, *or* a fan of the adult rock group Toto, you could refer to "The rains down in Africa," whilst playing a punchy little synth stab.

In the years to come, I find things have changed immeasurably. Listening to my now-teenage daughters talking with their friends about who they fancy, it's clear this is a generation that *has* created a new vocabulary of female sexuality. Looking at a picture of a party where the male attendees are lackluster, one will sigh, "Man, my eyes have malnutrition. There are no *nutrients* in that room." On spotting a single, fetching fellow, another will suddenly yelp, "Oh my *God*, look at him! I am filling a *paddling pool* here. Seriously—I can't walk. I'm going to *slip*." And they talk of "thirst" *constantly*—Bim Adewunmi and Nichole Perkins of the podcast *Thirst Aid Kit* do sterling work in promoting the tastes of "thirst buckets" and "heaux" in what *really* turns them on: Timothée Chalamet's eyelashes, Idris Elba's arms, Spiderman kissing Mary Jane upside down in the rain, Brad Pitt entering all our lives in *Thelma & Louise*, and clips of a love-wracked Alan Rickman moaning, "Give me an occupation, or I shall go *mad*." As the years go on, the lexicon for female horniness and vulval humidity swells bounteously. To slightly paraphrase Martin Luther King, the arc of the moral universe is long—but does bend toward fruitiness.

However, that is of no use to us right now, where, without a ready cache of "James McAvoy as Mr. Tumnus" GIFs, I am finding it hard to concentrate.

I stroke Pete's face, lovingly—for it's such a lovely face! What a lovely husband! So perfect—except . . . there's a blackhead on the side of his nose. Man, it's a *corker*.

"Hang on. I'm just gonna get this . . ." I say, going in to squeeze it, whilst squinting. He lies there, patient and noble—like Aslan on the Stone Table, as the White Witch cuts off his mane. We've been here before. He knows better than to protest.

"We could . . . leave it for now, and have sex?" he says, reasonably, after a minute, wincing in silent pain. He doesn't understand I'm grooming him – like monkeys do. This is a vital part of my matng ritual. I can't have sex with an imperfect nose!

"The water pressure in the bathroom's really low—I think we might need to bleed the radiators," I say, chattily, working my thumbnail under the blemish. "And I noticed some moss on the outside of the house, which suggests the gutter might be leaking? Also, the garden center's doing a flash sale on water butts. Could be good to get one? The two hundred and twenty liter one is only fifty pounds. I like big butts, and I cannot lie."

Very patiently, Pete takes my hand and says, "Your butt-talk is arousing to me. Shall we—have sex?"

"Yes! Yes! Sorry!" I say, starting to climb on top of him. Then: "Ugh! ARGH! Fuck! Soz—my hip's playing up a bit. The leg . . . keeps coming . . . out of the socket . . ."

I roll off him and lie next to him, banging the top of my thigh.

"It'll go back in a minute," I say, still thumping it. "It's my fault. I know I should do yoga, and probably some weight lifting—that's the new thing, isn't it?—but there's never *time*. Once I've finished helping Lizzie with this homework project on China, I could start doing yoga in the evening. Oh FUCK! *China!* Did you get the empty cardboard boxes—to make the Great Wall?"

Pete sighs. We both look at the clock. It's now 8:27 a.m. Sexy time is slipping away.

"Sorry! I'm going to concentrate now! I'm totally ready to have sex now!"

I stop banging my thigh. I think sexy thoughts. *Monkeys on At-tenborough. Harrison Ford, frolicking naked in a meadow of long grass. Long grass? Oh! I just remembered!* I look at Pete.

"And the lawn mower's broken!"

THE PROBLEM WITH women living with a permanent to-do list in their head is that . . . it takes a lot to turn it off and commence Cock O'Clock.

Over the years, I've been able to compile a list of all the tricks and techniques repeatedly recommended to those in long-term relation-ships; and I will now review their efficacy and practicality here, thus:

1. Role-play. Pros: It allows you to have sex with *hundreds* of peo-ple, *all* of whom are your partner.

    Perhaps it's 1898, and you are the proprietor of a cake shop, whilst your husband is the village doctor, come to cure you of "hysteria in your pants." Or maybe he's a sensitive sailor on shore leave, and you're the strumpet with a heart of gold, about to give him the time of his life. Who does not want to take part in a sexual story of their own writing? How could this go wrong?

Cons: In practice, unless you happen to be married to one of Britain's great character actors—Paddy Considine, say, or Jared Harris—suggesting role-play is likely to be an agony you will never forget. Your average forty-five-year-old's ability to convincingly play, without rehearsal or script, a "hot pirate" is likely to be quite low.

The role *you* will end up playing, then, after half an hour of self-conscious Scottish accents and hat-wearing, is that of a frustrated Hollywood director, saying, "Let me tell you a bit about Captain Sexington's *backstory*. I think it would help give you more *range*," whilst your husband sadly detumesces, and daydreams about becoming a member of Equity, so he can make a complaint about hostile working conditions.

Role-play really puts the "amateur" into "amateur dramatics." If you find it embarrassing watching the school's sixth-form play—they forget their lines! They look so mortified!—then sexual role-play is just as mortifying, but with the added horror of everyone involved being naked. It's essentially an anxiety dream, guest-starring a hopeful penis. And that penis will be *disappointed*.

2. Tantric breathwork. Pros: A much more expansive, intense, nay *spiritual* sexual experience than the average ten minutes of poking on the sofa.

Cons: Lengthy. Very difficult for asthmatics. Also: A great deal of deep breathing is apt to inadvertently come out sounding like . . . a tetchy sigh.

3. Sex toys. Pros: A rapidly vibrating item is never a *bad* idea; and there's a device for every preference: I once found a vibrator

that looked like the cute robot Twiki from *Buck Rogers*, and it was one of the best days of my life.

Cons: When it comes down to it, these are now just more bloody possessions that need dusting, and batteries.

4. BDSM. Pros: The odd riding crop flick across the flanks; a bit of old-fashioned spanking? All a smashing idea.

Cons: Until you realize how badly soundproofed your house is, and hear a child outside your door, going, "Mommy—why do you keep . . . *clapping?*"

5. Anal. Pros: It's intense. However pressing your to-do list is, you will almost certainly forget it when someone has wedged something the size of a Pret tuna baguette up your arse, then starts hammering away for the jackpot.

Cons: For someone of my age, anal feels a bit . . . I want to say *nineties?* I associate it with alcoholic lemonade, *Wayne's World*, and AllSaints. Things that everyone was into *then*, but that would seem a bit . . . *weird* if you were still into them *now*.

As the years have gone by, I have come to regard anal a bit like doing a wheelie. Really, it's a pastime for your teens and early twenties—when you have nothing to lose and are laissez-faire about the potential for having an accident and really hurting your arse.

Then you get a bit older, and realize it's just much more *comfortable* and *efficient* to pop both wheels down and ride the bike properly instead. Not least because, that way, stuff doesn't fall out of your basket.

And yes, that *is* a metaphor—for, by the very nature of the beast, it is impossible to do anal without, at some point, thinking about, worrying about, or indeed encountering, "something falling out of your basket," i.e., a poo. Anal sex is, I'm afraid, an unavoidably poo-centric activity. This is because the mechanics could be summed up by changing a few key lyrics from a Bob Dylan song, so that it isn't

"Knockin' on Heaven's Door," but "Knockin' on the Place Where All the Poo Is."

Given this, I find it generally takes the enthusiasm and sheer brio of a younger woman to ignore the undeniable poo problem that comes with anal sex, and just carry on regardless. In a way, you still have to be an incorrigible romantic to be into anal. You have to be able to be really *carried away* by the moment. "Up the bum" is strictly for romance novels.

There are ways, of course, to minimize the poo problem—you can time your meals carefully, and/or have an enema, to make sure the way is clear—but, really, once you reach this stage, you are less "someone with a bum-hole," and more "someone who is basically a full-time zoo-keeper for their bumhole's mad schedule of digestion and sex," and it can be hard to juggle the care of such a high-maintenance anus alongside children, work, and *Poldark*. Absently eat a hot cross bun at 3 p.m. on a sex day, and suddenly you've *either* got to pop a hose up your bum *or* cancel the whole shebang. *Hole shebang.* It all starts to become a bit . . . *adminy.* This is why, now, I have, essentially, put a sign on my bum that says "THANK YOU TO ALL OUR FAITHFUL CUSTOMERS OVER THE YEARS—BUT MY ARSE IS NOW CLOSED."

In recent years, I've noticed a reassuring trend for eschewing these more effortful and performative elements of sex—the post-*Fifty Shades of Grey* torture rooms and all-night anal discos—in favor of celebrating chilled, reliable vanilla sex, instead. In *Broad City*, the category of pornography Ilana loves the most is "Men with Average-Sized Penises." This celebration of normal, everyday sex gives me joy. It also, let's face it, makes sex more *likely.* In your life, the majority of your sexings will be Basic Shags with Average Penises. Learn to love that and, as Mary Poppins says, "SNAP! The job's a game!"

Hey, look—don't get me wrong. I am *totally* supportive of everyone's kinks. I am pro *all* the banging. The freakier, the better man. You do you—and everyone else you want to do, too.

But I do feel an ultimate loyalty to the Classic Shag—perhaps because it has become so unfashionable, in the pornographic age. I feel I need to stand up for its old-fashioned yet quintessential charm—possibly by getting the National Trust involved—so that future generations can experience the joy of having some sex, in bed, mainly vadge-based, with a bit of mouth and hand stuff to get things going. I worry that women feel pressurized to become some manner of ever-innovative Sexual Extremes Machines—a cross between a Fleshlight, a courtesan, and Barbarella—in order to not become sexually passé. Ladies—a Classic Shag will *never* be passé. You know what? If your man is tired of vadge, he is tired of life.

6. The "Oh, Thank God We're Not Them" Existential Gratitude Fuck. There are no cons to this at all—it's pro all the way if you, recently, have found it difficult to muster the will to shag, and the decades with your partner have somewhat dimmed their appeal. Then, my friend, what *you* need is another couple whose marriage is a car crash. Perhaps it's your parents, or in-laws—seething with undivorceable resentment after decades of misunderstanding and emotional unavailability. Or maybe it's another couple you know, whose red wine consumption is borderline terrifying, who trade spiteful barbs over the sound of another cork popping—real *Who's Afraid of Virginia Woolf?* shit. Either way, what you're looking for is two people who wince every time the other talks, have a brittle body language that always looks "pre-fight," and who say things like, "Look! He's *smiling* again. It's *absolutely unbearable.*"

In order to apply this couple to your lackluster sex life, simply visit them for the weekend, or book a cottage holiday in Dorset together. Within twenty minutes of watching their ill-concealed loathing of each other activate over "the best way to light a barbecue," or "the best route to get to Bridport," your previously humdrum partner will suddenly look like a glowing, joyous, love-infused sex god, and you'll be stroking their knackers under the table and winking, before running off to find a downstairs toilet you can have an urgent, life-affirming, filthy shag in, almost certainly ending in a simultaneous orgasmic cry of "Thank GOD we're not them!"

AND OF COURSE, no matter how fruity and experimental you are, practical things can still get in the way of your sex life. Dog owners, for instance, will often find that their beloved pet has some kind of sixth sense—a *sexth* sense, perhaps—allowing them to know when you are attempting some manner of Trouser Time. Many breeds of dog seem to respond to human sexual arousal by jumping on the bed and trying to sit on someone's head whilst looking confused, or by just barking dementedly and endlessly, as if an erect penis were by way of a tiny burglar who's just broken into your house.

This often exposes a rift in the marriage—with one partner ejecting the dog from the room and locking the door, in order to continue the sex; whilst the other, more easily manipulated partner says things like, "Oh, it's making sad noises!" and "It might get lonely!," as if you were some kind of inhumane Dog Rejector. Our family has what is now called "The Cockblockapoo," but I know others who have "No Sausage Dogs."

AS YOU CAN see, over twenty years of marriage, we have kept things joyful, experimental, and fruity. We have experienced highs, and lows. We are still, against the odds, having some Lovely Shags.

At exactly 9 a.m., Pete puts his trousers back on as I lie on the bed, giving him the thumbs-up.

"Thanks for the sex," I say.

"Well, thank *you*," he replies, buttoning up his cardigan.

"I would call that an absolutely textbook 'keeping things going' shag," I continue. We both sigh.

"How long do you reckon it is until the combination of work and children eases up, and we'll be able to bugger off for a dirty weekend in Venice—packing nothing but a small mother-of-pearl vial of MDMA powder and white, silk nightie?" I ask.

Pete calculates, on his fingers. "I think we could start safely planning that in . . . another ten years?"

He puts his shoes on. I get up and make the bed. We kiss for a minute—a sweet, half satisfied, half yearning thing—then pat each other reassuringly, and go about our days, post-shag. Less than a decade to go before we have dangerously amazing sex again! Not long now!

CHAPTER THREE

The Hour of Reflecting on a Good Marriage

9:00 A.M.

LYING ON THE BED, CHEERFULLY POSTCOITAL, I WATCH PETE LEAVE. I remember once reading about a man in his nineties with heart problems, who was admitted to hospital to be monitored on an ECG. When his wife of sixty years came to visit, the ECG went haywire: his heart still skipped a beat when she walked into the room.

I am lucky, because I think: I am that old man. Whenever I hear Pete's key in the door, my heart still skips a beat. And I know he feels the same. Customarily, I make silly noises when I hear him return, "Argh! Grargh! Waah! Gnuuuu!"

He will reply, "Fnrrrrr. Brrrr. Haaaaa. Lurrrrrr."

These noises mean: I would still choose you. I don't even need words anymore. I am glad home is *you*.

A GREAT DEAL of mad balls is written about love—and, more specifically, how to recognize it, when it arrives. Depending on what we're reading, we are told things about astrological compatibility, and birth order, and physical types, and shared values, and cultural sympathies. Love is often presented as something that can be recognized if you remorselessly grill your prospective partners with some kind of gigantic tick-list, which you need to hit a 70 percent like-for-like on ("I loved the second series of *Saved by the Bell*, too!") before you can safely say whether you really love someone or not.

Well, it's all balls. Now safely in my wise middle age, I can tell you the three vital—and, indeed, *only*—things about knowing you've found "The One."

1. The primary location for foolproof-love detection is in your nose. Forget about the heart, or the crotch—both of which are, sadly, idiot organs easily fooled by a bunch of flowers, or a vibrator. No—it's your nose you want to listen to. You can't fool a nose. Your nose knows what's going on. I can tell you right now, you will know you've finally found the love of your life because they just. Smell. *Great.*

    If, when you get near them, you find yourself huffing up great lungfuls of them—really snorting them down like it's Friday, and they're a nitrous oxide balloon, and you intend to do this *all night long*—then *this* will be the person you marry, whether they're an Aries with brown eyes or not. Do you find yourself sniffing the top of your partner's head so hard their hair *actually moves?* Do you frequently wedge your nose in their armpit and inhale them whilst going, "ARGH! SO GOOD!"? Have you sampled their body so thoroughly you could actually tell, in a blind smelling test, the difference between their tit sweat (oddly fresh) and their back sweat (more complex and earthy), but eventually concluded that "It's all good, man?" Does their body smell like a super-awesome combination of life, puppies, rain, hot cross buns, and "the good times"? Then congratulations—you've just found your true love. Pat your partner-selecting nose like it's a clever, faithful old horse, and enjoy the next decades of joy.

    There is science behind this—a combination of hormones, pheromones, and DNA can sense which partner would be optimal for you to reproduce with—but I prefer to believe that the nose is simply a solid-gold wizard, which knows magic when it finds it.

2. The Good Smell, when you find it, has a very specific purpose: to relax you. That's what love is, ultimately—being very, *very* relaxed. Look—you're going to spend the majority of your time with this person *sleeping*, so you *deffo* want to be looking for someone your subconscious is saying, "It will be good to be totally unconscious next to this person. Defenses are happy to be *down*. Brain is safely *off*."

And as for your waking time together—a good half of *that* will be spent sitting next to each other on the sofa, in silence, or in a car in a traffic jam on the road to Birmingham in the rain, eating M&S garlic and chili prawns from the container and listening to *Now That's What I Call Music! 42*. Although you will want *some* sparky bants and intellectual to-ing and fro-ing, the baseline for a long-term relationship should be making silly sounds at each other, for hours, in a meaningless fashion.

This is the primary effect of The Good Smell: It gets you superstoned. You're smoking this big darling like a massive doobie. As a consequence, you are sillier with them than with anyone else. When you guys are together, you *really* twat about. Silly voices, terrible puns. Laughing hysterically at your own jokes. Being able to find mending an overflowing toilet together *amusing*.

If you're the hard-assed CEO of a multinational corporation, and you know *for a fact* every single one of your employees would lose all respect for you if they saw what you're like when you're arse-ing around with this dude, then, again: congratulations. This one's a keeper.

3. Finally, true love is a bit . . . scared. Just *slightly*. Just a *tiny bit*. A pinch of salty fear, to season the dish. A soupçon of worry that, if you let your standards drop, and start taking each other for granted, all this delicious magic could . . . disappear. This fear means that, however much you're pissing around

and being relaxed, your true love never, ever drops its base-line standards of politeness. True love will always remember to say "please" and "thank you," and keep all communication super courteous. The people who will stay together forever are the ones who have proper, Aretha-style respect for each other. I'm minded of one of the most successful marriages I know, wherein a single, tinned pie was always kept in the cupboard of their kitchen.

"If you leave me, or make me leave you, that's what the rest of your life will be: eating a ready-made meat pie-for-one," she told her husband.

He treated her like a goddess.

True love always remains, at its core, *sexily deferential*.

So THAT's *LOVE*. That's the choosing someone lovely who you fancy bit. That's the bit we all talk about. Turns out, thanks to your nose, and the word "thanks," that's actually the *easy* bit. The *hard* bit is: *everyfuckingthing* else that comes after. Spending the rest of your life together, as a couple. Because *how* do you do it? What does "the rest of your life" look like? What's that schedule like? What's the template?

Unfortunately, as far as society is concerned, we have very little to go on. Humans are the only species to invent storytelling, and we came up with this in order to relay the most important information to each other, down the generations. But if you think of all our current stories, myths, and archetypes, most of them are about people *finding* love. They are about people in the *prelove* state.

HERE's THE THING about the institution of marriage. Before you get married, you can have revelations about yourself, form gangs, go on quests, save the world. You can jump off things, and scream, and be made over, and give speeches, and cry in the rain, and punch people or dragons, and press buttons in the nick of time, and *learn, learn, learn*. You are the exploding center of all things.

And then, at very end of the story—when you have completed all

your growing and learning—you get the biggest reward of all: You
are deemed complete enough to win the heart of the hottie and settle
down. There will be a wedding scene! And that—that is the ending.
Your story is considered told, now. You are done. You will now step
through the door of your house and cease all adventure. You will
not go anywhere, form any gangs, or save the world, now you are
married.

Indeed, it would be weird if you even *thought* about those things—
for you are presumed to have everything you need, inside that part-
nership. Like you built up a layer of emotional fat while you were
single, and now you can just live off that, until you die.

You have become replete—and also silent, now. Once the door
has closed on the marital house, no reports can emanate from it. If
the marriage is good, then the marriage must also be silent. That is
one of the rules. You do not gossip, you do not share. A good marriage is mysterious to everyone else around it. What *happens* in there?
Who are those people who walked into it on their wedding day, and
then pulled up the drawbridge? If a marriage is successful, you walk
in there in your teens, twenties, or thirties, and then only come out
again in a coffin—the partner who outlived you standing there, waving goodbye.

And whatever the mutual business of the marriage was, over
those years—the parenting, the caring for elderly relatives, the siblings having breakdowns, the friends divorcing, the politics that buffet it, the legislation that changed it—that, too, is seen as private.

For we don't write novels about long and happy marriages. We
don't have big blockbuster stories on how to raise children. We don't
show the endless, everyday business of domestica. We don't show the
house that becomes a refuge for relatives who are breaking, broken,
or unwell. We don't show how thirty turns into forty, turns into fifty;
we don't show towns as thousands of houses with thousands of silent
marriages in them. We don't show equal partners running a collabo-
rative effort. We don't show the adventure of keeping love alive until
we die. We have no template for that.

It is left, instead, to every household, on its own, to work out how that might happen: no useful role-model shortcuts; no helpful archetypes; not a single example of how you are supposed to make this work, in the twenty-first century, on a day-to-day basis.

When two people love each other very much—that's invisible. The world likes to pretend everything that happens in your world is your business, your problem, and to be kept quiet and solved by you and you alone. It is up to you to decide what your marriage is. Society ends on your doorstep. Marriage is a private enterprise. It's just you two, alone. That's the bad news.

But that's also the good news! Because it basically means *you and the person you love get to invent what marriage is.*

Here, then, are some scenarios you might recognize from your marriage, which you will not have seen in any story, and, therefore, have to improvise your way through on an *ad hoc* basis.

"WHO IS THE MOST BUSY?"

The majority of modern marriages contain two working parents. This is such a recent invention—just one or two generations old— that literally no one has yet had time to come up with any solutions for how to make it work. And the reason they've not had any time to come up with any solutions is they were too busy working! If you are in a marriage with two working parents, then, congratulations! You're part of a societal experiment with no precedents! Hurrah!

Casual anecdote suggests that the most common way to deal with this situation is a game called "Who Is the Most Busy?"

To play "Who Is the Most Busy?" properly, one must begin from the moment one wakes up. Within the first moments of mutual consciousness, one begins a version of "Scissors, Paper, Stone"—asking, "How did you sleep?" a question which you then must answer *at the same time* as your partner. No pause is allowed—both must reply in synchronization, thus:

"How did you sleep? *I didn't get off until midnight—*"

"*I was still emailing at 1 a.m.*"

However, like "Scissors, Paper, Stone," it's a best of three game: the 1 a.m. emailer has won the *first round,* but the second round is "Sleep Quality Evaluation": one offering, "I had a terrible anxiety dream about this report," as the other counters with "I had perimenopausal night sweats. My side of the bed looks like I've wet myself."

The decider is the description of how one feels at that moment: "My eyes feel like bags of grit," "I'm so tired, thinking feels like punching treacle into a sock."

Exhaustion Pecking Order now established, there's a brief side game of "Who Has the Least Time for Self-Maintenance?" whilst dressing—"Christ. Look at my arse. I haven't had time for a run for three weeks" vs. "Argh! Look at my *roots.* I haven't seen a hairdresser since July"—before breakfast is used to tackle The Schedule.

The purchasing of birthday presents; a child's braces-tightening appointment; the installation of a burglar alarm; an upcoming school concert; the car registration; the mending of a phone; the collection of a prescription; a hospital appointment; picking up a child's friend from school. These are listed out loud, and you and your partner take turns to divvy them out, according to ability.

The problems begin if there is imbalance in the divvying—if the divvy load weighs too heavily on one side. In this instance, the person who feels most overburdened can often opt to manifest this feeling visually by—as they recite what they will be doing today—loading or unloading the dishwasher in a noisy and overburdened manner, whilst sighing heavily.

However, caution must be exercised with this tactic, for if it is done in *too* self-sacrificing a manner, the unburdened partner might, correctly, identify what is going on—"You're being a bit of a *martyr*"—and you will lose half the points you have accrued so far.

In the worst-case scenario, the partner will then go on to say, "As you're obviously finding it hard to cope today, *I* will do *everything*. No don't worry—I don't want you to feel *burdened*," and start making terrifyingly effective calls to local servicemen whilst angrily typing emails *and* combing a child for nits—just to show how super-capable they are.

If this happens, it's checkmate, dude—you have overplayed your hand, and have gone from The Busiest (the winning slot) to The Most Ineffective (the losing slot), and you have to start again from scratch by doing one of the Big Ticket Awful Jobs, e.g., the clearing of the loft, or calling your partner's mother "for a chat." Just to prove you *are* an effective person, after all.

Never go "Full Martyr." Delegate as you would in the workplace. Every marriage needs a whiteboard in the kitchen with The List of Jobs on it, to be divvied up equally, no excuses. And if your partner feels you're "being too businesslike about all this," reply, "Dude, we bought a property together, we have yearly accounts. Do you remember when we signed those legal documents—even though I was wearing a mad white dress, and you were drunk? Marriage *is* a business."

WHOSE SURNAME WILL YOUR CHILDREN HAVE?

Indeed, what names will they have at all? Ostensibly, the mother should have the deciding vote here. If your vadge is about to be exploded by a head, it seems only fair you get to name the subsequent person the head is attached to. That seems like a fair exchange. Besides, often—in the preceding nine months—one might have had recourse to address the baby directly, as it kicks the shit out of your kidneys, or squats on your bladder, and one often finds oneself barking, "Okay, *Roy*, I get it. You're an active kid! But chill with the abdominal roundhouses, eh?" at one's distended, pulsing tum. You may already have started the naming process, just to establish a relationship with the beast inside.

However, we must admit something quite important, to wit: pregnancy hormones can often directly affect a woman's taste in names. In a bad way. Here, for instance, are some of the names I considered for my daughters, whilst heavily pregnant: Lettuce. Plum. Clove. Ambrosia.

Looking back now, I can see what was going on: I was just hungry. After all, I was about to name my child after (a) the ingredients of an unprecedentedly unpleasant salad or (b) tinned rice pudding.

Thankfully, my husband—who was *not* insane with hormones— deftly and gently encouraged me to think of names "that maybe *wouldn't* make their lives a living hell," and we settled for the more prosaic Elizabeth and Nancy instead.

Incidentally, when it comes to unworkably quirky names for your baby, I believe that the greatest possible argument against teenagers becoming pregnant is that the baby names you like when you're, say, fifteen, single-handedly prove you're not ready for motherhood yet. My teenage diary records that, had I had a child in 1988, I would have called them either Kitten Lithium, K. T. Blue, Tatty Apple, or Aloyious Jonst. Thank God my access to sperm was severely limited to the amount of none.

Surnames, though, are a whole other minefield. There are only three options: yours, his, or both of yours wedged together like a su- pergroup, like you've given birth to Hall-Oates or Simon-Garfunkel.

Double-barreling your surnames together has the effect of mak- ing your child automatically sound as though it's posh—either an advantage or disadvantage, depending on where they are, and what they go on to do. If you are comfortably middle class and liable to be around actual posh people, it can be helpful: The posh will con- fidently engage your child in conversations like "Was your first pony quite *naughty*?" or "Which is best: skiing or diamonds?" which means they have accepted your offspring as one of "them," and they will reap benefits such as "being invited to their cousin's castle in Carcassonne" and "being given a column on *The Telegraph*."

If you do not move in these circles, however, there is the chance your double-barreled child will be kicked up the bum by surly youths shouting, "Get your *butler* to stop me, Price-Waterhouse-Cooper!"— even though you live in a terraced house, and eat jam sandwiches for pudding.

If double-barreling is not an option for you, then you are a couple who has to pick just *one* family's surname to continue—which, when you put it like that, is brutal. The brutality of your situation explains how these things tend to end up being decided: Whatever your his- tory and sexual politics *as a couple*, things are usually decided on the basis of "whose set-in-their-ways father will *freak out* the most if his grandchildren do not have their surname?" Nine times out of ten, this means the kids are getting their father's surname.

Whilst this tends to leave female partners wildly resentful—and apt to whisper things at their children like "The minute Granny and Granddad die, you can change your surname to *mine,* okay?"—it does mean that, when and if you get a dog, your husband can't argue when you triumphantly register it at the vet under *your* surname, whispering, "Pulled one back for Team Moran." You take your tiny comforts and victories where you can patriarchy-wise. If the building of a matriarchy starts with the recruitment of dogs, so be it.

And remember—ultimately, whoever has the baby, has the power. All grandparents have to bow to the cradle—for life without their grandchildren is unthinkable. You have a pretty big unspoken bargaining chip. Especially if your child is called Chip, and he's really hefty.

WHAT I MEAN WHEN I SAY "I LOVE YOU"

"I love you" should be the simplest, most straightforward phrase in our vocabulary. It should mean, simply, "I, meaning me, love you, meaning you." There shouldn't be any weird gray areas, or double meanings, involved. It's a basic, yet classic, sentence.

But if I think about all the times I've said "I love you" during my twenty-five years with Pete, I have to admit that I have rarely meant, simply and purely, *I love you. I love you* has meant, over the decades, dozens of wholly different things, and been said hoping to prompt hundreds of different consequences. I chuck *love* around like it's vinegar on chips; like high notes in the third verse of a Mariah Carey song.

And that's before we get to the ways in which I have said it. I've sung it; I've shouted it; I've done it in the voice of Kermit crying; I've written it on my tits to be found, as a surprise, but also written it into a pile of mashed potatoes with my finger. Love is all around.

But love really isn't *all* you need—anyone who's dealt with the consequences of a child coming into the bedroom at 2 a.m., whispering, terrified, "There's something wrong with the toilet," will know that love comes second best to a plunger, a wet-and-dry vacuum cleaner, and good ventilation.

So: all the loves.

First of all, there's the fairly straightforward ones we all do: "I love you" at the end of a phone call, instead of "goodbye." I guess this also means "Don't die while I'm away, as the paperwork will be a nightmare and I haven't brought a front-door key with me, and I don't want to climb through the window again."

Then there's "I love you" in lieu of "thank you"—uttered when being presented with a baked potato, or a cup of tea. I guess *that* means "I love you for being a thoughtful person who knows what I like right now, and it makes me appreciate you."

Then there are the slightly more emotionally complex "I love yous"—when spooning at the end of the day, where it means a combination of "Thank God today's over," "You feel nice," and "I appreciate you donating your body warmth to my legs." "I love you" when we're in the bath together, and what I *really* mean is "And I would love you even *more* if you gave me a foot massage. Oh look! There's my feet! On your belly! What a coincidence!"

I say "I love you" not only when leaving the houses of unhappy couples, where it means "Thank God we're not them, please don't change," but *also* when Pete's done something I *would* like him to change, but I'm trying to sugar the pill. "I love you! You look so lovely! Do you think it's time we should treat you to some new trousers, perhaps?" or "I love you! And would it be okay if you rolled the pizza dough a little thinner? I essentially want a *cheesy crisp*."

Sometimes, "I love you" is a warning, which demands instant action—used instead of "This anecdote has gone on too long," or "Let's leave," or "Please take me away from this boring man." At a party, if I say "I love you," and slip my hand into his, it means we will be back in the car in less than five minutes. So, it means "goodbye" here, too—to everyone else.

When I'm hungover, or have been evil, or grumpy, "I love you" means "Please forgive me." When I say it, I feel like a drowned cartoon cat, hoping to be toweled dry of their shame. "Please cure me. Reassure me I have not broken the love."

Sometimes, and I am ashamed to admit this, "I love you" actually means "I love *me*."

"I *love you*!" I will say, quite violently, when walking into a room in a new dress that I feel amazing in. "I love you," I will say, after I've made a joke that makes him laugh, or I've cooked him something he enjoys eating, or if I've just had a sudden burst of joy. "I love you" here means "When I love me, I love you *more*—because we are kind of the same thing, now."

When I realized this, I started to understand why people who are unhappy with themselves often find loving others difficult—"I am *in* love" means just that: you are in the love *together*, and if you don't love yourself, you are confused as to why the other person likes you. You are standing *outside* the love, bewildered as to why the other person feels so happy.

During sex, "I love you" is a fucking minefield, and I need to sort it out as soon as possible. "I love you" can *equally* mean "You can come now—it's starting to chafe" *and* "Don't come yet—this is amazing. Let's do it for *five more hours!*" Even *I* don't know how you can tell the difference, and I'm the one saying it. Sex "I love yous" are absolutely demented bleatings from someone not at their intellectual best, and are probably best, in the long run, ignored.

Then there are the sad "I love yous"—said when I'm feeling down, or anxious, or bad in my body. "I love you" from a hotel room, far away, where I'm hoping for the reply, "And I love *you*— you work so hard, and we all miss you, and can't wait for you to come home."

"I love you" comes in a conversation when it's clear we disagree, and I want to end it before it gets brutal.

"I love you" comes when the dog's being amusing, or the kids are happy, or the house looks clean and shiny: then, it means "I love *us*. I love our family. I love our life."

As we can see, the poets were right: "I love you" *is* the most important phrase in the English language. It *does* mean everything. Just in a more complicated way than they intended.

COUGHING, SNEEZING, AND BEING SICK

When I gather with my women, and we discuss our brilliant, lovely, caring, emotionally expressive, gentle, burden-sharing partners, and rejoice in how we have found most excellent men, there is always a moment where—having spoken fulsomely in tribute to all we adore about them—we turn to the small, nigglesome things about them that astonish us. We presume they are in the pub doing the same about us ("She's a powerhouse high court judge with unequaled dance moves and an ass that won't quit—but *why* does she have a box in the bathrooms with 'EYEBROWS' written on it???" "Mate, my wife has a bathroom box with 'PORES' written on it. I'm too scared to ask why.") so we feel free to vent in a mutually respectful safe place.

And the topic that most commonly arises? Violent yet everyday physical releases. Coughs, sneezes, and vomiting. The coughs, sneezes, and vomits that we signed a legally binding contract to be married to—until death do us part—without really realizing all that would entail, but we now fully realize and find it difficult to handle without regular reporting to sympathetic ears.

Let me illustrate. For instance, when *I* sneeze in public, first of all, I try to suppress it—as I feel it ungentlewomanly to expel the contents of my head over other bus goers. Pinching the nose is very effective—you can subdue 90 percent of sneezes down to a minimal "P-*th*." If the sneeze is a surprise sneeze, and arrives too quickly to be mitigated, then it arrives as a slightly more strident "P-*thoo*." And that's it. That's *my* sneeze business.. It's over. Sneeze come, sneeze go. Easy sneeze. On with the day. My sneezing is *done*.

On the other hand, when my husband sneezes, it appears to be a lengthy, borderline berserk process that involves him, essentially, exploding—like a head in *Scanners*. I have witnessed sneezes that seemed to take up half the afternoon, would have been heard by everyone in our postcode, and which have left my husband so exhausted, subsequent bedrest seemed to be the only solution.

First, the sneeze announces itself—in the middle of a pleasant conversation, whilst chopping onions, say, my husband will suddenly stop talking, pull a face of impending horror, and look off into the middle distance—like one of the rabbits in *Watership Down*, on spotting a looming hawk. There will be a series of preliminary shudders and violent inhalations—"AH! AH!"—during which he will slam the knife down onto the countertop and, if I am near, *grab my arm*, as if he is trying to tether himself to something in advance of an impending storm. Sometimes, in this phase, he will utter a little, wracked groan of "Oh *no*" or "Oh *God*"—like those of Edward Woodward, just before he's burned alive in *The Wicker Man*.

Then there will be a tiny silence—as if the whole thing has suddenly, and miraculously, passed, which the unversed might unwisely use as a chance to relax—which is then followed by an eruption so mighty, the dog runs away.

"FWRARGH-*CHAAAAAA!*" he will scream—striking his foot down on the floor, as if warning everyone: "Evacuate! Unsafe area! SNEEZES ARE HERE!"

"FWRARGH-CHAAAAAA-AAAAA-AAAAA! FWARGH-CHAAAA-AAAAA-*ARGHHHHH!*"

Car alarms go off; children cry, "Are you *okay?*" down the stairs, in consternation.

In order to preserve my hearing, I will usually, at this point, have removed myself to the doorway, where I then witness a man who appears to have been pushed to the limits of physical endurance shakily mopping his entire head with a series of handkerchiefs and tissues, and then sitting down; drained of all life.

In 50 percent of cases, after a brief breathing space, the sneezing will start again—as if a portal to hell has opened up in my loved one's sinuses, and he is birthing a spiraling vortex of ebullient demons, one by one, through his nose, in a way that cannot be stopped until all his life force is spent. As my husband has hay fever, you may imagine what a yearly trial summer is.

Coughing involves a similarly involved and performative approach—a build-up of throat clearing and what can only be described as "intolerable nose noises," leading to mad hunching and barking, before tailing off in a minutes-long series of "HmmHHH-HHH, hmmmmHHHH" sounds, some of which can last, with slight variations, all the way through an episode of *Naked & Afraid*. The depth, variety, and sustain of these sounds are truly notable: it's as if the BBC Radiophonic Workshop had assembled a Men's Cough Orchestra, who are now making a pretty decent fist of re-creating the sound of a landing TARDIS.

As for vomiting—vomiting seems to strike terror in the heart of men. To them, it seems to be an unbearable physical voyage to a land of horror—like being deported to some manner of Puke Colony on the say-so of an evil king.

On the mornings my husband rises with a bug, he walks around the house looking as if he's waiting for a knock on the door that will see him press-ganged into a seventeen-month voyage to the Indies.

"I think . . . I think I might be *sick,* in a bit," he will whisper, every so often, in a manner that suggests that the whole house should pre-emptively don black mourning gear, before covering the road outside with sawdust to dampen the sound of horses' hooves.

This will go on for many, many hours, before the Time of Vomiting finally arrives—heralded by him wailing, "This is *it!,*" running from the room and throwing up in the toilet with a technique that makes it sound like he's *fighting* the vomit, even as it comes out.

"I *hate* being sick," he'll say, returning, clearly traumatized—hair on end, eyes red, breath still ragged.

I've studied this for many, many hours, in medical textbooks, and there is absolutely no physical difference between the male and female reflux system. The guts, throat, and spasms are all the same. I cannot, therefore, understand this massive divergence in male and female vomiting. Women puke easily, rapidly, and with minimal fuss.

We are very businesslike about it. When I am struck with a vomiting bug, and the moment of release approaches, I will slip out of the room, go to the bathroom, prop up a copy of *Cosmo* on the toilet bowl, and leaf through the "Recommended Summer Shoes" section whilst briskly hoiking up whatever needs hoiking. I might even take a pen with me, to mark a particularly fetching pair of espadrilles. On occasion, I have remained on Twitter throughout the puke—making lolz-some comments about e.g., *Sherlock* or Bear Grylls. To me, vomiting is a simple piece of admin I can tackle whilst going about my normal business. If I'm lucky enough to do it in a bathroom, I can make the experience comparatively luxurious—a nice folded towel for the knees, and another on the toilet seat to rest my head on, in between retches. There's no need to *suffer*.

However, I—like every other woman I know—would not be overly dismayed if puking struck when access to a toilet was difficult. Every woman I know is proficient in the "Lady Sick" or "Disco Vom"—that moment on the dance floor when you suddenly realize those five Jägers are sitting uneasily on top of your impassioned twerking. Who among us has not simply vommed into a pint glass, or a handbag, whilst still dancing—not even missing a beat? If we are dancing in a circle, we wouldn't even mention it. Not until the end of the song, anyway.

Vomiting need not interrupt your day. I once had champagne and oysters react terribly during a business lunch, and I simply carried on the meeting—occasionally leaving the table to wargh up my bad business, spray a bit of perfume, and then return to close the deal. You just crack on. I've had long, intense conversations at festivals with friends interspersed with several of us simply turning to the side, having a bit of a huey, and then continuing with the matter at hand. One friend, during appalling morning sickness, used to vomit into the sleeve of her coat, on the bus. It's scarcely any cause for drama.

I guess, in the end, it's all down to your baseline experience. Women are so used to things happening to us that would register as "illness"—cramps, bleeding, morning sickness, bloating, madly achy balloon tits from hell—that are, in fact, merely by-products of being alive; so that when illness comes, we do not fear it so much. Our bodies are constantly spasming and expelling things. We're like the fucking turnstiles at Wembley, bodywise. In and out, all the time.

By the age of sixteen, an otherwise healthy woman has, simply and unavoidably, experienced a thousand times more discomfort, pain, and random fluid than an otherwise healthy man of the same age—so a bit of a sneeze, cough, or puke is but a mere bagatelle. As Kristin Scott Thomas's character, Belinda, tells Phoebe Waller-Bridge in the second season of *Fleabag*, as they sit in a bar in their amazing outfits, "Women are born with pain built in. It's our physical destiny. Period pains, sore boobs, childbirth, you know. We carry it within ourselves, throughout our lives. Men don't. They have to seek it out, they invent all these gods and demons and things just so they can feel guilty about things, which is something we do very well on our own. And then they create wars, so they can feel things and touch each other, and when there aren't any wars, they play rugby. And we have it all going on in here, inside. We have pain on a cycle for years and years and years."

And if your husband isn't into wars, or rugby, he has sneezing, instead.

IN THE INTERESTS of balance, I ask Pete what mad, intolerable woman things I do that he has to deal with in our marriage.

"Oh, there's nothing," he said, not even looking up from the pile of vinyl he's sorting. "You're perfect."

"Oh, come now," I say, leaning in the doorway. "That can't be true. I must do *loads* of berserk and irritating things. *Millions.*"

"No. I have absolutely no complaints. You can't attribute a single critical quote to me about your behavior as a wife." He pauses for a moment—creating a breakaway "Birmingham reggae" section—then continues. "Which means, when you write this up, I will look like the far more tolerant, pleasant, easygoing partner in this marriage. The one who adores his wife, no matter what.

The one everyone sides with. The good guy. The—dare I say it?—*winner.*"

I whistle, admiringly. This seemingly mild, amiable, mad-sneezing man is actually a gold medalist tactician and mind-fucker. We are totally equally matched. I can best him at nothing. The game continues.

CHAPTER FOUR

The Hour of Vulvas

⤌⤍

10:00 A.M.

THE THING IS, IF A MARRIAGE IS STILL GENERALLY A MYSTERIOUS AND unchronicled thing, it is a rigorous Ordnance Survey map of inner London compared to "the bodies of women." Even though we're walking around in them every day, they're still madly secret and baffling to both us and the wider world. Even at this point in the twenty-first century, a woman's body is basically a map of problems—most of it still only roughly sketched out, by guesswork, and appended with a series of ?????, or crude drawings of perimenopausal dragons with HERE BE MONSTERS—WE KNOW NOTHING ABOUT THEM written underneath, and by actual fucking experts. I assure you I am not exaggerating. Go and talk to a consultant about endometriosis—a condition where, every month, various parts of your body, up to and including your *lungs* and *brain*, can start menstruating.

He'll be like, "Whoa, that sounds harsh. I can . . . take your uterus out?"

That's not a *solution*, dude—taking away my fertility and entire hormonal apparatus. That's like me complaining about the terrible congestion problems in the Coventry one-way system—expecting a chat along the lines of "more buses" or "car sharing"—and hearing back, "I dunno. I could . . . *bomb it?*"

I want you to *make it better*—not *chuck it in the fucking bin.*

But women's bodies are, still, largely—like Coventry—a mystery no one wishes to solve.

Example: It's 10 a.m. Pete and the children have left the house for school. The building is empty. This, then, is my chance to have a bath without being interrupted by someone falling down stairs, asking for help to build a Great Wall of China for homework, coming in and doing a poo, or crying, "I THINK THERE MIGHT BE DEMONS UNDER MY BED. PLEASE SEND HELP I.E., YOU."

I pop on the radio—nothing like a bit of Melvyn Bragg's *In Our Time* to start the day. Cor! It's about Hildegard of Bingen! RESULT!

I run the bath. I get in. I wash. I get out. I dry myself off. Melvyn tells me how Hildegard managed to get away with writing and preaching ideas no woman in the twelfth century would otherwise have got away with, simply by claiming everything she said had come to her "as a vision from God." I make a note of this: "Could be useful re. putative American 'evangelical feminist' wing?" I get dressed.

And then, ten minutes later, as I put on my makeup, and with no warning—some water comes out of my fahnita. What is it? I smell the subtle yet unmistakable fragrance of Radox. Yes. There's no two ways about this—my genitals have honked up a good five hundred milliliters of bathwater, held onto it for ten minutes for reasons unknown, and now gently ejected it into my pants.

Now, I'm aware that my vadge, although a plucky thing, has had a great deal of wear and tear over the decades. You have two children and, as Indiana Jones says in the *Temple of Doom*—another possible title for a book about my vagina—"It's not the years, honey, it's the mileage."

In its life, I, a series of lovers, my children, and sundry GPs and gynecologists, have treated it in a way that, were I to witness them treating a handbag in the same way, I would shout, "Hey! Careful! You'll rip the lining!" It's been chucked around. It's been overstuffed. It's had things rammed into it, and things yanked out of it. I can't claim, with absolute certainty, it hasn't had a pot of yogurt burst in it, at some point.

And yet, it's had in no way an *unusual* life. Nothing that's happened to my vadge would make the six o'clock news, or even a mention on the local roundup on Radio WM. I refuse to believe I'm the only woman this has happened to. But, still—I have never heard of this bathwater thing happening to anyone else.

I do not tell anyone about this sudden development for ten years. *Ten years.* For a whole decade, I continue to witness this mysterious translocation of bathwater, and never mention it to anyone. I never hear of anyone else mentioning it—and I have a Google alert on for this kind of stuff.

The first time I finally speak of it is in 2015 in front of two thousand people. They've gone along with all the stuff I've said so far, so I suddenly, recklessly think, *maybe I'll launch the "Bathwater Mystery Story."*

There is a momentary gasp from the audience—where I think, *Oh God, I've fucked it. I've* finally *gone too far. It's* only me *with the bathwater! I have projected my unique vaginal sluice system onto the rest of womankind! No one else has a capillary muff problem!*—and then there is, thankfully, a massive bark of recognition that turns into a solid two minutes of laughter.

Wave upon wave—perhaps literally, depending on how recently *they* had had a bath—of women acknowledging, with relief, that this happens to them, too. You may imagine how reassured I was.

I felt that I could then go on to relay the worst time it happened to me—a year before, at 8 a.m. at the Hay-on-Wye literary festival, when I'd had a hasty, hungover bath, then come downstairs to do an interview on BBC *Breakfast.* Just as we were doing the countdown to going live, to millions, I felt the familiar *splooooooosh*—and looked down to see my lovely royal blue trousers telling a postbath story of their own. Thankfully, as it was a middle-class literary festival, I had come appropriately dressed—I was wearing an M&S 50 percent cashmere pashmina around my neck.

As we went on air, I simply draped this Trouble Curtain over my crotch and went on to be very eloquent about the fight for female equality—all accompanied by the relaxing fragrance of Badedas bubble bath, from the impromptu diffuser in my pants.

So here we have a genuine, unreported phenomenon, one that happens to many women, which has never been recognized or named. Having always wanted something slightly shaming named after me, I am keen to try and claim this one as my own. My dream scenario has always been a situation where my children are having to tell an official who their parents are.

Official: "Moran? As in . . . Moran's Bathwater Front-Bum-Bum Syndrome?"

My children, proudly, tearfully: "That was *our mother!*"

There are other suggestions, though; after gigs, people would approach me with their own views on what it should be called: The Punani Tsunami, The Bridal Wave, The Fud Flood, The Reverse Bidet. Or—and I think this one wins for me—The Vagina-Monologue Flume.

ANYWAY. THE REASON I'm giving my vadge a rinse is because today is a special day: it is Cervical Smear Day. As this isn't my first cervical smear rodeo, I'm aware there are ways to prepare for it that are to your advantage.

For the Smear of 2008, for instance, I foolishly wore a jumpsuit— meaning that, when I had to undress for the old Spatula of Curiosity, I was entirely naked, save for a bra. I was so cold and shivery I had to pop on my duffel coat. This meant I then lay there on the gurney, legs akimbo, looking like a weird, porno Paddington, who was encouraging the nurse to smuggle kitchen equipment somewhere awful.

The Smear of 2005 was enlivened by the fact that, the night before, I'd used a battery-operated pelvic floor exerciser, to strengthen my pelvic floor—only foolishly to put it in the wrong way and, somehow, severely electrocute my birth passage.

As a consequence, the next day, everything was still quite tender when the spatula went in, and I exclaimed "YAROOO!," like Yosemite Sam sitting on a porcupine..

And one does, of course, want to make one's vestibule seem vaguely habitable. You don't want to turn up with a wodge that looks like a Wookiee's dirty mitten, saying, "Sorry—got lucky last night.

Tell you what—you got any wet wipes? I can give it a quick going-over for you."

Consequently, and particularly since I've just had sex, I have a sub-To-Do List on my To-Do List, concerning today. It reads: "Rinse vag, good knickers, SEPARATE TROUSERS AND TOP."

Five minutes later—with my vagina on sparkling form, contained inside reasonable underpants, and accompanied by jeans and a shirt—I leave the house, to have my minge professionally surveyed.

ALTHOUGH SHE DOESN'T know it, Mrs. Adams, the nurse at the sexual health clinic, is my mortal enemy. I don't know which Sorting Hat gave her the job of "sexual health nurse," but it appears to have been faulty—as she has a weird vibe around vaginas. Every time I've had to offer mine up to her, for medical inspection—AS REQUESTED IN A VERY FORMAL-LOOKING LETTER FROM THE NHS—her reaction is as if I've just rocked up and randomly whacked it out, for no reason. There's a slight wince, a raising of the eyebrows—and then a sigh, as she politely tries to make the best of a bad situation. As if she's generally an elbow nurse, but she will humor my mad genital scheme today as part of her Hippocratic oath.

"Morning," I say, cheerfully, after my knock on her door is greeted with a weary "Come in."

"I've come to ruin your day with my Genital Safety Check!" I say.

Silence.

I enter the room and wait for her guidance on what to do. *Chair—or bed?*

She doesn't look up, just continues typing on her computer. I close the door behind me.

"Shall I sit down, and bring you up to date with all my vaginal gossip?" I ask, still hovering. "Or just hop on the bed, and bring out The Big Gun?"

She looks up—pained. She really doesn't like jokes. This is difficult—because I am a person who, if I am in a situation where

I am showing someone my genitals, *will* make jokes about it. Every single one of my nine ex-lovers can confirm this—plus my friend Caroline, who accidentally saw it, when she popped round unexpectedly to borrow a DustBuster charger.

"On the bed, please," she says.

I obligingly start to take my trousers off.

"No! Let's have some *privacy*," she says—springing up to draw a curtain across the room. "Oh, don't worry! I don't mind!" I say, cheerfully. "Once you've had twenty medical students watching you give birth, the idea of privacy dies." I don't want her to go to any trouble.

"It's for the *best*," she replies.

It's clear that the curtain has been deployed so my naked buttocks don't offend *her* eye. My arse is bad news.

Subdued, I take off my shoes, socks, and trousers, and pop onto the bed.

She appears from behind the curtain and surveys my half naked form.

"Put your heels together," she says, bringing out the speculum and applying a microscopic amount of lube to it.

"I'm happy to go for a second helping on that," I say, eyeing its potential dryness warily. "You can treat me. Date night."

She ignores me, and starts to pop it in. To all those who worry about getting a cervical smear, it's fine, really—just like having a narrow medieval scroll inserted into your flaps. And who hasn't done that? I do my relaxing deep breathing, in order to help it on its way.

"I saw, from your records, you're ten months overdue for this," Mrs. Adams says, disapprovingly.

"I know! I know! I'm so sorry! I feel terrible! But you know what it's like. I'm busy, my *vagina's* busy. It's hard to find a time when we can get our schedules to match," I say—but her chiding, plus visible wince at the word *vagina*, have made me tense up.

"Relax!" she says.

The only way I know how to relax is to be chatty, and so I start some chat that I think is appropriate to this time and place.

"As a medical expert," I say, as she slides the speculum in, "would you say I have a more than usual prominent mons?"

"I'm sorry?" she says, pausing.

"Camel toe. Do I have a massive camel toe? You've seen millions, I guess—so you can tell me where on the spectrum I land. Or, indeed, where on the *speculum* I land."

She looks at me like I'm losing my mind.

"It's like, I never see a mons like mine in popular culture," I continue. "When magazines do a swimwear special, it chooses models with special 'thin vaginas' that don't even fill a thong. But as you can see, I'm essentially *well hung*. If you did a swimwear special with *me*, I'd be filling the codpiece the guy from Cameo wore. On a good day, in the *right* trousers, I have to make a decision to dress to either the left or the right."

Whilst I muse on this subject, the nurse engages in a bit of argy-bargy with the speculum and my cervix—for thirty seconds, she apparently stirs my innards with a spoon—and then pulls the speculum out, before handing me a paper towel.

"You don't need to come back for three years," she says—making it sound less like a medical guideline and more like a personal plea.

I can't deny that I feel quite deflated. Ostensibly, yes, I'm here to just give her some cells—but, surely, it's great if I give her the odd chuckle and a bigger issue to ponder on, too? Seemingly not. She disappears back behind the curtain, sighing as if she's incredibly unhappy.

"Thank you," I say, quietly, and reach for my trousers.

I am middle-aged, and I have still not found a way to talk about my reproductive system that is acceptable. Or, to rephrase this, the medical system still has not yet realized that "having a ripe sense of humor" is actually medically vital for practitioners whose workplace is your genitals.

AT A CURSORY glance, one would believe that Western society has no problems with the reality of the female body. After all, no one is ever going to cry, "But where are all the scantily clad sexy young ladies and explicit acts of pornography! I can't find any anywhere! Perhaps we are running out of them!"

There are bums and boobies *everywhere*. You could put all the glistening, lithe upper thighs in a line and reach to the moon and back.

And yet . . . whilst we have the pictures, we don't have the *words*.

Whilst things might, admittedly, not be as bad as they were in Victorian times—where women were basically "a dress" with a head on top—one can see just how far we still have to go, as women still struggle to find an acceptable word for their most fundamental and defining part: their genitals. In 2012, Michigan Congresswoman Lisa Brown was banned from further debate in Congress after saying the word "vagina" *in a debate about contraception*—with Republican Congressman Mike Callton, saying the word is "so vile, so disgusting, that he could never bear to mention it in front of women or mixed company."

Whilst we might struggle to understand how lawmakers could debate human reproduction without mentioning the body parts *used* in reproduction—it's a bit like having a debate on the timber industry without mentioning the word "trees"—the sad fact is that even the "poshest" word for a woman's genitals is still a fudge. We have fought so hard for "vagina"—I bow my head now, in respect, to every feminist in the world who has spent the last ten years wedging her vagina into every conversation she can; amused by the reaction it causes. I see you all, women! You did good, good work!—but "vagina" isn't even the correct word. The Vagina War has been fought over the wrong territory.

Vagina describes the *inside* of your genitals—not what most of us mean when we hobble into a pub, wincing, order a double gin and cry, "I had to climb over a wall and banged my vagina!" Unless it really has been an exceptionally bad day.

Vulva is the correct word for the external genitals—but it's rarely, if ever, heard.

And how can we battle for equality—even invent a new thing or two—if we are still misnaming our fundamental physical attribute?

As a thought experiment, imagine how weird it would be if you read, in history books, how Alexander the Great insisted on referring to his penis as "my balls." He never, ever referred to his cock—he found the word horrible. Instead, everything in his pants was referred to as "my knackers." *You know what it's like—when you're pissing out of your knackers.* It just looks mad. A man who misnames his defining body parts looks like a man whose whole worldview suddenly becomes questionable. *How* could a fully grown adult man call his penis the wrong thing? So confidently? And the world just accepts it, *and* does the same? We would read history books whilst crying laughing.

Consequently, I've done the math, and I've estimated that—taking into account the mechanics of how linguistic change occurs—globally, we will have to say "vulva" a *billion* times, in public, for it to finally catch on. A billion vulvas. That's our target. That's the number at the top of the Vulv-O-Meter, in this week's Minge-Renaming Telethon. We need to wedge in at least one "vulva" a day—during a meeting, or whilst giving a reading for the gas meter on the phone—in order to affect proper genital progress.

In order to affect carefree ramming of the word into everyday conversation, I would draw your attention to the "Name Your Vulva" game that was so modish in 2018. The rules are simple: You ask everyone to reveal the title of the last film they saw—and that becomes the new nickname of their vulva. On the day we played it, Cecy's became *Carol*, Jen's was *Let the Right One In*, Nadia's was *Paddington*, and mine was *Mamma Mia! Here We Go Again*. All of them were oddly fitting.

CHAPTER FIVE

The Hour of Physical Acceptance

~☙~

11:00 A.M.

I STAND IN FRONT OF THE MIRROR AND LOOK AT MYSELF IN IT, NAKED.
Through some mad quirk of fate, I am a middle-aged woman with a
nonperfect body who still, nonetheless, *likes* her own body. My initial
instinct, on seeing my naked reflection, is to wave at myself whilst
smiling.

"Hiya!" I say, still waving. "How *you* doing?"

I wobble everything around, to amuse myself.

"Hurrah!" I say, to no one.

I can see all the parts of me that belong only in "before" pictures in articles about plastic surgery—the Womble-nose breasts
that point downward, one larger than the other; my C-section
scarred belly; the Malvern Hills of my hips and thighs—and I'm
fine with them. I've got some outfits it all looks good in, and I'm
reasonably certain I'll never be stopped in the street by a swimwear company, forced into a bikini, and then judged out of ten by
an international jury of Bum-and-Tits Inspectors—and so I can't
bring myself to be anything other than "generally supportive" of
my body. It's a friendly looking beast that gets the job done. That's
why I've just done it the favor of getting a smear test—got to take
care of Old Faithful!

The idea of *hating* it seems incredibly unkind; wildly out of pro-

portion to any crime it's committed—primarily, breaking wind—
and, yet, I know I am in a minority.

As far as I can see, for most women, disliking your body is the
default.

I can't work out why I don't have this default.

I regularly read features by women with bodies far smoother and
more symmetrical than mine, bewailing their horror with their appearance. They talk about themselves with something bordering on
terror—even as they stand there, looking unbelievably lovely. I feel I
must have missed an important meeting—one where my awfulness
would have been officially pointed out to me. I just haven't had those
feelings for decades now. I know that if I appeared on e.g., *Newsnight*,
and cheerfully said, as part of the conversation, "I think I look *ace*.
I'm pretty hot! I genuinely like my body!" that a huge proportion of
the people watching would think, *But—why? How?* and would then
take to Twitter to kindly point out to me how, with my saggy tum and
puddingy thighs, I am, simply, *wrong*.

It seems to be absolutely part of being a modern woman to feel a
constant *despair* over your own body. Every feminist comedian I have
seen launches into a familiar body-hating riff, which seems an almost
obligatory part of connecting with their audience—that it must be
established that however successful, funny, confident, and clever she
is, she has an Achilles' heel—her Achilles' body. There are a couple
of exceptions to this: the *Broad City* girls take it in turns to rhapso-
dize over each other's bodies—Ilana worships Abbi's brilliantly average arse—and, in more recent years, pop star Lizzo has demanded
joyous respect for her bounteous tits, thighs, and bummage.

But, by and large, otherwise badassy girls still insist they are literally badass: in that they have a "bad ass."

This is, fundamentally, bad lady juju—for it feels as though we've
got stuck halfway through a process. Admitting that—in a world
dominated by images of female perfection—we feel like we don't
come up to scratch is a useful and vital piece of truth telling. Of *course*
we feel inferior compared to supermodels and Instagrammers! And,
of *course*, it's amusing and relieving to describe or reveal the truth of

your own, imperfect body, in some manner of bonding ritual with other women who feel bad about *their* bodies, too.

But it can't, surely, just end there—for, once having admitted you feel bad about your body, the next thing to do is, logically, for the sake of your own happiness, find a way to feel better about it. All we are, at the end of the day, are bodies and minds—and if your mind is pained by your body, then you are, fundamentally, split down the middle: at war with yourself. It came as a mind-blowing revelation to me, in my late twenties, to realize that is an eminently possible option to decide that you just . . . love your body. After all, it's gonna be with you until you die. It's stuck with you, through literal thick and thin. It's on your *side*, man. It's where you keep all your . . . *you*. You just have to become a die-hard fan of it—like you are of, say, David Bowie. You love Bowie whatever he does. You acknowledge that he's done some shady shit—the Nazi salute, the mullet, Tin Machine— just as your body has done some shady shit, like cystitis, and "going floppy," and never looking good in cycling shorts. But you still *love* it. You need to be able to get drunk and rant about how amazing it is to your mates: "It lay naked in the garden yesterday, in the sun, and absorbed all this vitamin D like a fucking *boss*; and then it totally dug a border for an hour feeling all butch and *glorious*; and then it made this like *sweaty smell* that was oddly compelling, and I just had to keep sniffing how *awesome* I was?"

And then prompt your friends until they, too, admit that they love taking their body for a bit of Zumba, and then giving their body this fucking *amazing* apple, which it ate with all the joy of a pony in a field.

If we love giving a pony in a field an apple, we must love giving *us* one. Are we not as glorious as ponies?

Of course, it's little wonder women have so many problems with their bodies, when there are so many body parts that are seen as problematic. Indeed, the amount of body parts that can be problematic grow year on year.

For whilst we still might not yet be able to name body parts that do exist—the vulva—we appear to be creating names for body parts that *don't* exist at an astonishing rate. There are incredibly common words and phrases that you come across every day—online, in magazines, or in conversations—even though the things they are talking about *aren't real.* They're just not actual things. Can I say this any more emphatically? *It's entirely fabricated balls.*

Thus, the "muffin top" brings up 103 million results on Google—including the claim that drinking neat vinegar for breakfast will eliminate them, which suggests the writer is confusing "muffin tops" with "limescale."

One hundred and three million results are weird, because *muffin tops don't actually exist.* It's just your hips and belly. Just your hips and belly in some too-small trousers. Believe me. Look in *Gray's Anatomy.* Muffin tops don't exist.

Similarly, "back fat." It's not "back fat." It's just your back. It's literally just your back. It doesn't need a separate name, *because it's not a separate thing.*

"Knee overhang?" Allow me to clarify: no. It's not "knee overhang." It's just a knee.

"Cottage cheese thighs?"—them's your thighs, sister. That's how you be.

"Bingo wings—I mean, if they actually *were* wings, that would mean you would be the next stage in evolution, which would be something to be globally celebrated, and not covered with a Matalan shrug. As for "cankle"—well, even though calling a woman you hate the "Archbishop of Canklebury" is *momentarily* amusing, I think we can all admit that, in the long term, by using it, you're just ruining ankles for yourself and everyone else. Dude, ask not for whom the cankle tolls—for, one day, after six months in a posturally incorrect wedge and/or a good Christmas, it may toll for thee. It's just too *risky* to live in a world where you might, one day, look at your own ankle and think, self-loathingly, *That is a cankle! Shit! I have* cankulated!—for then, you have allowed *someone else* to be the voice in your head. *Someone else* has put a little explanatory caption beside the beautiful collection of things that are your body, and that is the beginning of a terrible process that can end up with you walking around, wholly alienated and distant from your body, and at risk for many self-loathing behaviors, ranging from self-harm to wearing midlength culottes.

Women slagging off other women for perceived physical imperfection is like farting in a spaceship: everyone on board suffers, including she who dealt it. I do not think you can truly love other women if you do not love your own body. It is urgent, urgent work—for both yourself, and womankind—to learn to love your own adorable legs and fully functioning arms. And you must *never, never, never* allow yourself to start seeing your body as a collection of separate, problematic items—cankles, muffin top, bingo wings, camel toe—for that is the tactic of a far-right polemicist: dividing a glorious whole into a series of sad, isolated ghettos, and then pitching them against each other *(I can't decide which is worse—my back fat or my bra overhang)*. It's all *you*, and it must, urgently, become your lifelong friend.

OF COURSE, AS any eager historian knows—and by "eager historian," I just mean anyone able to Google "Rubens"—what is considered a "desirable" female body is always a matter of fashion. Any one of a dozen feminist #bodypositive hashtags will show you side-by-side shots of a Juno masterpiece, or the Venus of Willendorf next to Ashley Graham or Tess Holliday—illustrating that what might be a "controversial" body shape now would have simply been described with an admiring "hubbana hubbana" in centuries gone by, or on a different continent. There is a growing awareness that there's no such thing as the "wrong" female body—just the wrong culture, or century. This is one of the reasons I'm glad there is finally a female doctor in *Doctor Who*. If, at any point, someone tries to belittle her about her legs, nose, or tits, she can simply fuck off in a time machine to an era where they're hot.

And the thing about certain body types being fashionable, is that things can change so quickly. For instance, in my lifetime, what constitutes a desirable bum has done a complete 180. When I was a teenager in the 1980s, the bum everyone gunned for was, essentially, the "Invisibum." Anything bigger than two boiled eggs in your jeans' back pocket was seen as something to despair over—every aerobics video showed some woman with a flammable, dry perm wielding the kind of microbum you could fit in a cup.

And then: the Kardashians. We could spend the rest of our lives analyzing the exact societal pros and cons that have come with the Kardashians becoming the most influential women on earth—*is spending eighteen seasons of a reality TV show crying into gigantic salads good or bad for women?*—but one thing we can absolutely credit them for is the rise of the Big Bum Empire.

The Kardashian sisters have taken sibling rivalry to a new and very specific place, in that there appears to be some kind of arms race—or, more accurately, a "bums" race—between them, in order to have the largest bot. Within the Kardashian milieu, the bigger the bum, the greater the power. It's almost as if the bum is a proxy for their wealth—like their arses are actually made of cash. Every season, they get bigger. To be a Kardashian is to be a Bum Farmer—raising a yearly crop of buttocks and taking them to market (Instagram) for "likes." And I can't pretend my massive bum hasn't been a beneficiary of all this. In the twenty-first century, I can say to my teenage daughter "My bum is *bigger* than yours," and she will cry, "Don't rub it in!" For people of my generation, this is, truly, a miracle.

What I find most vexing about the ebb and flow of "fashionable" female body types—suddenly being made into some physical extreme of one sort or another—is that we still trail wildly behind men in glorifying "normal bodies." In 2015, an American psychology undergraduate, Mackenzie Pearson, wrote a blog that coined the phrase "Dad Bod," in terms of an affectionate and celebratory lust.

"The dad bod says, 'I go to the gym occasionally—but I also drink heavily on the weekends and enjoy eating eight slices of pizza at a time.' It's not an overweight guy—but it isn't one with washboard abs, either." The dad bod, she notes, is the preferred physical type for her female friends.

"We call ourselves the 'dad bod squad.'"

The phrase went viral, is now in common parlance, and regularly prompts "Top Ten Dad Bod" charts, in which Seth Rogen, Matt Damon, Leonardo DiCaprio, and Denzel Washington are featured.

Personally, I'm really moved that a young woman—of the gender that has been dealing with impossible physical ideals for its entire existence—reached out to a generation of men becoming increasingly worried about *their* physical appearance, and said, "Guys! We've been here! Don't fall for it! We love you as you are! You had us at 'a reasonable level of fitness, but still up for spag bol!' We're even going to come up with a term to describe this kind of body, and then write endless blogs talking about how we like to put our hands on your round tums and go 'Wubba wubba wubba!' You will *not* feel as unhappy about your bodies as we do! We're going to do you a solid favor!"

"Dad bod" has genuinely changed the metrics on male attractiveness, and in the loveliest and most supportive way possible.

But this leads to a question. MEN! THIS PHRASE WAS COINED, FOR YOU, FIVE YEARS AGO. WHY HAVE YOU NOT RECIPROCATED WITH AN EQUALLY LOVING PHRASE TO DESCRIBE THE AVERAGE FEMALE BODY? WHY IS THERE NO "MOM BOD?" WHY, IF I HAVE TO DESCRIBE MYSELF PHYSICALLY, DO I HAVE TO RESORT TO "I'VE GOT A LADY DAD BOD?" WHY ARE THERE NOT HORDES OF YOUNG MALE BLOGGERS HYMNING THE PRAISES OF WOMEN WITH SLIGHTLY POUCHY BELLIES, BUMS LIKE A WOBBLY CUSTARD, CHUNKY MONSES, AND ADORABLY BATTERED TITS?

Don't leave us hanging! In 2019, John Legend—another man who scores high on the dad bod charts—was voted *"the sexiest man in the world."* And yet I can guarantee you there isn't a single chart of the sexiest *women* in the world that includes, say, Kate Winslet when she was a bit chunkier, or Meryl Streep in her dungarees in *Mamma Mia!* It's an absolute failure of both lexicon and chivalry, and I find it frankly *rude* that women are going around the internet captioning pictures of Jack Black in his underwear "HELLO FUTURE HUS-

BAND!," whilst men stay resolutely silent and uncreative about loving Amy Schumer in shit leggings.

Men need a to-do list, and they need to put this at the top—possibly ahead of world peace. Because there will *be* no world peace whilst 50 percent of the population feels bad about just having a body.

CHAPTER SIX

The Hour of Housework

꩜

12:00 P.M.

So, AWAY FROM MY BUM, AND TO THE OUTER WORLD: THE RUNNING of the household.

My brother Andrew lives with us now, for when life gives you Technically Homeless Sibling, you make Put a Sibling in the Attic-ade!

It matters not that I am a middle-aged woman steeped in nineteenth-century literature, with two children and two jobs; whilst he is an eighteen-year-old *Star Trek* fan studying for his A-levels. A sixteen-year age gap, and its ensuing cultural disparity, are but a mere bagatelle—for do not many of my male heroes regularly *marry* women much younger? So it must be, like, *fun.* Having a teenager in the house will be a unique opportunity to learn about a different, younger generation. I will gain a whole new set of reference points and skills. The cultural clash will be enlivening. It's like the beginning of a long-running sitcom. *Teenage Boy About the House. Very Different Strokes.*

The youngest of my seven siblings, Andrew is six feet four, with a shoulder-length bouffant mane of hair, and usually clad in a floor-length black leather coat—which I frequently have to steal while he's asleep, and Febreze all over, because floor-length black leather coats are very badly ventilated. The first thing I learned when Andrew moved in is that everyone in *The Matrix* would have ponged super bad.

WE MOVE HIM into the loft with his four bin bags of possessions—two of clothes, two of books—and he seems delighted.

"My *own* bathroom!" he exclaims. "Now I won't have to flush all the time!"

I gently explain to him how much plumbers cost in London, and how flushing *is* mandatory in the twenty-first century.

"You are financially responsible for all your own blockages," I conclude. "Your shit is on you. Possibly literally, if the toilet overflows."

This is an important lesson for any young adult to learn.

He Blu-Tacks his *Lord of the Rings* posters on the wall and stacks up his math and physics textbooks by the bed. His dumbbells are next to them. My loft office is gone. It is now a teenage boy's room.

"Pity about the old running machine," he says, sadly.

We declined to bring his secondhand running machine with him, as none of us could even get it out of my mom's house—let alone carry it up the four flights of stairs to our loft. It weighs approximately the same as a whale.

I'll have a gentle stroll on it, whilst watching Antiques Roadshow, my mother had said, eyeing it warily.

The next time I visited her, it had gone the way of all running machines—it was rammed up in the corner, draped with damp washing.

Our lives together are enlightening. He shows me how to slaughter Thrall's Horde of Undead Forsaken in *World of Warcraft*, and I show him the Toilet Duck bottle. He explains the Kanye West "fish dicks" joke on *South Park*, and I explain to him the problematic nature of intersectional racism and homophobia. In the evenings, the whole family gathers to play *Mario Kart*, and once we've explained to him that he can't shout "Motherfucker!" in front of the children whenever they run him off the road, it all goes swimmingly. I greatly improve my performance. Sometimes, I come seventh out of eight contenders.

The main thing I learn, however, is how different we are. Bewilderingly different.

TODAY, I'M IN the kitchen, trying to work. I'm very tired. Lizzie is ill, with a cough, and so, last night, as is often the case these days, I worked until midnight to hit all my deadlines. Today, having a cogent thought is like trying to push a marshmallow through a keyhole. My brain is floppy and peevish with exhaustion.

Andrew, however, is chatty.

He's standing by the oven, repeatedly dropping a tennis ball on the floor.

"Did that look like that was just falling straight to the floor to you?" he asks, excitedly.

"Yeah?" I say, staring at my laptop.

"Well, *you're wrong*. When it fell from my hand, its speed was actually *zero*. But as it fell to the floor, it *accelerated. Acceleration due to gravity.* Watch!"

I press save on the document. Andrew drops the ball again. I observe, patiently.

"I've got to say, it definitely looked like it was moving when it left your hand, dude."

"That's because it's only falling a *short way*. If I could drop it *a mile from Earth*, you'd notice the difference. Maybe I should drop it out of the bathroom window?"

He looks eager.

Andrew is preternaturally gifted at physics. All day, he sits at the table doing math equations using symbols I don't understand. Every so often, he tries to explain the symbols to me. He has tried, on many occasions, to teach me the basics of algebra. As I'm someone who didn't even learn their times tables, he might as well be explaining Mozart to the cat. I'm a words person.

"It's like *another* language," he says, helpfully—drawing things on the whiteboard as we try to eat dinner. "Once you crack the codes, you see the *entire universe* differently."

I can't crack the codes. I can't see things how he does.

MOVING IN WITH a family must be hard for him—for here, in my house, day-to-day, I am not the person he used to know.

When he was just a visitor—coming for Christmas on holiday—I was someone else. Off-duty me, having fun times, putting a keg of cider on the table and kicking back with chilled anecdotes.

"Do the dishwasher in the morning—we're on holiday!"

"Who has an anecdote about a cyst bursting? Me! I'll go first!"

When I made my offer for him to come here, he must have thought he was basically coming to live in the party scene from *Animal House*—albeit one with much nicer soft furnishings, and two small children incongruously hanging around in the background.

Now he lives here, and the holiday/party John Belushi-sister has disappeared. Day-to-day, I am no fun at all.

Instead, there is this slightly uptight woman who spends all day staring at her laptop and sighing like she's losing the will to live— and, yet, she doesn't seem to appreciate attempts to cheer her up with the intriguing conundrums of physics or algebra. If you try and suggest maybe she should take a break—"Go for a walk, or play *Mario Kart* for a bit. You deserve it!"—because she clearly needs one, she puts on a very pained air and says, "I won't be able to just 'go for a walk' for at least five years, Andrew. I'm working my way through an ever-lengthening to-do list," and then goes back to staring at the laptop, visibly pissed off.

Or, if she's not at the laptop, sighing, she's walking into the room with her lips pressed really tightly together, like she's trying not to shout, and says, "Well, *today* is end-to-end bullshit," and talks about how busy she is—but then does something weird, like paint oil onto all the kitchen worktops, or go and repeatedly stab the lawn with a garden fork, shouting about "drainage."

In the evenings—sitting in the perfectly nice front room—she'll suddenly leap up, and go, "WHO put the big overhead light on?," angrily click it off, and then spend four minutes going around turning on half a dozen tiny lamps, instead, muttering about "flattering sidelighting enhancing the mood." If she's so busy, why would she do that? It makes no sense.

Likewise, when she gets mad about the Stairs System. She's *obsessed* with the Stairs System. It's fucking *crazy*.

Every so often, there will be a bellow of outrage from the hallway—and then she'll come into the kitchen and say, in a way that's supposed to be humorous, but is clearly motivated by fury, "*Why* can no one get their head around the Stairs System? It's *perfectly simple*. If there's something at the bottom of the stairs—shoes, new loo roll, books—and you're going *up* the stairs, *take them with you*! Likewise, if there's something at the *top* of the stairs, and you're going *down*—take *them* with you! It couldn't *be* any more basic! It's like a funicular railway of *stuff*! Stuff goes up—stuff goes down! UP! DOWN! DOWN! UP! Why does *no one* but me *get this?????*"

And you, and your two little nieces, and your brother-in-law, will stare at her, and wonder why she's *so uptight all the time*.

Why is she worried about so many things? Why doesn't she just concentrate on work, and then chill? She just seems to . . . see things differently.

I SEE THINGS DIFFERENTLY.

IN LATER years—whilst still galloping up the stairs, my arms full of shoes, loo roll, and books—I have a sudden revelation about why my rants about the Stairs System meet with blank eyes from men; whereas, all the women I know yelp, "Yes! Yes! I do this too! The Stairs System! Why do men not *get it???*"

It's because we have been brought up in two utterly different worlds.

Living with my little brother allows me to see this—for, unlike previous boyfriends or my husband, I *know* what his life has been like. We were brought up in the same house, on the same income, in the same town. Really, if anyone were to see the world the same as me, it would be this man, whose DNA and upbringing I share. We come from *the same world*.

But we do not—even though we shared the same parents, and toilet. From birth, men and women are installed with *different software*. We are given different information. Our worldviews have totally different frameworks.

If you compare the pile of books and magazines by our beds, you see how this happens. When Andrew was thirteen, the floor by his bed was heaped with gaming magazines, and books about physics. He liked physics, his Xbox, and he read books and magazines solely about how to be good at physics—and about how to play Xbox.

He had no choice in this—there are no "general interest" magazines for teenage boys. A boy in a newsagent is faced with specialist titles—on music, gaming, fishing, film, martial arts, etc.—and so gains a worldview dictated by mono-interest, clannish communities, dedicated to becoming good at "a thing." In newsagents, this is made clear by simple categorization: "men's magazines" are racked together under the title "Men's Interests." Men have *interests*. You pick your thing; you dedicate yourself to it. You see the whole world through your specialist subject. You concentrate on becoming good at your thing—and that is how you become successful. This is the way of men.

By way of contrast, the newsagents' racks for female periodicals are titled "Women's *Lifestyle*." Men have interests—women have *lives*. Lives they must strive to *perfect*. As a consequence, the magazines heaped by *my* bed were there to guide me through a world where it was presumed I would have to become knowledgeable about a whole range of things that would give me not an *interest,* but a *life*. And a *stylish* life, at that. And *that* is how you become successful if you are a woman. By curating a whole *life*. By identifying problems in your house, wardrobe, body, job, relationships, and existence, and learning how to solve them.

Like most teenage girls, I was being given kind but firm information on a panoply of skills, which it was absolutely presumed I needed to master in order to succeed in the world—some lighthearted, some serious.

Here are the things I remember reading about, and regarding as deathly vital, in magazines bought from jumble sales like *Cosmo,*

Woman's Own, the *Lady,* Elle, *Sugar,* and *Jackie*; at the same age, Andrew was almost solely dedicated to learning to get to Level 47.

- How to get shiny hair by rinsing it in vinegar.
- How to protest against arranged marriages.
- How to calculate which Btu rating of radiator you need.
- How to give a good blow job.
- How to use leftover cabbage in six delightful suppers.
- How to deal with childhood eczema.
- How to arrange chairs in clusters of three, to encourage "informal chitchat."
- How to be wary of Scorpio men if you're a Cancer.
- How to get a "work-life balance."
- How to choose the best kitchen flooring.
- How to dress "day to night."
- How to get blood stains out of cotton.
- How to break through the glass ceiling.
- How to firm up your bust by splashing cold water on it, after a bath.
- How to counsel a friend through a broken heart.
- How to prevent pregnancy.
- How to get red-wine stains out of a decanter using a piece of lead shot.
- How to have a delightful collection of crockery that will bring elegance to a dinner party.
- How to grow a miniature garden in a bottle.
- How to report a rape.
- How to bathe a room in delicious, golden sidelighting that will make everyone feel amazing.
- How to curtsy.

At no point would Andrew have ever read anything about any of these subjects. And so, he has grown up in a world where he simply doesn't see these things.

In some ways, it's been a massive benefit to him—he, unlike several female friends of mine, has never decided not to date someone perfectly nice, just because they're a Libra. And his ability to dedicate himself solely to the things that he's good at, and which interest him, have meant he's really good at physics and Xbox. He's been accepted to study for a degree at UCL, and on *World of Warcraft*, he has a winged, armored horse, which is apparently a really big deal.

But the problems begin when men and women—raised in these different ways—start to interact with one another. We live in totally different worlds, with totally different aims and frameworks. The rules and objectives are at mad variance. We just don't have a fucking clue what the other guys are on about.

Yesterday, for instance, Andrew—a man—came home with a single, new cereal bowl that he found in a charity shop, and did not understand why I—a woman—was *furious* that he'd broken the Crockery Rules I *had* to learn when I was fifteen, reading *The Lady*.

"THAT BOWL—IT'S BREAKING UP MY CROCKERY SCHEME, ANDREW," I say, with a tight smile, as he holds it aloft in awe. "IT DOESN'T MATCH ANYTHING I HAVE. BUT NEITHER IS IT A DELIGHTFUL PIECE OF VINTAGE THAT I CAN BUILD A NEW COLLECTION AROUND. IT'S JUST A FUCKING WHITE BOWL, ANDREW. WHY IS IT HERE?"

"But . . . it's just the right size for my Shreddies," he says, confused. "And it was only one pound. I like it."

"BUT WHERE'S IT GOING TO GO, ANDREW?" I say, opening the crockery drawer, and dramatically pointing inside. "WHERE'S IT GOING TO GO? IT'S TOO BIG FOR THE 'SMALL BOWLS' PILE, AND TOO SMALL FOR THE 'BIG BOWLS' PILE. WE'RE GOING TO HAVE TO START A NEW PILE, ANDREW. A *NEW* PILE. FOR THE ONE ROGUE WHITE BOWL ON ITS OWN. THEY DON'T HAVE DRAWERS WITH ONE ROGUE WHITE BOWL IN THEM ON PINTEREST, ANDREW. I URGE YOU TO LOOK. THERE IS NO SOCIETAL TEMPLATE FOR THIS."

"I could . . . keep it in my room?" he says, looking both confused and frightened.

"I THINK THAT WOULD BE FOR THE BEST, ANDREW. YES. KEEP THE ROGUE BOWL IN YOUR ROOM."

Of course, for "single white rogue bowl," you can substitute "horrible La-Z-Boy armchair," or "disgusting pair of sneakers," or "horrible coffee table that matches nothing," or "mad choice of last-minute skydiving holiday." "Wrong" things that men will pick, which will infuriate the women in their lives—because the women have been reading expert advice on armchairs, sneakers, coffee tables, and holidays since they became sentient.

Women do not make sudden, snap decisions about things. We have been taught to believe there is a best practice for everything that needs to be done—that there are *rules*—and that adhering to this best practice prevents problems further down the line. We will have worked out our "armchair personality type," constructed a Pinterest board of our favorite kinds of armchairs, got advice on armchairs from Mumsnet, and planned to buy the perfect armchair in two years' time—*after* we've redecorated the front room. We will have found out the (a) safest, (b) easiest to clean, and (c) most versatile type of armchair, and be slowly working toward it, on a long-term plan.

Whereas men just see a thing—on sale, or possibly in a dumpster—think, *I like that. It will do,* and it would never occur to them that their girlfriend/wife/sister has been thinking about armchairs since she was thirteen, and has a long-term armchair plan, which he has now just utterly set fire to, with his spontaneous shit chair. For who thinks like *that?*

WOMEN. WOMEN THINK LIKE THAT.

If you are a man reading this, and you want to test if this is true or not, go up to any woman—*any woman*—and ask her if she has, say, a particular "aesthetic" about cushions. Or what her "beliefs" are about coat hangers—*no wire hangers. NO WIRE HANGERS!!!* Or which school of thought she comes from re. towels. White, colored, patterned, tasseled—or, Monica from *Friends-style,* a complex categorization system that matches a particular towel to a particular guest, room, and/or task?

Never try to do something spontaneously "for the house"—

women have been planning that shit since before you were *born*. They are working toward a to-do list they started in their teens. A to-do list that will lead to a perfect life.

I tried to explain this to another brother, Eddie, when he came round to my place, six months into his first relationship.

"Women are always doing mad things—like hoovering curtains, or . . . moisturizing their elbows," he said, bemused and also slightly alarmed, sipping on a beer. "It's just *weird*."

As he said it, I could see why these things seemed random. Men have *never* been taught to look at a curtain, or an elbow, and think of it as a problem. They don't live in a world of five-page to-do lists.

That is their power.

That is also, sometimes, their downfall. Because life is long, and it involves . . . other people.

I AM, IF I'm honest, constantly, quietly furious with Andrew—*for being Andrew*.

When he moved in, I had a wonderful vision of how life with him would pan out. His advent would mean the addition of a third, magical, part-time parent—quietly seeing what needed doing, in the day-to-day running of the house, and lifting some metaphorical weight, when he'd finished cranking his actual thirty-kilogram dumbbells.

That there would be days I'd come downstairs, exhausted from a night of tending ill children, and find he'd magically tidied the kitchen and laid the table.

The evenings where I'd finish work and find him taking some oven chips and Quorn nuggets out of the oven, saying, *Welcome to Andrew's Café!*

The weekends he'd come into the front room—where I was hunched over a pile of paperwork while the kids were hitting each other with cushions—and say, "What say old Uncle Andrew takes the young uns to the zoo! Kids—fancy getting some hot penguin action?," and I would weep with fond gratitude as he ushered them out of the house for a few hours.

I'd even imagined him coming home with a bunch of flowers, one evening—going, *Daffodils! How jolly! And only a pound! Who knew you could buy such radiant beauty for a single coin of the realm!*

I have imagined such a brilliant Andrew. I have imagined a brilliant, *female* Andrew.

I have imagined, basically, *me* at his age. In my teenage years, I was basically a third parent to my seven younger siblings. I roasted my first chicken when I was ten; I mowed the lawn every week (except for the sad month after I accidentally mowed a frog's leg off. Did you know frogs scream when they have a leg mowed off? They absolutely *wail*. I was like Clarice with the lambs. Haunted. The lawn grew very long before I could shake off the trauma and wield the trusty old Flymo again).

I made soups, stews, and bread; I experimented with turning leftover spaghetti into Spaghetti Pancake-ios (a dismal failure, in need of much cheese and ketchup). I took the kids to the library, the park, and into the field at the back of our house to play hide-and-seek in the hay. I told stories and made magazines; I stopped tantrums and night terrors; I made birthday cakes and threw birthday parties; I cleaned toilets; I bought stocking fillers from jumble sales and made endless mince pies; I got a job at sixteen and bought bunk beds, shoes, coats.

I did what girl-children have done since time immemorial—I took over what parts of running a household I could, as soon as I could, because I had read all the books and magazine articles about how to do this, and learned the tricks, and I then took pride in making things better. I saw problems, and I fixed them.

Yes, some days—mopping the kitchen floor, wiping mouse poo out of a cupboard, scrubbing the tannin stains out of the stainless steel sink—I would do some Cinderella-like sighing and think of all the American teens I saw on TV, who spent most of *their* sink-scrubbing time fretting about the prom; but I had been raised on *Jane Eyre, Anne of Green Gables, Little Women*. I knew to be a girl was to work in the home because homes do not make themselves. They must be made by someone. So why not take that power, and be the one who changes things, for the better? I took pride in being a thirteen-year-old girl who knew how to nurse a toddler though a fever; mend a torn buttonhole; make a gloomy, overcrowded bedroom look cheerful by stringing up some fairy lights, pushing all the mess under a younger sibling's bed, and then threatening them if they made a fuss.

I knew all these skills would be useful later in life—when I had children, and a household of my own. I knew that "running a home" was a complex mechanism, with a million different tricks and knowledges to it, and I felt a bone-deep security in knowing that none of it was mysterious to me. I could do *all* of this. I was capable. I enjoyed being capable. I liked making things better—for pets, for children, for "The House." I liked seeing how I could improve things. I knew none of this practice would be wasted.

When I went to other people's houses, I saw them for what they were: a million decisions, purchases, problems solved, routines. I quietly applauded them in my head, for that gently glowing lamp, that pan that was exactly the right size, the prize-winning coziness of their curtains, that exemplary shoe rack, bath-time routine, herb garden, dog.

But when Andrew walks into a house—specifically, *this* house—he does not see this mechanism. He might see how gravity works on a falling orange—but he doesn't see how the carpet stays clean. He can imagine, and describe, an event horizon two hundred million light-years away—its formation, its consequences—but he could not imagine and describe how his two nieces have learned, over endless months that felt as long as two hundred million light-years, to say "please" and "thank you." There are no books and magazines, or blogs for teenage boys explaining this. He does not understand how this world—the world of domestica—works. And so, everything that both wearies me, and makes me proud, is invisible to him. He does not see what I do. Ninety percent of what I am does not exist to him. This is what feminism means when it talks about the "emotional workload" and the "second shift." These jobs that women see and men, largely, do not.

And in Andrew—in this inability to see the ultraviolet spectrum of house, home, garden, and childcare—I can see my friends' boyfriends and husbands, when *they* were teens. Living with a worldview that will abruptly clash when they enter into long-term relationships. Andrew just accepts everything domestic as "the way things work," without understanding or questioning—in exactly the same trusting way I accept gravity and event horizons existing, without questioning or understanding. We are different.

This revelation reminds me of the fourth, and last, unspoken mystery that happens within the sealed citadels of marriage—the mystery of "What are you thinking? *Really?*"

WHAT ARE YOU THINKING? *REALLY?*

This is, perhaps, the question I ask Pete the most—outside of "Is the boiler *supposed* to be making that noise?" and, on the phone, "Are you near the shops?"

Whenever he is quiet, or thoughtful—whenever I see him staring into the middle distance, or frowning at something—I utter the most recurrent phrase of wives everywhere: "What are you thinking? *Really?*"

Here we are just last week, driving up to see his parents in Birmingham. I am in the car, feet up on the dashboard, and I am aware Pete hasn't said anything for half an hour. He has a look of deep concentration on his face. He is, clearly, giving me a signal that he is thinking about something. I am going to find out what, like a good wife should!

"How you doing?" I say, to open proceedings.

"Good. Bit rainy."

"Do you need anything?"

He thinks.

"Can I have another plum?"

"Of course!"

I give him the plum, from our customary Travel Bag of Plums, with a flourish. I leave another pause. Then:

"So—what you thinking?"

"That these plums are nice?"

I look at him. He still has the look of deep thought on his face, and has been silent for *so long*. I prompt him again.

"You can say *all* the things you're thinking, you know. I'm ready for it. It doesn't just need to be about plums. I'm ready for a heated debate!"

"That *is* everything I'm thinking!"

He seems almost indignant at my accusation that he is withholding his true feelings.

I, on the other hand, now feel edgy. This *can't* be all he's thinking. It can't! He's been silent for half an hour—he must have had *nine thousand* thoughts in that time. And if he's not sharing them with me, they must be . . . *secret* thoughts. Or ones that need cajoling out. By me, his extremely loving and now slightly paranoid wife.

"Are you . . . *worried* about something?"

"No. It's quite rainy, that's all. I'm having to concentrate on the road."

Fucking hell—this guy is really holding out on me. Deliberately. This is some mad mind game. I'm not going to engage. I'm now withdrawing.

"Fine," I say, a little too briskly, and turn the music up.

"Have I done something wrong?" Pete asks, alarmed. "What have I done? I'm just driving! There's nothing going on! I swear! I just like plums!"

"*It's fine,*" I say, singing determinedly along to Aztec Camera, and feeling . . . like I so very often do. Like he's obviously not telling me what he's *really* thinking.

"WHAT ARE YOU *really* thinking?"

Women are constantly asking men what they're thinking. And their reply never makes us happy.

For the first decade of our marriage and parenthood, I would regularly ask Pete, "What you thinking?"—mentally clearing the next half hour to engage enjoyably with his reply—only to feel terribly let down and uneasy when he would reply, "That it's a lovely day!" or "That I am happy!" or "I think I will be . . . hungry in half an hour?"

I simply could not believe these answers. Clearly, they could not be true—they were obviously tactical, defensive replies, which indicated Pete was not ready to say what he *really* felt *yet*. I must *dig deeper*—making it clear to him he was in a safe space. He could now spill the fears, dreams, secrets, and plans, which he had repressed for decades, until now—in this queue for the cheese counter at Morrisons, where he could open up to me, his loving wife.

And so, for the first ten years of our marriage, my tender, engaged inquiry of "What you thinking?" invariably heralded a tense half hour or so of me meeting his "That I'm a bit sleepy?" with "Okay! *Now* we're cooking! Do you think we should get a new mattress? There's a deal on at the moment. I can order us one now! Or, do you think it's more *psychological*—and that you're worried about the kids? Three nit infestations in a month *is* quite high," and he would reply, confused, "No: I just woke up for a piss at 3 a.m., and it took me a while to fall back asleep."

And I would be convinced he was lying.

This tetchy, mutually bewildered impasse continued for years until, one day, we watched a Jerry Seinfeld stand-up DVD, and his bit about "What men are really thinking."

"I know women don't understand men," Seinfeld says, amiably pacing the stage. "I know they're looking at me right now, going, 'I wonder what's going on in that brain?' I bet women would like to know the honest truth of what men are thinking. I bet you'd like to know *right now*. *Well,* shall I tell you what men are *really* thinking?"

The audience roars—men and women alike, high and low whoops. They wait. *Here it comes! This is the big one! What's he going to* say?

"*Nothing,*" Seinfeld says, standing stock-still, and staring out at the audience. He looks at them for a long, long pause. "We're not thinking . . . *anything*. We're just . . . walking around, looking at stuff."

There is a small pause—and then a huge, deep, bass affirmative man roar from the crowd. A truth has been spoken! Jerry has spoken the truth! The men rejoice! The high sounds of women, however, are missing. They are, clearly, in total shock.

"This is the only natural inclination of men!" Jerry continues. "Just kind of . . . checking stuff out. We work because they *force* us to, but other than that—this is really the only thing we want to do."

The men in the audience were still wildly applauding, and the women in shock, when my husband paused the DVD, then pointed— dramatically, for him—at the TV screen.

"It's true!" he said, in between relieved, hysterical laughter. "It's TRUE! That's it! We're just dogs, sniffing around! We're not thinking *anything*! Oh, Jerry, I love you."

He pressed play on the DVD again, and we carried on watching, and laughing. I felt enlightened—if this really *was* true, and it seemed to be, this solved a massive mystery; *plus*, saved me another three decades of harassing my husband, in the car or at the cheese counter, to tell me secrets he didn't actually have.

But as we continued watching, I was also aware that this posed a whole new question: why do all women who *haven't* seen the Seinfeld routine presume men are sitting there, heads bursting with a billion secret plans—thinking, thinking, thinking, ceaselessly, and surely eager to, finally, say all these things out loud?

The answer is quite sad: It's because *we* are. Ask a woman about *anything*—crockery, Scottish camping holidays, the best way to train a dog, how to get home from Vauxhall at 2 a.m. safely, what her plans are in the event of the total breakdown of society—and you will prompt a lengthy, thoughtful speech on her tactics, beliefs, experiences, research, and future plans. On a million subjects—some big, some small; some serious, some utterly ridiculous—women are always thinking, thinking, thinking. It never stops. Show me a woman frowning whilst hoovering, and I will show you a woman thinking about how best to set up an ISA for her niece, in case her unreliable father runs away with that strange woman she saw him with at Walmart last week.

We don't daydream. We *dayplan*. We think, think, think, and plan, plan, plan, *endlessly*—because we know women must. We are aware that we are the half of the world that is generally poorer, and weaker, and busier. We know we so often only get one chance to prove ourselves—one hour to achieve something, one opportunity to change things—and so we want to be *absolutely ready* for it. We don't want to be caught on the hop, because we don't have the time, money, or power to rectify a mistake further down the line. We know that when a door opens, it usually only opens once—study after study has shown that women, along with people of color, are far more likely to be demoted, or fired, when they make a single mistake compared to white men. And that when disaster hits, as with Coronavirus, it's women who are disproportionately affected: precarious, part-time jobs—the majority of which are done by women—put them most at risk. Domestic abuse rising. Children to be fed, educated, amused, and counseled through their fear.

This is why we game plan *everything*. It's why we know our future children's names when we're six, and the wedding we want at ten, and what kind of cottage we want to retire to by the age of sixteen.

We are preparing because, when the crisis comes, we know it is women who will usually be the ones confided in, will be the ones asked for money, or shelter, or advice, and we must always be ready to spring into action.

We know that when a child, or friend, opens up, we need to be attentive, on point—mumbling, "Wow, I don't know what to say—I've never really thought about this" could prompt them to clam up again, and the opportunity will be lost.

Women plan years into the future—*because they have to*. Our lives are big, slow-moving ships, laden with responsibilities and consequences—pregnancy, attack, abandonment, demotion—and so our constant thinking, thinking, thinking is because we are always ready for the alarm bells to ring, or our moment to come. We were raised like this. We know no other way. We are so used to thinking like this that we think it's normal. And it is—for 52 percent of the population. We are, essentially, in a constant state of alarm. Panic. *Readiness*. It's why, in an emergency, it is almost always the women who step forward, take over, say: "I know what to do." When the world falls apart, it's women who put it back together again.

I think, often, what we really mean when we say, "What are you thinking?" is "Ask *me* what I'm thinking." If they have the time to listen to the entire contents of a woman's head spill out, like a piñata, in a never-ending monologue that lasts from London to Solihull.

Thankfully, Pete does have that time. Now I've said all this to him. Now I've explained to him what *women* are thinking when they ask, "What are you thinking? Really?"

CHAPTER SEVEN

The Hour of Missing the Children

1:00 P.M.

FIVE HOURS. THAT'S ALL IT TAKES. JUST FIVE HOURS.

At 8:30 a.m., I am desperate for the children to leave the house.

By 1 p.m., I miss them again.

This is the push and pull of young children. Wishing them away. Wishing them back again. It's either too much—or never enough. Parenting small children often makes you feel like Richard Burton married to Elizabeth Taylor. She drives you to distraction when you're with her—always *wanting* things, always arguing, always creating drama—but, every time you get divorced, you end up staring out of the window, sighing, "You know what? I miss that crazy bitch. It's no fun without her."

AND OF COURSE, both your child and Elizabeth Taylor, are the most beautiful things in the world.

I LEAVE MY laptop to go to the loo and, afterward, without even realizing what I'm doing, I find myself wandering into the girls' bedroom, like a lovesick homing pigeon.

The floor is covered in Barbies—all rammed into Pete's shoes, in lieu of proper Barbie cars. There are *Doctor Who* stickers all over the windows; a small Dalek in a dress; and, taking up half of Lizzie's bed, a giant bear she won at a fairground. We call it, privately, "Inconveniently Fucking Massive Bear." She calls it, perhaps more leniently, "Teddy."

A child's bedroom when the children are gone is a melancholy affair. This is because, when they are here, it's a room full of *action* and *incident*—small people leaping off beds, bursting out of cupboards, putting the entire contents of your jewelry box onto their heads, making cauldrons of "potion" with shampoo, and starting sentences with "Imagine that . . . that whole wall is on *fire*, right."

So when they are gone, it's like an abandoned film set, when everyone's left for lunch. Everything paused. Everything empty. Everything silent. The animating force has left the puppet dragon in the corner. The stars have left the building. You fully feel the velocity of their lives when you look around the empty shell they leave. The only thing that cures this sorrow is when they return.

But, two hours after you greet them, hungrily, on the doorstep—as one starts weeping about an aching leg, whilst the other demands you find their storybook and do *all* the voices, and the pot on the stove boils over, and the emails stack up—you are back into the frenzy of despair again that it *Just. Doesn't. Work.* There is something inherently, structurally unstable about parenting. It's a circle that can't be squared. The children are the problem, and the cure. They are the thing that makes the sadness—and the only thing that can relieve it. All your other comforts, and support mechanisms, have been blown away. They are the alpha and the omega. They are everything.

I think of how Pete's dad constantly nags us to go and visit him, in Birmingham—then retreats to his shed an hour after we arrive, moaning about the noise. "It's too much!" And then how, when we try to leave, we find him fussily, inconveniently changing the oil on the car—desperately trying to delay our departure by a few more minutes. "Drive carefully! Do not speed!"

In this messy vignette, you see how your children's presence and absence is still unmanageably dementing—even when you are seventy-two, and your child is fifty.

It's too much. It's never enough. And yet, at the end of a day where it has been "too much," you finally lie in bed, and try to work out *why* it was too much—and you can't really remember what actually happened, or why it was so dementing. On paper, you simply woke them, dressed them, fed them, played with them, washed them, and put them to bed—but at the time, it felt like you were some kind of explosion farmer, barely coping with a constantly detonating field. Why is it so intense? What is *happening* in those hours?

I lie on Nancy's bed, and have a small mom cry about how much I miss her—inhaling her greasy puppy smell from her pillow—even as I look at my watch, in fear, and realize she will be back in two and a half hours, and two and a half hours isn't enough time to do what I need to do, which is everything. *Go away! Come back!* Who is it that can say these things, passionately, within seconds of each other, and mean them both equally? Parents, and children.

Also, shepherds with their dogs, of course—but I don't want to confuse things here.

SEVERAL YEARS LATER—WHEN the children are teenagers, and I have fractionally more time for luxurious things like "thoughts"—I look back on the years of having small children, and realize what this paradoxical situation most echoes: drug addiction.

No one really talks about the chemical elements of parenting—but when you think about it, it is what underpins everything. Humans are, essentially, bags of chemicals. We chose our mate on their smell—their hormones subliminally whispering to us in a Neanderthal grunt, "This man make good babies with you."

Then, when a women gets pregnant, what is created in her uterus is, essentially, a living hormonal implant emitting random amounts of fuck knows what into her system, rewiring her entire body and brain in a massive hormonal pyroclastic blast that she never fully recovers from.

Oh, all the videos, and books, and movies, show a gradually swelling woman being kind of cute in her new weirdness—eating fifteen bananas a day, crying at adverts with baby squirrels, and falling asleep in the middle of dinner—and just go, "Ho, ho, ho. New mom!"

But if you put all those actions into a movie about Jonah Hill going on a drug bender, or Cheech & Chong hitting the doobies, you'd see New Mom Stuff for what it is: someone absolutely off their face. These are movements of someone who is *wasted*. Mom just smoked a baby.

Studies are only just starting to delve into the chemical relationship between children and their parents. A recent one showed that children emit such powerful chemicals that you don't even have to get pregnant with one to get high off it—the more time fathers spend with their children, the more prolactin and oxytocin they produce, and the more their testosterone levels drop. In short, children chemically induce gentleness and love in the people around them. The plot to *Annie* is true! We're *all* Daddy Warbucks—going from "snarling Wall Street titan" to singing "And how she was almost my baby / Maybe" whilst holding her nightie. Kids are like MDMA with arms and legs. Children turn all your emotions up to eleven. As author Elizabeth Stone said, "Having a baby is to decide forever to have your heart go walking around outside your body."

And so, it surely correlates that the cold, fretful, empty sadness you feel when you are apart from your child is down to missing out on those massive oxytocin blasts. Your kids have got you properly addicted to that warm, opiated, "Everything is all right so long as I can sniff your head" feeling—and when they're gone, you are, essentially, going cold turkey. By my reckoning, you start jonesing for your kid roughly two and a half hours after they last hit you with those sweet, sweet hormones. When you go into their room and sniff their pillow, you're essentially like a junkie, licking an empty wrapper—desperate for just a taste of that baby calm. It's funny how parents have to pretend they are the sober, sensible ones in a parent-child relationship, when in reality, we are absolutely, chemically hooked on them. They are the dealers to your *soul*. Your child is your The Man.

This is also why, even though days with small children feel so hectic and intense, when it comes to actually relaying what happened, you get a minute into your anecdote, falter, and go, "Ah—maybe you just had to be there." Stories about caring for children are *exactly* like stories about when you're on drugs. You're trying to describe a *feeling*. Nothing really *happened*. And whoever you're telling the story to is bored senseless. Unless they are another addict, too. That's why parents can only really ever talk to other parents. We're just junkies, swapping stories with each other.

The thing about children being drugs, though, is they're not just *one* drug. It's not *just* the oxytocin—the physical, *dreamy* highs and crippling comedowns. No—for the aspect of pregnancy and motherhood I find to be least chronicled is what an intensely *psychedelic* experience it is. Honestly, gestation, birth, and early motherhood are as wiggy as drinking ayahuasca in the rainforest, naked, wearing a headdress of feathers and mud. It is *crackers*. Anything Hunter S. Thompson has ever described—as he drove across America, spending thousands of dollars on drugs, and hallucinating insects—is dwarfed by the average pregnancy, birth, and early childcare years experienced by millions of seemingly normal women, all currently wandering around and touching the bootees in JoJo Maman Bébé.

Really, it is one of those things where one wonders, anew, at just how great women are at Dealing With Things, Keeping Their Mouths Shut, And Keeping Their Shit Together—that all the imagery around motherhood is, still, flowery dresses, reasonableness, and calm—rather than the reality: some lysergic mix of *Alice in Wonderland, Yellow Submarine,* and *Trainspotting.* You literally lose your mind.

During my Baby Breakdown, I oscillated through many exciting possibilities—including a six-month conviction that we should move to Swindon; the belief that new, new baby might have been sent to save the world: just in some *minor* way, like "by inventing a new kind of electricity"—and the simple knowledge that I *had* to purchase a 14' x 4' canvas, and then paint on it, in oils, our garden, in all four seasons.

My husband found me weeping over the canvas at 11 p.m., distraught that I'd already painted in all the tulips: "I should have started with all the evergreens first—they're the backbone of the planting!"

"You do know," he said gently, "that you are a completely mad bitch right now, don't you?" He prised the brush and palette from my hand, then sent me to bed.

After we had our second child, I knew I didn't want to get pregnant again—but became convinced that we should adopt a whole family of five children, "So the siblings weren't split up between other families."

"I know what it's like to come from a big family! *You have to keep brothers and sisters together!*" I wept, looking at photos of children in care in the local council's magazine. Five children. I wanted to adopt five children. This emotional state of "too much" ended when my husband—a continuingly wise man—bought us two kittens from Battersea Dogs & Cats Home, and I poured all my excessive mothering instinct into making them a two-story "cat palace," which they roundly ignored in favor of unfailingly wishing to sleep on my laptop keyboard instead.

This is why there is a rule that should be enforced with iron—never to judge a woman who has a child under the age of three. However dizzy, unreliable, or straight-up weird my friends are, if they gave birth within the last thirty-six months, I absolutely give them a pass. You're not in your right mind.

And of course—how could you be? What *is* normal? What *is* your right mind? You've no way of knowing! You grew *a whole human being, right next to your liver, then pushed it out into the world through a hole that's clearly not fit for purpose!* And then, right, *your tits turned into food.* Your brain's baseline for "normal" is absolutely shot to shit. You *are* Alice in Wonderland. Motherhood is literally the practice of doing ten mad, impossible things before breakfast. Your Overton window of sanity has been inverted, painted orange, and relocated to the ceiling.

And the psychedelic aspect of motherhood—that temporary, LSD-like, absolute destruction of your sense of "self"—is a key part of the whole process because your baby *has* to rewire you. Every element of who you are needs to be blasted into the air, and then the pieces reassembled in ways you never imagined. Previous neat freaks *have* to be remolded into people who can buff poo off a tiny bumhole whilst singing a song; introverts *need* to be able to make small talk with twenty other mothers at toddlers' birthday parties; the rigidly modest *have no choice* other than to whop out a massive tit on a bus, in order to stop a tiny person wailing themselves inside out on the 261 up Holloway Road.

You might have made another human being—but they, in turn, make you into a mother. You are being reassembled around them. *They* are your center now. They're at the very heart of your system; they're your core processor. It's a symbiotic relationship conducted entirely, for the first few years, through chemicals and screaming. Your mentor weighs eight pounds and doesn't know any words—and yet they are training you to be what is needed, now; or else they will become endangered, or even die. They're like tiny Yoda on Luke's back, in the swamp, hitting him with a stick, and telling him to use the Force.

GIVEN THAT THIS is an easily observable fact—which has been going on for tens of thousands of years, in the lives of billions of women—it is bizarre that there is no storytelling archetype for this. Whilst writing this, I spent hours trying to think of narratives that touch on this—in the same way we have folktales, fairy tales, novels, and movies about, e.g., falling in love, coming of age, rebelling against tyrants, or going on journeys of discovery.

Why is there no cultural shorthand for how absolutely motherhood changes you? The physical and mental rewiring—often spectacular, and deeply strange—that allows us to become something patient, inventive, and strong enough to give ourselves utterly in service to those whose lives depend on us.

It's only now—frying onions whilst ordering secondhand curtains online—that I suddenly realize: this story *does* exist in our culture. Indeed, it's the most popular and overused story in twenty-first century Hollywood—it's just you won't notice, because they switched the genders. They make it happen to men, instead. Because it's the plot of every superhero movie ever made.

Consider the structure. An otherwise normal man experiences some substance—something radioactive, or else some mysterious thing, from space—and suddenly undergoes a massive physical transformation. He can make web shoot from his wrists, or shoots lasers from his eyes, or becomes incredibly strong.

Well, there is no other human experience in which a person absorbs a substance, and is then *turned into something completely physically different*, than pregnancy. Once a woman absorbs that spunk, she grows an extra *organ*, and another pint of *blood*; her heart swells. Instead of being able to emit web, or lasers, she starts producing *milk*.

The similarities continue: Superheroes know that, with great power, comes great responsibility. They all realize that their transformation means they must, now, become the protectors and saviors of humanity. Everything else—romantic relationships, jobs, personal lives—must, now, be put aside, at great cost, in order to be on call for weaker, troubled human beings 24/7. OH MY GOD—THAT IS BEING A MOTHER.

Superheroes regularly suffer seemingly crippling injuries that would stop anyone else in their tracks—yet somehow, mysteriously, carry on. OH MY GOD, THAT'S YOUR FOURTH-DEGREE PERINEAL TEAR!

Their work is never finished—there is sequel after sequel after sequel after sequel. OH MY GOD, THAT IS WHY YOU ARE SO FUCKING KNACKERED. BOTH A WOMAN'S WORK AND BATMAN'S IS NEVER DONE. THERE'S ALWAYS SOME FUCKING JOKER YOU HAVE TO VANQUISH.

Superheroes can only really hang out with other superheroes, as they're the only ones who understand what they're going through: YOU ONLY REALLY TALK TO OTHER PARENTS NOW!

And the mission of *all* superheroes isn't to gain power, or learn who they are, or find new things—but, simply, to protect innocent human life. I mean, it couldn't be any more obvious. Humans are babies, and superheroes are mothers. Their only purpose in life, ever, is to save the stupid breakable human children-babies, who keep doing dumb things.

The most poignant similarity is that no human ever knows who superheroes *are*. They *never* know how hard they work. There they are, saving millions of lives, every day—but the inhabitants of Gotham or Los Angeles never *thank* Superman or the Hulk. They have to keep their heroism absolutely secret from people—they have to assume the persona of a slightly idiotic buffoon, or an eccentric, in order to not blow their cover. THAT'S YOU, YES YOU, THE ONE DRESSED UP AS A FAIRY—WITH YOUR FACE COVERED IN STICKERS—SINGING, "THE WHEELS ON THE BUS," EVEN THOUGH YOUR DAY JOB IS RUNNING THE BANK OF ENGLAND!

Observe the relationship between Lois Lane and Clark Kent—where Lois thinks Clark is a lovable idiot, and frequently rejects him; yet, he watches over her and saves her life, time after time, without her even knowing—and you are watching Hollywood's mad homage to the relationship between mothers and small children.

So this is why the mothers of small children feel weird at 1 p.m., when the children have gone, and you have time, but not time enough, and you can't work out why it all feels so impossible, yet so intangible. You are Spider-Man, lying on the bed of the thing that built you, and to which you are cripplingly physically addicted—but when people tell your story, they pretend it all happened to twenty-one-year-old Tom Holland, instead. Mothers are all superheroes. But it would never work the other way round—Batman could never, *ever* potty-train twins.

CHAPTER EIGHT

The Hour of Working Parenting

❧

2:00 P.M.

THIS IS, OBVIOUSLY, THE EASY BIT. I DO WORK, FOR WHICH I AM PAID, and where I deal with adults who thank me when I do something, and don't—most of the time, anyway—lie down on the floor and cry if their piece of cheese gets "broken." This is, really, my leisure time. Work. Work is the fun time for women!

In between the work, I fill in the passport forms; put on the tea; kill clothes moths in the coat closet by hand; email a child's friend's mother about a "playdate," i.e., "child dump"; get as far as measuring the stairs for a new carpet; load the dishwasher; fill in a voting census form; tweet a petition about the NHS; order an inflatable mattress for Christmas (you can never start the prep too early!!!!); pour boiling water down the bathroom basin, because it's issuing a "bummy" smell; then, take the U-bend off and remove a slimy, rat-like fist of hair, phlegm, soap, and toothpaste because the boiling water has just "cooked" the bummy smell; book a time to donate blood; yadda, yadda, yadda. The doorbell rings. The phone rings. Often, it will be a child—oblivious to the notion of "mommy being at work"—asking me if I can "swing by" the school and "drop off" a folder they "forgot." During these kinds of days, I always think, with merriment, about how legendary the story is of Samuel Taylor Coleridge beginning to write "Kubla Khan" in a fever dream before being interrupted by "a person from Porlock," and then becoming furious at "losing his vision" forever. I think it is so repeatedly mentioned—as one of the "all-time" stories of frustrated literary ambition—because it's the only instance in history a *man* was interrupted whilst doing some work. Women have fifteen "person from Porlock" a *day*.

Anyway, I won't give you the full list of my day's tasks because you, too, are probably a working woman, and this list will be giving you PTSD, a reminder of what you were doing twenty minutes ago.

I do all this now because, at 4:30 p.m., when the kids arrive home from school, I will be too busy being a parent to be a housewife. The wife, the employee, the mother, and the housekeeper all take it in shifts. You're more than *a* woman. You are many women. You're every woman. They're all in *yooooooooooou*. It's kind of cool. You get to live many lives. Who doesn't want to do that? That is the ultimate dream of mankind!

The only niggle is that they all happen at once.

"COULD THIS BE any easier?" I ask myself, every working day—trying to ram "motherhood" and "earning money" into the same tattered, bulging, inadequate twenty-four hours. "Have I learned *nothing* that would make it fractionally less impossible?"

Whenever I am asked for advice by working mothers—and it has happened three times now—I feel I invariably disappoint. What is longed for, I think, is some detailed advice, along with specific links to websites for clothes you can purchase, companies you can work for, phrases you can use, techniques you can employ, and magic flying nannies you could hire that would make it even 1 percent easier. There must, surely, be a powerful, silky Stella McCartney blouse you could wear, and a conversation you could have with your managing director—*Did you see the match last night? Coh! PS please let me work flextime. And pay me the same as the men*—that would allow you to both pay the rent, *and* not feel like a terrible mother.

Unfortunately, if this advice exists, I don't know it. I don't have a Stella McCartney blouse; I still don't know how to bond over football; and the first time I asked for a pay raise, I, shamingly, wept throughout: "I'm sooo sooo sorry"—hiccup—"but I have two children now, and just need more money—or I *can't do this*." Thankfully, my boss at the time was a lovely man who handed me a box of tissues and agreed to my suggested sum.

"My wife cried the first time *she* asked for a pay raise," he said, calmly. Good male bosses who have wives that work are a blessing you will never forget. And if you have a female boss who gets where you're at, give thanks to God every day.

I give thanks also to another good man, who gave me two useful truths before I went to ask for my pay raise. As I agonized over whether I should ask in the first place—It's too *cheeky!* They say they love me, but what if asking them for a pay raise makes them so angry that they *fire me???* If I deserved a pay raise, surely they would have just *given it to me!* Oh, I *can't do this!*—he looked me in the eye, and told me two things: "Firstly, people *never* just give you money, or power. You *always* have to ask. *ALWAYS*. And, secondly, the way big institutions show that they *really* love you is with cash."

Over the years, I have thanked him, again and again, for telling me vital things at such a young age. I have borne them in mind in every business meeting I've had, and not cried since.

However, the single piece of advice *I* have to give is much simpler, yet harder, and more basic than this. It is: do not marry a cunt.

When I gather together with my Janets, and we talk about what we would tell younger women—if we did not worry that we would come across as yet another instance of older women seeming to rag on younger women—it would be this: nine times out of ten, a woman's life will only be as good as the man or woman she marries.

I don't *want* to say this! I don't *want* it to be true! Because it feels, on first analysis, to be unfeminist to tell bright, hardworking, joyous women that it doesn't matter *how* incredible they are, how many degrees they get, how many businesses they start up from scratch—if they then shack up with a self-pitying woman or man called Alex who's not very good at replying to texts; "freaks out" when they have kids; doesn't use the washing machine because "I'm just not good at stuff like that"; always has to see the guys on the weekend to "wind down"; and flies into terrifying rages (e.g., he or she can't find their favorite suede jacket)—they are doomed.

We *want* that woman to do well. She *should* still get promoted, be happy, and succeed in life—because of her sheer determination, hard will, and charisma. But she almost certainly won't.

Life is an experiment that bears this out. I'm forty-four now. Of all the married women I know who have children, all the ones who are successful in their careers (and are happy) are—*without exception*—the ones who married, for the want of a better term, "good men" or "good women." Gentle, clever, kind, funny people, usually in cardigans, who just *show up* for everything. Ones who at a *bare minimum* cut it fifty-fifty with the housework, childcare, and emotional upkeep.

Furthermore—and again, *without exception*—the women who have done the *best* in their careers, and are happiest, have partners who do *more* than fifty-fifty. The more their partners do—the more they engage in childcare and housework—the more those women fly.

It's amazing that this shouldn't be an obviously known fact—the equivalent of knowing if you marry a butcher, you'll have a lot of sausages; or if you marry a lighthouse keeper, you will live *really close to the sea*—but the math is simple: If you have children, you can only have as much career and happiness as your partner will help make for you. You *are* dependent on them. Because all you have is your time. And as we all have such short, finite lives, every tiniest increment counts.

Even a partner who does 40 percent of the childcare and housework (who you'd think was a good guy! 40 percent! That's *nearly* half!) is leaving 10 percent of *their* shit for you to sort out. Their trousers to wash, their kids to raise, their meals to prepare. Here's what that would look like, if it were a picture: a woman pulling a sled on which were her career and her children, with her partner occasionally jumping on—10 percent of the time—"to chill."

This is why, of all the things young women say, "I'm into bad boys/girls" makes older women wince as hard as if they had just said, "I'm into heroin." No, girls! Do *not* want a bad boy or girl! If you find yourself saying that, you go and get cognitive behavioral therapy (CBT) *right now*—or else say out loud, "I formally renounce all my plans for a career, and happiness, in order to marry the wrong person and spend all my time feeling tired."

Because if she wants children and a job, a woman's life is only as good as the man or woman she marries. That's the biggest unspoken truth I know. All too often, women marry their glass ceilings.

FOR HERE'S THE thing: If you and your partner have jobs and children, then every day you are, essentially, both in trucks on a road laden with the day's deadlines—*driving them at each other.* Whoever blinks first, and swerves off-road, is the one who will be looking after the children that day.

Given what a risky situation this is, you *really* need to know the guy in the truck coming toward you is a good, sensible, altruistic person, who can realistically assess who is best positioned to swerve that day, and who is rigorous about taking turns for who stays on the road, so that you might both not get fired.

The trucks metaphor is a useful one, because it accurately conveys how fucking stressful it is to both be working parents. It also explains why so many women—shattered by adrenaline and pressure—feel inclined to give up work completely to look after the children. In the short term, it can often feel like the only answer. The peaceable solution.

Of course, everyone's circumstances are different, and I do not proffer myself as an infallible wisdom broker. You must do what you feel in your gut to be right.

But the other piece of advice I would give you, in my older years, is that if it is at all possible, do not give up your job. Do not become financially dependent on your partner. I am at the end of observing a solid decade of divorces in my social circle, and I beg you to consider that there is a one-in-three chance you are going to end up divorced. *One in three.* As the woman, you will almost certainly get primary custody of your children. And this will mean that—in the middle of all the heartbreak and pain—you will end up in a financial media-

tion meeting with your soon-to-be-ex partner, being mortifyingly or-
dered to make a list of everything you spend in a year, and essentially
begging someone you have fallen out with to give you money for gas,
bread, and shoes for you and your children. There is nothing quite
like being convulsed with the humiliation of having to ask someone
you are trying to get away from for an extra twenty pounds a week so
you can, say, feed the dog.

Unless you're divorcing some cash-bloated oligarch, and you
have amazing lawyers, you are about to become quite poor. You will
almost certainly have to get a job anyway to make up the shortfall.
And you will now be trying to find a flexible job, that you can fit in
around childcare, with a CV that has huge gaps in it, i.e., the magical
dream job you would have been looking for *anyway*, had you decided
to remain in work.

Statistically, whatever choices you *think* you're making about being a stay-at-home or working mother, in the end, you'll probably end
up as a working mother *anyway*—so you might as well painfully grit
your teeth and stay in the game.

As a gender, women are not generally blithe about their futures.
We know it will be tough, and we're prepared for a fight, and we do
not shirk from hard work. But, before you have children, there is
one fundamental misconception almost all of us have: that we will
somehow find a way to make motherhood work that is different than
everyone else. That it won't be as difficult as everyone says it is. That,
if you are *really* clever, you'll find a way to avoid all the things that
older, haggard mothers complain about. *Even though* I was the eldest
of eight children, and took on a huge part of their childcare—sharing
a bed with one, teaching another to read, almost fully parenting a
third as my mother was recuperating from a difficult birth—I still
swaggered into my first pregnancy *convinced* I'd find a work-around.
I believed I'd somehow have *more* time than I did before I had children. That I'd put the baby in a box under my desk, when it was
asleep, and knock out a book in its long, calm hours of snoozing.

What I discovered, immediately, was that however much mothers might complain about motherhood, they're still not telling you

the *half* of it. Not even a quarter. No one has *ever* conveyed how *long* it goes on for. This is possibly because it's longer than a human can actually conceive. It's soooo looooong. You simply don't have a temporal reference point vast enough. I caaaaaaan't convey how very looooooong it is. It's. So. Looooooooooooooooooooooooooooooooooo ooooooooooooooooooooooooooooooooooooooooooooooooooo ooooong.

Imagine if I just carried on there and wrote the word *long* with so many *o*'s in it that it filled this book. This entire book, just *o*'s. And you had to read *each one*—no skipping! You must read *every single one*, individually. Out loud. With due care and attention. No matter how tired or busy you are. ALL THE *O*'S.

No one else is going to read those *o*'s out. It's just you. Doing the *o*'s, every day. You. You through fever, you through menstrual cramps, you through mourning, you through rainy days when you just can't be fucked. *O* every day of your holiday, on Christmas Day, on your birthday. On *Mother's Day*. Enjoy *that* sweet irony. On the toilet, on a train, in your sleep, in the bath, at your desk. Does it bore you? Do you wish you could do something else? Do you think, even now, *Fuck those* o'*s! I wouldn't spend eighteen years reading* o'*s! I don't have the TIME! That system sounds like it's for* dummies*! I'm clever! I'd find some work-around, to make it better—I'd find some other letter to read! I'd get* help*! I'd have* breaks*! There* must be a work-around. We wouldn't design a system where you spent all that time doing something so enragingly,* maddeningly repetitive and dull.

Guess what? We haven't. This *is* it. This is what you're working with. There's no way out.

Read Michelle Obama's book. She'll tell you exactly the same thing. If even Michelle Obama—insanely clever, emotionally intuitive, incredibly rich, strong of arm, married to a president—hasn't found a way out of this, then we're all fucked.

THIS IS WHY the third piece of advice I would give for working mothers is this: campaign for systemic change. We need a government-led initiative on the practicalities of childcare for working parents, and one of the simplest would be allowing working parents to pay non-working partners childcare fees—so that they might still be financially independent—and for *all* childcare fees to be tax deductible.

At first, this idea seems outrageous—*pay* the parents of a child *to look after their own child?* You're *supposed* to look after your own children! That's 101 parenting! What next—tax credits for having *sex?*

But childcare *is* a job—millions of people are paid to do it—and so why should we not pay the person who most loves the child to do it? Why does love suddenly exclude you from earning a living? We can't constantly quack on about how important a parent's love is to a child—but simultaneously say it's worth nothing. *Big institutions show you how much they love you with cash.* Currently, British parents pay the highest childcare costs in *the world*—with 68 percent of the earnings of the second earner, usually the mother, going to childcare. If you were to be blunt, you would say, simply, that the British government shows no financial love to working mothers and their children.

And governments also show you just whose lives they *see,* and whose lives are mysterious to them, in the taxation policies. When I finally became well-off enough both to need and afford an accountant, I was *astonished* at the things I was allowed to claim, because of my "media" career: clothes for television appearances, accountants (of course), magazines, first-class travel, hotels, taking clients to lunch, *golfing lessons.* All of these have been argued as necessary to the continuation of people's careers—the appearance, the schmoozing, the research, the travel.

This tells us that the person inventing the tax laws knew a lot of "media" people, who were able to lobby successfully for sweet bonuses to *their* accounts—but knew *no* working mothers who could chime in with a mystified, *Erm—childcare? Why can't we claim for childcare? FUCKING HELL YOU THINK GOLF IS MORE IMPORTANT FOR PEOPLES' CAREERS THAN WHO'S LOOKING AFTER THE KIDS????*

This isn't about "treating" working parents to something "lovely"—it's about the foundations of society. Stressed, working parents—either together, or divorced—both scrambling to earn money *and* raise their children are less able to cope when something goes wrong. They have fewer resources to get help. We have to remember the absolute, bare minimum, core mission of parenting: It's not giving children a delightful childhood, or having an enchanting time—much as we dearly wish to do those things. It's raising children who are loved, cared for, and safe, and who have all the tools to thrive in later life. A recent US report showed that providing just $3,000 per year in benefits to working, low-income families boosted their children's future earnings by 17 percent. There is a powerful economic argument for helping families—for, every time we make things easier and better for parents, we make things easier and better for society. Relieving some of the financial burden on working parents won't solve everything—not even close. But it wouldn't do a single piece of harm.

So that's my main advice to working mothers, really: Don't marry a cunt, and totally change society. Given what you're dealing with on a day-to-day basis, you should be able to manage it *easily.*

And finally, in those early, tired, fractious years, when you're negotiating with your partner over whose career is the most "important," and therefore must be "protected" from the majority of childcare, beware any man who suggests that their work, and earnings, are somehow more vital to them than you. Who seems unhappy, or alarmed, if you suggest *they* go part-time, and *you* become the primary breadwinner—*because I've just got that old-fashioned "male pride" thing of wanting to take care of the family.*

They might say this firmly; they might say this apologetically. They might even say it putting ironic quote marks around it. But let me tell you something that will be useful to both of you. *There is no such thing as "male pride" about work and income.* It's not produced by some gland in their balls, which you don't have.

Instead, "male pride" is this: fear about being poor and unvalued. A fear of having no money or power. A fear of becoming unemployable.

And as soon as you call it that, you realize, quite obviously, that *duh—women have that too. We're* scared of having only twenty-seven pounds in the bank, no career prospects, and having to ask our partner for ten pounds for the pub! We're scared of falling off the career ladder! We're scared of being broke, and over! It's *literally* the same thing! It's just because men would, generally, rather die than say they're scared of something that they invented "male pride"—a sore, warning phrase that suggests they would somehow be *fundamentally wounded and belittled* by it in a way women are too amazing to experience. A phrase that suggests, unnegotiably, "Back off—this is a conversation that could end with me losing all sense of who I am."

No. Absolutely not. All genders are equally scared of being poor. Insist on calling it what it is—fear—and start again from scratch.

CHAPTER NINE

The Hour of Parenting Teenage Children

◁━◁

3:45 P.M.

I AM IN THE MIDDLE OF AN IMPORTANT WORK DEADLINE—AND SO, obviously, on my knees, trying to winkle a swollen lemon pip out of a hole in the dishwasher spray arm with a pin—when my daughter, returned from school, comes into the kitchen.

"What do you think?"

I look up.

There comes a time in every young woman's life when she must experiment with expressing her sexuality. When mine came, it was July 1992, I was seventeen, and got on the 11:43 a.m. Wolverhampton–Birmingham New Street train in a black-lace negligee, with a black-lace dress over the top, and torn tights.

My friend Matt—who was two years older—refused to sit next to me on the train, because he "couldn't handle the hassle" of me "dressing like a hooker," and, in the end, insisted I wear his raincoat "to cover up the epicenter of the problem. Because I can see your epicenter in that dress."

"I'm dressed like Madonna in the *Justify My Love* video," I said, indignantly, buttoning the coat up.

"Yeah, but Madonna wouldn't wear that to the Bullring Shopping Center to buy a secondhand sleeping bag, would she?" he said, quite reasonably. For this was, indeed, our quest for the day.

A small part of me was grateful—(a) it was very cold and (b) the cheap petticoat was ferocious with static electricity—it clung to my legs whilst making the odd crackling sound, as if Michael Faraday had moved into lingerie. I was quite happy to cover it up.

Another part of me, however, was deeply shamed that *he* was shamed by this first, tentative outing for my burgeoning sexuality.

My understanding was that there comes a day where a young woman's hotness must be exposed to the world—her Cinderella moment, where she appears at the ball, or Wolverhampton train station, and the assembled people gasp: They had *no idea* the sexiest woman in the world lived here! Tales of this day will be told for generations to come! GASP! Excitement! Worlds changing! The princess has *arrived!* She is a woman now! The best *kind* of woman—a sexy one!

There is *no* telling of the Cinderella story where she turns up at the ball, and the guests all just sigh, "Put it away, love," as had just essentially happened to me. I was confused. In some ways, I still am.

And now, here, today, in what feels like the mere blink of an eye, I have gone from "young woman dealing with the turbulent expressing of her sexuality" to "old woman dealing with a young woman dealing with the turbulent expressing of *her* sexuality."

And, as it turns out, my *full* descriptor is "old woman dealing with a young woman dealing with the turbulent expressing of her sexuality—and doing it very badly."

"Oh!" I say—a sound that I issue when desperately stalling for time to think.

"Honest opinion?" she says, twirling.

She's wearing torn fishnet tights, white ankle boots, and a very short dress which is—I can see now that she's twirling—backless, and so reveals her bra. She is fourteen and is going to an after-school science lesson.

"*Very glamorous,*" I say. "Very . . . *edgy.*"

I can hear what my voice is doing. It's saying the words *glamorous* and *edgy* like the sentence is actually, "Very *inadvisable.* Very *dangerous and terrible.*"

"You're doing it *again,* Mom," she says. I have deflated her Outfit

High, which has made her feel vulnerable and now, therefore, angry. "This is just like the photo shoot, all over again!"

"The photo shoot" was a series of pictures she posted on Instagram last week. As part of an art project on "fragility," she did a shoot where she was naked from the waist up, smeared red lipstick across her face, and wrapped POLICE LINE DO NOT CROSS tape around her breasts.

"You could—pop on a cardi?" I suggested, tentatively.

"Mom!" she said. "Don't you *get* it? It's appearance as political comment—because a woman's body is so *often* the scene of a crime, yeah?"

Shit! *Shit!* You see, this is the problem with raising strong, clever, argumentative feminist daughters—the first person they practice being strong, clever, argumentative feminists on is *you*—and you are so much more tired and worried than them.

"Darling, I *love* the statement, and I'm *totally* down with it from a political point of view," I said. "Right *on*. But, as your *mom*, I want you to think about who's going to see those pictures on your account, and what *their* response will be to them. Because most people googling for pictures of teenage girls with tape around their tits aren't looking to debate the semiotics of crime-scene accessories, juxtaposed with fragile female physicality. They just want to have a wank."

It was a cunty thing to do. There's absolutely no need to say *semiotics* to a fourteen-year-old girl during breakfast. Indeed, I would say that is my first piece of advice for parents of teenage girls: Never use the word *semiotics* during breakfast.

I was trying to crush her with big words and phrases.

And of course, if you try and crush someone with big words and phrases, they will try and crush you back with some big words and phrases of their own. The guns are out! It's a Lexicon Standoff!

"Don't slut-shame me!" she had said then, as she says now. "You're slut-shaming me! *And you say you're a feminist!*"

And now, as she did then, she runs back to her room, and slams the door behind her.

I stare down at the dishwasher. Where the fuck do all these lemon pips come from? And what psychopath invents a rotor-arm with no service hatch? It's basically a rotating cul-de-sac of bullshit.

"DON'T SLUT-SHAME ME!"

IF YOU HAVE twenty-first century teenage girls, you are going to hear this. A lot. And almost certainly roughly twenty-four hours after Pay-Pal informs you that someone in your household that isn't you—or, as far as you're aware, your husband—has spent one hundred and forty-seven pounds on body-con dresses at asos.com.

When it comes to matters like this, it's useful to regard things in two time frames: the short game and the long game. The long game is that, of course, it should not matter what a young woman wears to jaunt around town or buy a secondhand sleeping bag. When the Feminist Utopia happens, everyone will be able to wear exactly what they want, without fear of judgment or reprisal. It will be understood that a teenage girl, on a hot day, wearing short shorts and a crop top, is no more demanding to be catcalled, harassed, and assaulted than a toddler, dressed up for Halloween in a nurse's hat and apron, is volunteering to give passersby a tetanus booster and a leaflet about cholesterol.

However, the problem with being a hard-core feminist teenager is that we *don't* yet live in a Feminist Utopia. We live in a world that contains many, many arseholes. You, as an elderly hag mother, understand this. Your child does not.

Years later, I have a better understanding of these first feminist-on-feminist standoffs that are a hallmark of raising strong girls who read jezebel.com. Of course, personally speaking, I was absolutely not trying to slut-shame her. As far as I'm concerned, any and all of my children can come down for spaghetti bolognese in a gimp mask and three bits of tinsel, and I would just be like, "Wipe-clean PVC! How practical!," and then pass the parmesan. No one can be too slutty in my house. When the cat licks its nunny, I'm like, "You get in there, girl. You have your time. Have a good old rootle around for me, dude."

However, part of the job of being a parent is to be by way of a proxy for the outside world. *You* are the invisible, loving membrane between your offspring and the world they will eventually be in, alone, and your job description contains passages that could be titled things like "Breaking it to them gently that not everyone is as lovely as Mommy and Daddy" and "Allowing them to test-drive aspects of their personality on the private racetrack of your home, before they join the mad, old Motorway of Life."

Of course, if you're a teenage girl in a tiny dress—looking for affirmation that you look newly sexy and amazing—it's hard to grasp that the parent in front of you is *not*, when they talk to you, being your parent but is putting themselves in the shoes of imaginary pedophiles online in Cousinfuck Idaho. Or some bloke in a white van who's going to drive past you shouting, "Nice tits, love!" Or some boy at school who's going to pass round a picture of you on his phone whilst sniggering—because there is *always* a boy who will do this. Every school is provided with one by law.

As a parent, it is a dereliction of your responsibilities to allow your children to leave the house wearing an outfit that will provoke responses they are just too young, and inexperienced, to handle.

I can't tell you how many awkward mornings and evenings I had, standing in the hallway, watching a girl I loved cry as she put on her coat, because my response to her outfit had been "Personally, I love your knickers—but I don't want anyone else you meet today to be able to say the same thing."

In the event, what made our "slut-shaming years" end happily was the discovery of *RuPaul's Drag Race*. On the show, Mama Ru— the world's first supermodel drag queen—loves and nurtures all the contestants but also doles out affectionately acerbic critiques of their outfits and endeavors.

As drag is the art of taking the signifiers of femininity and turning it into a competition, it's the perfect thing to watch with girls who are themselves engaged in learning what "being a woman" is, and deciding what to reject, and what to embrace. It's all there on the screen! Each episode is a lesson!

It was watching *Drag Race* with my girls that made me realize what this phase of parenting is. In essence, you have to become the door bitch of an edgy nightclub, testing the punters to see if they are sassy enough to handle what's happening inside.

Post-*Drag Race*, when my daughters came clip-clopping down the stairs in some "challenging" new outfit, I would assume the persona of RuPaul and throw the kind of comments at them they might expect to receive, once they left the house.

If my, "Hey! Sweet-ass!" provoked instant weeping, and a retreat to the bedroom, we all knew it wasn't, perhaps, the right time yet to be wearing it.

But as soon as the reply was "That's *Dr.* Sweet Ass to you—I am fully qualified in having both a left and a right buttock, and hold a professorship from the *Kiss My Ass Institute* of Massachusetts," we knew it was time to let the hot bird fly the nest.

OF COURSE, IN many ways, dressing sexy is an aspect of becoming a woman wholly disproportionate to its eventual usefulness. There are, obviously, times when "looking sexy" is the right and necessary thing to do. How will you know when those times are? It's when you absolutely know you have to look sexy, right now, because that is the thing you want to do. I can't stress how important it is that we recognize "because you really, really want to" is absolutely enough reason for a girl to do a thing. When you're going to the right place with the right people, and you know looking like Absolute All Hotness is at the top of your to-do list, there is no valid argument on earth against it.

What *is* useful is being aware of how surprisingly few times there are when "being a sexy lady" is actually fun. Sexy schoolgirl, sexy business lady, sexy hen-night crew, sexy shopping look—nine times out of ten, twenty minutes after you've left the house, you will feel a sudden, weary rue for the look you chose. Why? Because it's quite *exhausting* to be sexy. Sexy shoes require a strut, sexy dresses need a wiggle, and sexy makeup needs an air of "Yes, I *am* a goddess." If your sexiness has its logical effect—making people look at you with an air of "you look sexy," or coming up to you saying, "hello, sexiness"—you suddenly have some admin to attend to: deciding whether to encourage or rebuff these responses. That can take up time you had otherwise put aside for dancing, talking, falling over, etc. It can absolutely shank your schedule—particularly if it includes multivariable calculus.

On the days where you don't have the energy to do this, you end up being the girl who's constantly trying to pull her dress down over her legs, and up over her tits, and hobbling in her heels until she finally takes them off, and spends the rest of the night padding around in her tights, wishing she had flip-flops.

Speaking as The Sexiest Person Alive, I would estimate the amount of time I find myself with the right amount of energy to spend all night being A Hot, Sexy Bitch is around four hours a month, tops. Your mileage may, obviously, vary, but the reason it's important to be honest about just how infrequently you will be able to engage fully with "being supersexy" is because "being sexy" is often the default option. Prom? Sexy. Party? Sexy. Clubbing? Sexy. It often seems like the only other option is "sensible," which involves dressing like e.g., a sparrow.

This is why—episodes of slut-shaming aside—I spent a great deal of my parenting years passionately marketing some other clothing options to my girls: "jolly" and "comfortable." In a world so loaded against female physical comfort—a world where *comfortable* is *never mentioned* on fashion websites, or on the front covers of women's magazines, or even in conversation—to instinctively discover and embrace comfort shows you at your best: confident. At ease. Finding your own things. Ready for anything. That's why *comfortable* is one of the two greatest descriptors of what a woman is wearing.

And "jolly?" Why is "jolly" good? Because "jolly" shows you're choosing happiness as the main thing you project. *Jolly* means that, against all the odds, you radiate joy that you are *you*. You like your *foundations*. You have a vague idea where you're heading. And that your instinct—your bright, correct instinct—is that the person who enjoys that journey most is not coquettish, or red-carpet ready, or heroin chic, but just . . . *comfortable*. *Jolly*. "Comfortable" and "jolly" take no energy to project; they find no unwelcome responses. "Comfortable" and "jolly" make the wearer, and all those who see them, do only one thing: smile.

A couple of years after Slut-shaming-gate, my daughter attended her school prom.

My girl wore a hot-pink trouser suit with hot-pink hair and carried a pink, fluffy clutch bag with pictures of Selma and Patty—Marge Simpson's sisters—on it.

When she came downstairs, I was on my knees, trying to get a swollen sunflower seed out of a hole in the rotor-arm of the dishwasher with a pin. Keeping those nozzles free is a goddamn full-time job.

"What do you think?" she said, twirling. "Because I know how I feel: comfortable and jolly."

She beamed, like the sun.

Then she opened her jacket and showed me the black push-up basque underneath.

"And *this* is for when the vogueing starts," she said, grabbing an apple, and leaving.

I knew my work was done.

THE MICROBREAKDOWN

I am on my knees, trying to remove a dead mouse from under the fridge. On the one hand, I'm kind of pleased—I *knew* I could smell maggots! My ability to detect a flyblown mammal corpse remains top-notch! Bitch still got it!

On the other hand, I'm unhappy, because I am removing a dead mouse from under the fridge. My daughter enters the kitchen. She appears to be made of rain clouds and sorrow.

"Oh, Mama—everything is *terrible*. All my clothes are wrong, I feel fat even though I'm not, I think my friends secretly hate me, I've got too much schoolwork, the duvet in my bedroom is depressing me, I don't even know who I'll vote for in two years' time, and all the whales are *so sad*."

THIS IS "THE microbreakdown"—a common occurrence in the teenage years. It's not to be confused with any long-term, lingering problems—which we'll come to later—but to be recognized for what it is: an acute *yet temporary* state of affairs. The "microbreakdown" is the dolorous psychological equivalent of "the minibreak": it's not a proper holiday breakdown, merely a weekend away in extreme self-loathing.

Usually lasting no more than twenty-four to forty-eight hours, a parent's handling of a microbreakdown requires an understanding of three major principles. The first is that nine times out of ten, your child is not having a nervous breakdown at all—it just needs a nice cup of tea and a biscuit. As soon as you hear your child's "micro-breakdown voice"—and you will know it: it has a sad, baaing quality, like a lost lamb on a hillside—you need to put the kettle on, and get the biscuit tin out. Don't say a word until they've finished their first Bourbon—just nod, whilst squeezing the teabag. Teenagers often simply don't recognize when they have low blood sugar, or that they're hungry, or tired. It's not actually the end of the world—it's just the end of the *day*. Feed them. Also, remember that *you* often still don't know when you've got low blood sugar, and have melt-downs exactly like this, and you're forty-four. Really, Fitbits should be telling us this shit. What's the point of having robot overlords if they aren't telling you, at the point where you start crying to EE Customer Service because your 4G is "feeble," that it's really time for a brew?

The second is *just keep nodding*. Just keep nodding in a sympa-thetic, slightly dumb way—like you're a stereotypical mom in a sit-com, for whom, as usual, the writers could not write any interesting dialogue or characterization. I'm sorry to break this news to you but, when your children enter their teenage years, what they need—in many ways—is for you to become quite stupid, yet loving. Imagine a lovely Jersey cow called Buttercup, wearing some Whistles jeans. That's you, now. Are you actually a dynamic, alpha, problem-busting lawyer with martial art skills and the ability to quote apposite passages by Auden when the occasion demands? My friend, you must bury that woman, for a while. Amal Clooney is *not* the droid you are looking for right now.

Being a brisk, practical, and problem-solving maven—an intellect that truly bestrode the world—was the correct thing to be when your child was seven, and crying because their art project papier mâché pig was still soggy. You used your gigantic brain to pop the pig into a low oven, then sat back and enjoyed a world where crises could be solved with action.

When your child reaches its teens, however, being a dynamic, alpha, nigglebuster is a character trait you need to unlearn, or else die of the ensuing arguments. Your child does not want you to be a clever problem solver anymore.

The reason why is obvious: This is the time where *they* have to turn into a clever problem solver. If someone else in the house already fills that role—and has an extra thirty years of experience, to boot—then they can't step into those shoes. They will have to remain in a state of childlike dependency—always running to you for answers. And that will make them furiously resentful. You know all the arguments you have when your child comes to you with a problem, you provide the solution—sitting back smugly in your chair, puffing on your pipe, like a lady Sherlock Holmes—and they suddenly and ferociously start explaining to you why your solution is shit? And you're like "What? What is going on here? You came to me with a problem! I sorted it! THE FUCK?" And then they start saying mad, wild shit: "You think I'm stupid," or "You always think I'm messing things up," or "Your pipe is smelly, and I hate it when you play the violin." And you're like "But I was *just* trying to *help*."

Well, the rules have changed, now. You can't help by helping anymore. *Your* job, during these years, is to be a calm, benign sounding board to their *own* problem-solving. For when you provide your child with a solution to their problems, you kind of *are* saying that they're stupid—because it seems you have no faith in them being able to solve it themselves. I know! I know—they looked like they wanted you to sort things out. But they don't. They want you to help *them* sort it out.

So, three: triage the situation. As they drink their tea and eat their biscuit and tell their tale of woe, you need to address the primary problem that they feel bad. Acknowledging that they feel bad is half the solution—you need to be aware that sitting around your kitchen table are you; your child; and, on the third chair, their anxiety or despair.

"Oh mate, this all sounds fucking horrible. I can see how worried you are," takes half the heat out of the situation immediately. Often, their body language immediately shifts from "I am going to throw myself *off a cliff*" to "I am going to throw myself *off the bottom two stairs*—maybe *onto a beanbag*."

Then you need to, sympathetically and succinctly, repeat their situation back to them: "So, your best friend is freaking out and you want to go and see her—but you also have a lot of homework. Man, that's tough."

This both shows you've been listening and allows them to see the simple facts of their problem. Nine times out of ten, when a teenager has their problem repeated back to them, they instantly start coming up with solutions: "I guess I could do one more hour of homework, then have a sleepover with her" or "I could do my homework during playtime tomorrow, and go see her now."

At this point, you just need to nod at them in a wise yet delighted manner—as if they have just started singing an amazing song of cleverness—possibly ending with a little round of applause, and a "I *knew* my girl would sort this out."

With a solution now decided upon by the child, you will now, as a parent, actually be *able* to help them—because their solution almost always involves getting a lift to Kensal Green, being lent a tenner, or borrowing your nice Acne boots "for reasons of morale." Your full job description, at this point, is sounding board, chauffeur, cooperative lending society, wardrobe, cheerleader, tea lady. That's what "being a mother" means now.

———

IN THE TENTH instance—when repeating the question back to them results in "Don't repeat the question back at me, you shriveled, old hag! Help me! Break into the DVLA and change my test results to 'pass,' or else I swear to God, I will set fire to everything that has ever existed"—you are within your rights simply to leave the house, go straight to John Lewis, and touch all the folded towels, which is always very soothing.

The third option—if everything else fails—is to shout "EMER-GENCY CHRISTMAS!," make everyone put on their pajamas, get under a duvet on the sofa, and watch *Elf*. There isn't a microbreak-down alive that can withstand seeing Will Ferrell caught in a revolving door wearing green tights.

AN EXISTENTIAL CRISIS

The dishwasher is, for once, working; so far today, no mice have died; and I've got a Cauliflower Cheese Surprise in the oven, a sweet ten minutes away from being done.

I am now, therefore, sitting on the sofa, on a supertight deadline, trying to write a 3,000-word think piece about what Benedict Cum-berbatch's face *means*, when I see the sadness trudging into the room. I internally sigh, and close my laptop.

One thing I have learned about teenagers is that—unfairly but inescapably—their unhappiness is like one of those rare plants in the rainforest, that live for a thousand years, but only bloom for twenty minutes every decade. A child can be unhappy for a long, long time—but remain utterly mute as to its cause.

When their misery does finally bloom, into something now speakable, it's for the briefest period—and you just *have to be there*, or you miss your chance to bear witness to it. I finally understand why my friend, who was very high up at *The Times*, resigned when her children hit their teenage years.

At the time, I had very young children and was utterly confused by this.

"But the teenage years are the *easy* years!" I said, almost crying. "Surely! They can make their own breakfasts, they can shit without involving you in any way, you don't need to stop them falling down the stairs. For the love of *God*, tell me those are the easy years. The thought of that is all that's keeping me going right now."

"The teenage years are when they *really* need you," she said, clearing her desk. "*You.* No one else."

Now my children are teenagers, I get it. No childminder, or after-school activity, can deal with an existential crisis. You just have to be there, hanging around—so that when the sad flower finally emerges, the right and sole expert is on hand to deal with it. The time is now—and now only. The cure is you, and no one else. It is the ultimate heavy privilege. It's the proof you are parenting well. You must congratulate yourself, even as you put your laptop away—only briefly and bitterly thinking, *I bet Ernest fucking Hemingway never had to stop midsentence because his kid had a "sad emoji" face.*

"You're sad," I say. "Say what you see, and keep it simple" is rule one of dealing with unhappy teens.

"You'll think I'm stupid," she begins, in the tiniest voice, hugging the cat.

"Well, that goes without saying, you big bum . . . but tell me anyway."

There is three minutes of silence, and then, finally, a sigh.

"I'm just . . . *ugly*," she says.

Her voice is factual, and sad. Like a newsreader would be, when they said, "Sir Richard Attenborough died today. He was ninety-one."

I am so astonished I am silent for a minute. This is the *wrongest* thing ever said!

"You are *not!*" I finally say, outraged. "Who said that? Who do I need to kill?"

That was the wrong thing to say.

"Stop thinking I'm a *victim*," she says. There's another few minutes of tension. I remain silent, and stroke the cat, hard, as it's the only thing I can do. (We're going halves on the comfort animal right now.)

"I'm sorry. I'll shut up. Just . . . tell me."

She takes her phone out of her pocket. Ah. Someone has been cyberbullying her. She's going to show me messages. In my head, I've already written to her teacher, the head of pastoral care, her headmaster, Childline, and the Minister for Education. I've run a successful campaign to bring back the death sentence, and whoever has sent her this message is going to be electrocuted, tomorrow, in advance of me dancing on their grave. I will happily take the time off work to do all this. I am ready to go to *war*.

She hands me the phone. I am braced to read something abusive, which I will refute every line of, and show her the truth—that she is *unbelievably beautiful*—and we'll all be eating cauliflower cheese in ten minutes. Thank God—the next few minutes will be sad, but the worst is nearly over.

Then I look at the phone. It's a picture of her and her friends. They're all in the playground, posing for the camera. Her friends— clearly ready for the picture—are all pouting, but she is just smiling a happy, guileless child smile. Her eyes are scrunched up in happiness, and her beam is as wide as a pumpkin lantern. She looks joyous. She looks—

"—ugly. In that picture, I'm ugly. I'm so confused—because I didn't think I was. But now I know I *am*. I'm clapped."

And she sits there, looking utterly deflated. I look again at the pouting girls, and then the smiling girl at the end. I look again at the picture that has broken her heart.

In Neverland, whenever a child says "I don't believe in fairies," a fairy dies from sadness.

I think whole cities of Neverland fairies would die, instantly, if they'd ever seen a good, good smiling child—the kind that wants to save the world—say, "I am ugly." The world would end.

My girl thinks she's ugly. And I know this isn't a problem you can solve in ten minutes. That cauliflower cheese is going to go cold.

———————

I THINK, AS a mother, you fear your daughter saying, "I'm ugly" more than you fear them saying, "I'm in love with a boy called Emo 'Knife' McMurderer" or "I'm pregnant."

If they're pregnant, and they don't want to be, it's a problem that can be resolved. However unpleasant it may be, there is a way through. You can pick up the phone and fix things. You can change things, for the better, very quickly. You can stop your girl from feeling like her life is ending.

And if she has a bad boyfriend—well, you'll just frame him for a crime he didn't commit, and then move the whole family to Canada. These are problems that can be remedied.

But if your daughter feels they're ugly? If, every time they look at a picture of themselves—of their happy, smiley face—their hearts break? It's like that bit in a horror film, where they go, "The call is coming from *inside* the house." The call is coming from the inside of their house. Their *inner voice* tells them they are ugly. They are bullying *themselves*. You are both facing an enemy who has hidden in the one place neither of you can attack it—inside your kid's brilliant, brilliant bones.

What are you going to do? What can you fight? Who can you call? You're now just some impotently furious person who wants to pick an argument with 10,000 years of history; every book, movie, and magazine in existence—for it's a problem that circles the entire globe. All over the world, *girls right now* are thinking they aren't beautiful enough. It is an emergency and a stain upon our souls. So, what are you going to do, when this wrongness comes to *your* house, and your girls? Hijack the entire earth, drive it into deep space at 10,000 miles per hour whilst screaming, "I swear to God, I will not return you to the Milky Way until you re-evaluate your entire value system for women!"

You don't have time. Your kid's crying. Otherwise, that plan would totally work.

I can tell you what *doesn't* work, though: sitting on the sofa and telling your sad kid they are beautiful. They're very logical about this. Although you *will* say, "You are beautiful"—how can you not? It's impossible? *They are!*—it won't do any good. Watch.

"Oh my love, that's just *wrong*. You are so, so beautiful. So beautiful, my heart *bursts.*"

Sad, young woman in the darkest tones ever: "You *have* to say that—you're my mother."

"That doesn't mean I don't know what's beautiful," you reply. "I *totally* know. Look: Judy Garland in *Meet Me in St. Louis* equals beautiful. Nigel Farage having a poo equals not. I'm *qualified.*"

"But I don't look like *this*, do I?" they say, scrolling through their Instagram, and showing hundreds of pictures of girls with kissy mouths, and Gothic-arch eyebrows, and immaculate olive skin, living in the kind of bodies—tight, long—that go with everything. God, these women have such confidence and grace.

She pauses on one, who appears to have been built by some kind of award-winning tit-and-bum architect.

"But she's a supermodel, babe—she's *paid* to look like that," you say, comfortingly.

"That's not a *supermodel! That's a girl from my school!*" she howls.

"Fucking hell—how old is she?"

"Fourteen! She's called Anna!"

God. *I* feel intimidated looking at her, and I'm both her economic superior, *and* on acquaintance terms with e.g., Dan Stevens from *Downton Abbey*. How can a fourteen-year-old cope with being around someone so beautiful?

Fucking Instagram. Fucking contouring. Fucking Kylie Jenner's lip fillers, and the belief you can have no pores, and the battle between the Kardashians about which is the hottest sister. Fucking twenty-first century. Fuck this woman-hating world. It has never been more difficult to be a young girl.

IT's 1989. I am fifteen. It's the twentieth century. My parents are hippies, so we live in a house with no mirrors. There's no internet, no Instagram, no contouring, no lips of Kylie Jenner. Neither pores nor eyebrows are yet "a thing."

And yet—I am ugly. I know I am ugly. My face is very round and pink—"Like a planet made of ham," as Caz says, helpfully, one day, as I struggle for the words—and there are no round-faced girls in movies or on TV. They all have *oval-shaped faces*, instead. That's the shape a girl's face should be. My lips are quite thin, and my hair is neither one color nor another, and, when I smile, my eyes crinkle up, leaving just a couple of lines—exactly like the eyes on the worms in the Mr. Men books. And the smile makes my mouth stretch wide, like a pumpkin lantern. I've seen it in photos. When I am happy, I have Mr. Men worm eyes and a pumpkin mouth.

The photos kill me—because, all the rest of the time, I can pretend I am a beautiful girl. But when I look at photos where I am happy, I know what category of girl I would be filed under.

I know I am a smiling, ugly girl.

And I know exactly what that means.

WHY IS IT important for a girl to be beautiful? Because it *is*. You know it is. Having people believe you are beautiful is like having money—it's *always* useful. What's the first thing we say to baby girls? "You are beautiful!" Whenever a woman is introduced on TV—whether it's on a comedy panel show, or to give an award at a ceremony—the MC will always say, "And now, the *beautiful* Emma Watson," just after he's called Ben Affleck, "The talented, the dynamic, the one and only!"

"Beautiful" is so common, when it doesn't turn up, the absence looks like the product of a very harsh, existential meeting, followed by an outright declaration of war. I once watched a panel show—I think it was *Have I Got News for You*—where the young female comedian was introduced as "the beautiful!," but fellow-contestant Germaine Greer, in her seventies, was not.

This raises all manner of questions. Why? Why? Was Greer not called "beautiful" because of her age? Or was it because she was a feminist—and it might be seen as "non-PC" to call a feminist beautiful? Or was it because they just didn't think, when they looked at a seventy-year-old woman sitting on that chair, that she was beautiful? Would that imaginary conversation have taken into account that Greer *had* been objectively beautiful, once? For, as a younger woman, Greer was, by any index, indisputably and ragingly hot. That conversation would, then, have logically had to cover exactly when it was that Greer had *stopped* being beautiful—which, if made public, might well help us compile official guidelines on when, exactly, women tip over into "hag," *unless* they are Helen Mirren or Dame Judi Dench, who simply become, as they age, "luminous," instead—like a talented and incredibly well-respected lamp.

There isn't a workable alternative for women to being beautiful. You just . . . have to be beautiful. If you're not beautiful *now*—if you have not managed it by eight, or ten, or twelve—then you certainly must be beautiful *later*. Your arc is to work toward the day that you do something new to your hair and take off your glasses, and walk into a room, and everyone says, "But—you're *beautiful!*" Beauty always has to happen *in the end*. That's the only story, for a girl. To either be born beautiful, or to become it. There are no stories about ugly girls, plain girls, normal girls who stay ugly, plain, and normal all their lives. Or at least, there aren't stories where those girls are at the *center*. There is *one* place an ugly girl can be, and I know where it is.

This is why, at fifteen, I am wild with fear—because, if I am an ugly girl, the one place I will exist is at the end of other people's jokes. That is the only place we see ugly girls. You get to be the punch line. You get to be the girl in the montage of some guy's terrible dating history—before he meets Meg Ryan. The girl in the gang of school losers the heroine momentarily has to hang out with, when things are going wrong. You get to be someone else's disappointment. The booby prize. A thing no one wants to win. You have no market value.

THE IDEA OF what makes a woman beautiful is cruel—because so much of what we deem to be traditional beauty is down to luck. And, even if you are lucky enough to be born with it, it's down to yet more luck if you can keep it. Hormones, acne, a broken nose, alopecia, stretch marks, growing "too tall," or "not tall enough." So much of what makes us sad about not being beautiful is, actually, a deeply buried, righteous anger: an anger about not being able to control our faces and bodies. *An anger about not being able to control other people's judgment of you.* An anger that the world made up its mind, a long time ago, about what beauty is—and you didn't get to sit on that committee, and neither did any of your friends. You did not get to put a value on yourself, or what *you* hold admirable. *That's* why we're angry. *That's* why we cry, i.e., beauty is a tax we are asked to pay, in a system we have no vote in.

"You *are* beautiful," your friends will say, and mean it—but what use is that if they can't change other people's minds? If they don't get to make films, adverts, TV shows, and catwalks where what *they* think is beautiful is represented? If they can't change things so *everyone else* thinks you're beautiful, too?

Or, perhaps, they will say something else: "Beauty is in the eye of the beholder"—but that is a useless thing to say to a girl who is sad. What? You will only ever be thought of as beautiful *by people who love you*—thus, making one task (being beautiful) suddenly double in size (got to make someone love me *as well*)? Fuck my life.

But there is a trick to this. It is saying something that is true as soon as you say it. It is, I think, the single most magic sentence a woman can hear. Are you ready? It's this:

You are the beholder.

Realizing *you* are the beholder is a spell that sets you free.

You are not the beauty. YOU ARE THE BEHOLDER.

You are not to *be* "beautied"—you are to *see* it. *You* are the one who gets to point at beauty, define it, ENJOY IT. To write about it, photograph it, sing about it, rejoice in it, and see it in others. Isn't it more fun to *look* at beauty than *be* it? To be beautiful often causes problems. To *look* at beauty causes none. To decide what is beautiful gives you *power.*

I say this to my daughter, and every other woman in the world: *People don't need you to be beautiful. It is not necessary for the functioning of this world that you be hot. You affect literally nothing if you don't look like a model.* As author Erin McKean said: "You don't owe prettiness to anyone. Not to your boyfriend/spouse/partner, not to your coworkers, especially not to random men on the street. You don't owe it to your mother, you don't owe it to your children, you don't owe it to civilization in general. Prettiness is not a rent you pay for occupying a space marked 'female.'"

You are the beholder. Your job is to go and behold stuff.

And once you realize you are the beholder—once you become the eye, instead—then the whole power structure of beauty dissolves, because you *decide* what beautiful is. That's *your* job now. That's part of becoming an adult.

And when you have decided what beauty is, this is where the magic of makeup and clothes and hair become wholly joyous and benign. Who do *you* behold to be beautiful? I would guess you would pin on your wall Frida Kahlo, and Siouxsie Sioux, and Tess Holliday and Zadie Smith, and Phoebe Waller-Bridge, and Lana Del Rey, and Billie Eilish, and Barbra Streisand, and Lizzo, and Cleopatra. You would have your friends on there, and your aunts, and your grandmother, and your cat. Pictures you just *found* of a woman with an amazing nose, a tilt of the jaw, fierce eyes. And it wouldn't be just *people*—you would put beautiful *things* there: pictures of a lilac tree, a blue lake, slate in the rain, a minaret. You amass wonderous *thoughts:* the quotes, lyrics, and poetry—the deathbed confessions and declarations of love—that make your bones fill with electricity and light when you read them. You collect what *you* wish to behold on your bedroom wall; it would be personal to you: for a bedroom wall is by way of a blueprint for your future, a map of how you wish to get there, and a chronicle of your heart and soul.

If you want to see what a teenage girl is, look at her bedroom wall. *That's* what she is, or what she will be. These are the tools that she has found, with which she is building herself. What she sees, then, in the mirror is a *curator of beauty*—not the beauty itself. She is constructing her own judgments and standards. Her own laws.

I SOMETIMES THINK that it is too complicated a question to say, "What is a woman? How should she be? How can she make herself?" The words *girl* and *woman* are so freighted with a million different arguments, meanings, and history that it feels like a terrifying endeavor to embark on at age eleven, twelve, or thirteen. To become a *woman?* A whole woman? A thing that bleeds, and births, and works, and thinks, and fights, and loves, and plans—a thing that has so many assumptions and rules bound up in it that you do not even know where the invisible lines, boundaries, restrictions, and taboos lie until you bump up against them—often shamingly, or humiliatingly, in front of others?

These days, when I talk to young women about the task of constructing yourself, I find that it's a calmer, easier thing to suggest you begin thinking of yourself as a small museum, instead. One of those small, private ones that started in the Age of Enlightenment, perhaps—little more than a townhouse where an individual started to amass all the curios and wonders they had encountered, during their travels. You are your own museum, and you exist for your own inspiration, comfort and delight.

And now, as you wander around your museum, you might see things in your collection that you wish to manifest on yourself. Perhaps, you would be oddly satisfied if you had a green skirt printed all over with woodland leaves; perhaps, you wish to smell of roses yourself. Maybe you will do your hair like this statue of Nefertiti or this woodcut of Grace O'Malley, Queen of the Pirates.

And, when you look at your pictures of the women you love, you see many who take joyful delight in a bright headscarf; a round Afro; a red lip; a tramline of eyeliner; hair dyed blue, black, or red.

And because now *you* are the beholder of beauty—now *you* are the committee that decides what is beautiful, and what is not; now *you* are the one who calculates value—you can adopt these things you behold as your own, if you wish them. You can cut your hair short or curl it; you can paint stars under your eyes or put opals in your ears. You can paint your lips red, blue, or pink, or leave them as they are; wear your skirts long or short; wear overalls, or boots, or tights covered in stars. There is nothing destructive in a woman wanting to be beautiful *if she has decided what is beautiful* and knows *why* it makes her heart sing. If she is paying tribute to those who inspire her; if the things she does are cultural signifiers, to say: I love *this* singer, and *that* artist. Look! I wear a gray streak in my hair, so you know I love either Susan Sontag *or* the Bride of Frankenstein. Or, powerfully, *both*.

How you look is the first silent communication you make when you walk through a door, if you wish it to be. The way you choose to be "beautiful" says, "These are the things I love," *not*—as so many people mistakenly think—Love *me*. Once you know this, all the pressure disappears. You are free to enjoy being yourself, whatever you decide that may be.

These are the conversations I have with my girl, in the weeks following her sad declaration that she is ugly. No matter how clever, a mother cannot give an answer, or a solution, to the heartbreaking statement "I am ugly!" But she can give a question, instead: "What do *you* find beautiful? What would you like to collect around you, and on you, that gives you joy?"

"IF YOU THINK you're ugly—and you're *wrong*—then what would you *like* to look like?" I say, as we both continue to stroke the cat. "There are a million things we can try and do."

"I tried wearing makeup once," she says, still looking impossibly small and sad. "But I think I got it . . . wrong. A boy said I looked try-hard and fake. And some girls said I was a hypocrite."

"*What?*"

"They said, 'You keep saying you're a feminist—but makeup isn't very *feministic*, is it?'"

I ask for these girls' name, and then put them into my mental feud jotter. They, too, will die. This is one of the things no one ever tells you about motherhood—that you will have to become by way of a part-time assassin. Oh, the knives and crossbows I will have to buy! I will need a bigger handbag.

"One said, 'Why are you wearing makeup?'" and I said, "Because I want to?"

"And did they leave you alone? Did that work?"

I don't need to hear her answer—which is, inevitably, "no." A woman saying, "Because I want to" is *never* enough. For every decision she makes—even if it's putting on mascara—she must have a carefully thought-out manifesto with citations and quotes, ready to be brought out in front of any self-declared committee at a moment's notice. Being a woman is like writing a GCSE coursework essay on *Macbeth*. You can't just read it and enjoy it. You have to be able to pull it apart and show how it works—despite the fact it's successfully been *Macbeth* for five hundred years. Oh, how the world would change overnight if a woman saying "Because I want to" was *enough*.

"I didn't really care about the boy, because . . . *boys*. But the girls . . . is makeup not feminist? Is makeup fake?"

Is feminism against makeup? No! How could it be? I wear makeup, and I'm a feminist, because—how could my makeup be against the social, political, and economic equality of women, when I apply it for the simple reason that I want to look like charismatic seabird the puffin? For that is what my go-to makeup look—bright, iridescent blue eyelid, thick black eyeliner, and super-super pale skin—is attempting to do. It is a homage to a creature I feel a great affinity toward, due to its adorable waddling gait, love of sardines, and fondness for laying eggs on cliffs.

Most of the time, I wear makeup because I like *colors*. I want to look pretty like a garden, or a seashore, or a sunset. I can't see how feminism wouldn't want me to look like a sunset. *Or* Elizabeth Taylor. Feminism, surely, loves both Elizabeth Taylor and sunsets. How could it not?

And if feminism feels like it needs one last reassurance that makeup isn't a tool to oppress women, then let us consider David Bowie. If it is wondrous for David Bowie to wear makeup—if we adore drag queens, Adam Ant, Boy George, RuPaul, and Matty Healy from The 1975, who kohls his eyes until he looks like a Persian prince—then it is good enough for me. In the twenty-first century, the best feminist argument for the magic of makeup, and dressing up, is that if powerful, funny, clever boys are rejoiced in for wearing it, then surely twelve-year-old girls should be, too?

"Let's try some of Mommy's MAC eyeliner," I say to Nancy. "Whose eyeliner do you like?"

"Amy Winehouse," she says.

I pause for one second.

"Then—let's Amy Winehouse you."

And I draw a line across her lashes and out, out toward the freckle on her temple. And she smiles. We have decided what beautiful means. We have a vote in the system now. We can cut off the call that is coming from inside the house. When the existential crisis came to call, we could reply: "Not today. Not in this house. Not in this girl."

CHAPTER TEN

The Hour of the Ancestors

⤸

4:00 P.M.

OF COURSE, IT MIGHT NOT BE CHILDREN YOU ARE GUIDING THROUGH an existential crisis. For the day is moving on—it's afternoon now—and there are so many who need you.

I am lucky. My parents, so far, do not need caring for. My mother is still sprightly enough to have painted her entire house purple, and filled it with dream catchers—*gotta catch those dreams! Don't want them sailing out of the window!*

My father, meanwhile, is continuing with his lifelong quest to buy every *nicky-nacky-noo* that the jumble sales of Sussex have to offer. For those who do not know what a *nicky-nacky-noo* is, it's a category of item into which falls small glass animals, faux art deco mirrors, tiny Buddhas, bead necklaces, and Womble figurines, which can be stared at, appreciatively, whilst listening to jazz. Sometimes, I think of the fact that he had eight children—all rammed together in a tiny house—and think, "Were we just basically *nicky-nacky-noos*, too? Was he *collecting* us? Was he . . . *hoarding children?*"

My parents' divorce, after thirty years of marriage, seems to have given them a new lease on life—a fresh source of energy with which to argue over who owns which photo album, who was the best parent, and who the best jazz drummer was. Currently, they need no care at all.

But within my social group, I am almost the only one in this position. Half the friends I have can speak for hours about social services, nurses, the fitting of chairlifts, the purchasing of oxygen, the opiate ramblings. The funeral plans.

The other half are in a kind of in-between world—their parents aren't yet dying, but they are not quite living as they used to, either. Their abilities are slowly eroding—a window is stuck; a front door key misplaced; lids cannot be removed from jars. A phone call will come, late at night, or too early in the morning—a sudden worry, or sadness: "I get too tired walking the dog. Am I being unkind, only taking her around the block?" "My hands feel achy." "I think someone's been trying to climb over the back fence."

Or, perhaps, they won't *say* anything's wrong, but you can hear how quiet the house they're calling from is: the sound of silence that has had hours, or perhaps even *days*, to bank up before being broken by this phone call. Your parent's voice sounds a little rusty from lack of use.

And, so, the 4:57 p.m. London to Preston. This is where so many of you are, now, every other Friday night. Coach H, seat thirty-two—you are a creature of habit when it comes to rebooking these trips to your old hometown. Eighty-nine fifty pounds there and thirty-one fifty pounds back—because it's always harder to go than come back, as Avanti West Coast darkly, philosophically acknowledges in their fee structure.

Four fifty-seven at night—two hours and thirty minutes, two hundred and thirty miles. Cramped in your reserved seat with your healthy salad (the food of a sensible middle-aged woman) and your unhealthy half bottle of red wine (the drink of a sensible middle-aged woman), which you are obdurate isn't really alcohol, *really,* but merely "journey juice"—a potion that eases the jet lag of landing back in the city you fought so hard to leave, so long ago.

Hometowns, you muse, are so often like Glenn Close in *Fatal Attraction*—they chase you around, no matter how much you try to get away. They come alive and grab you in the final reel, when you're just too old and Michael Douglas to fight back.

You're going back because your mother is on her own now—divorced or widowed, it doesn't matter which—and ailing, but will not leave her home.

"It's my home," she says, simply. "All my stuff is here. The cat won't like moving. And I'm not going to go and live in some OAP prison, eating cabbage and being *spied* on."

And so here you are, on this train, every other week, "caring" for your mother for twenty-four hours, before traveling back again. How much care *can* you give to someone in twenty-four hours? You cram two weeks' worth of housekeeping into that time: the light bulbs that need replacing, the bed linen needs changing, the freezer that needs to be restocked. Nails to be clipped and medication to be doled out into pill sorters, cats to the vets, and duvets—hopefully not sodden—to the launderette. A tin opener that's easier to use; new glasses picked up from the optician—you blitz through that list like a motherfucker, even as she says, "Sorry!" or "Thank you!" or "There's a letter from the council I don't understand." It's a full-time job you magically compress into one day and night—like compressing a month's worth of clothes into a tiny suitcase.

But it's the easy part. The difficult part is the . . . *emotional Sherpa-ing.* The conversations. The bright face you have to put on. The exclamations of "You're looking well!" and "It'll get better soon!" and "The house looks cozy!"—which make you feel like some traveling huckster, trying to sell your parent a happiness you yourself don't quite believe in.

For there comes a point in every aging parent's life when you, and they, realize that a new mechanism has kicked in: They have begun, ever so slowly—perhaps over *years*—but inevitably, to travel toward death. This is the next big thing that will happen in your family—and, just as they brought you into the world, you will be there as they leave.

And of course you're never ready for it, and you don't have the words for it, and you don't have the time for it—who ever schedules the end of their parents into their lives?—but you must be, and you must have, and you must do.

And so, you get on this train, every other week, to never talk about this, and to pretend you're just there to wash the windows and see the cat.

OF COURSE, THERE are a million variants on this situation. It might be your father, not your mother. They might still be together. One might be ill, and the other just *old*—someone increasingly frail themselves caring for someone even more frail because . . . they have to. They might hate each other. They might hate *you*. You might have had a fractious relationship—each visit carrying the extra burden of a lifetime of resentments, and featuring inevitable bitching and crying.

Maybe they *would* leave their home, actually, to come and live with you—but that's something you just can't bring yourself to offer them. Your house is too small, your marriage too precarious, your children at the wrong age, your friends too used to hearing you say, "If they lived with me, I would go *stark staring mad*," before counseling you through your drunken, tearful guilt.

This will all only have become an issue because of some kind of crisis. Six months ago, two years ago, five years ago, they were *fine*—still active, seeing friends, hosting Christmases. They'd come to your house and mend a broken lock, hoover your curtains, go to your local shop and marvel at how expensive everything is. For fuck's sake—they went on holiday to Sardinia four years ago.

But then "The Sudden Bad Thing" happened—the list of plot twists that enter at this age are endless. An injured knee, a crumbling hip, galloping blood pressure. Diabetes, a stroke, a fall. A heart operation or a failing kidney. Anxiety. Depression. The early mists of dementia—gently erasing first the playful margins of conversation, before picking up the pace and eating right into the heart of sentences. Deafness, cataracts, something distressing about going to the toilet that you both try to be cheerful and matter-of-fact about—"There are things we can buy!"—even as you both try not to wince or cry.

And so now you are the one caring for them because family

history is what it is, and everyone's roles are what they are, and so you—good, capable, overworked daughter—are on the train, or else driving, to fit something in your schedule that, on paper, doesn't fit at all.

If you are a middle-aged woman with aging parents, chances are you'll be the one to care for them. In the US, 62 percent of women provide more than twenty hours of parent care each week, compared to 38 percent of men. In the UK, 86 percent of "sandwich carers"— those looking after both children and aging parents—are women. Why? Every family varies, but I have noticed that, more often than not, behind every tired middle-aged woman laden with responsibilities and caring for aging parents, there's usually a brother or two not pulling their weight. We just don't raise men to ride to the rescue when a family-caring crisis hits. "You're better at this stuff than me," or "I wouldn't know what to do," or "She wants you more than she wants me."

You're not, of course, any "better at this" than your brother. The one thing you *are* better at than him is seeing how your mother— parenting a son without all the modern feminism you have access to—was the very one who raised him *not* to come to the rescue.

He's from the last generation of boys raised as princes—allowed the luxury of believing his life and career must not be troubled by family problems.

You—scrabbling at your laptop to pay bills and answer work emails on the way to your mother's house—were not.

You're "just more capable." Should you explain feminism to him? It would simply end up being another thing on the to-do list. It's easier to go to Preston, every other week, on this train, with this wine.

THE PRACTICAL SIDE of caring for aging parents is one thing—how so few employers allow for flexibility or leave for carers; how badly women's careers are affected by it; how society has still not yet come up with *any* solid plans for caring for an increasingly aging population. It's an unspoken presumption that we will simply carry on as we are, with women carrying the burden, unpaid.

Of course, with every generation of women who take a hit to their career—forgoing promotion to care for aging parents—we compound the future problem: When *these* women reach old age, they, too, will not have the financial resources to take care of themselves independently. A purpose-built apartment, a cleaner, a physio will be out of their reach.

And so, they will have to lean on *their* daughters—and so on, through the generations. It's a baked-in financial inequality. It's also a tax on love—for if you are the gender that, traditionally, loves and cares, by offering a service that saves the state billions, you are put at a financial disadvantage.

But the second aspect of having aging parents is more . . . existential. The only comparable life event is having children—an evolution into someone else, entrusted with someone else's well-being in an exhausting process you cannot stint or swerve on.

There are, of course, dozens and dozens of books about mothering your children—how you relate to them, how you assert control, how you soothe them, and develop into a master tactician with the gentle patience of a saint—all phrased with the battle-weary camaraderie of parents counseling other parents. We know what a mother *should* be, even if we fuck it up half the time.

But there is pitifully little written about how to deal with your parents aging and dying—despite the fact it is equally transformative. We have no template for what woman you should become *now*. For when you start caring for an aging parent, something seismic happens: You swap places. Your parent must, slowly and carefully, climb down from the top of the family tree to a safer, lower branch, whilst you gradually ascend to take their place. You must climb to the top. It's your turn. The simple passing of time has pushed you up there.

At the end of their lives, parents turn back into children, and you must now mother your father or mother, or both.

And yet, this momentous, inevitable occasion has no name. It's an unacknowledged changing of the guards: an unchronicled, permanent body swap. You must become the new matriarch, even as you tend and mourn the passing of the former queen. You arrange the Christmases, settle the family arguments, fret over errant nieces and nephews, become the first port of call for those in trouble. You become mother to a whole, extended family now—because someone must, and it's you.

Perhaps it's a power you want. Perhaps it's a power you wish you could give away. But that's where you're headed, eventually—steeling yourself on the 4:57 p.m. with your wine. And I salute you, even as I know, one day, I will be on that train, too.

CHAPTER ELEVEN

The Hour of "What About the Men?"

~≈~

5:00 P.M.

HAVING DEALT WITH FIVE EXISTENTIAL CRISES BEFORE DINNER, I come into the kitchen to check on some emails. Andrew is sitting at the table on his laptop. I serve him his Cauliflower Cheese Surprise—the surprise is there's kale in it, too!—sit down, and sigh.

"Man, it's hard being a feminist, raising feminist daughters," I sigh. "No wonder Germaine Greer just raised some geese instead. Imagine if all I had to do every year was manage a migration to Africa and a bit of random honking. It would be a cinch."

Andrew grates some more cheese onto his cauliflower.

"I don't know," he says, pausing to tap the back of the grater. "I just think that maybe feminism has . . . gone too far?"

I blink. No—there is my brother, sitting in my feminist house, grating my feminist cheese on his feminist cauliflower, with five feminist sisters and two feminist nieces, suggesting that feminism has gone too far. I look down. Yes—once again, he's rammed his feet into my feminist slippers, stretching the sheepskin. It's like a massive, ironic metaphor.

"What?" I say.

He carries on grating. "It's just gone too far," he says, conversationally. "Everything's about women now, isn't it? But, in the twenty-first century, I think it's actually harder to be a young man than a young woman. *What about the men?"*

SINCE WRITING *How to Be a Woman*—a book about women and feminism—there is one question I have been asked more than any other. Whether it be an interview, Q&A, or informal advice on the street, one question is asked ten times more than "How do I deal with sexual harassment at work?" or "What are the biggest problems feminism faces in the twenty-first century?" or "Why, why, *why* did you have to write so much about masturbating whilst thinking of Chevy Chase?"

That question is "But what about the *men?"*

At first, I was pretty dismissive. I am, after all, primarily gunning for the ladies. I am avowedly "Team Tits." I have very publicly specialized in one topic—so don't ask me about the *men! I* don't know! I'm concentrating on the other 52 percent of the population! *I'm busy!* It would be the ultimate irony of feminism, would it not, if—having once solved the problems of women—women then had to solve the problems of men as well? FUCK OFF WITH MEN! LET THEM SORT IT OUT! JESUS CHRIST!

Over the last decade, however, I have had a long time to think about this, and now I find myself in the wholly unexpected position of asking, "Yes—what *about* the men?"

It's a question that feminism *should* be asking, because feminism is a very simple thing: The belief in the social, economic, and political equality of the sexes. *Equality.* And when we talk about what it is to be either a man or a woman, we can see there is bullshit on both sides.

Yes, we women know that one in four of us will be sexually assaulted and raped; we know we still get paid less; we are judged harshly on our attractiveness, age, and manner—to be old, unsexy, or "bossy" is still a death knell. Ask Hillary Clinton.

But men—men, you suffer from gender presumptions, too. You know you do—that's what "What about the men?" means, surely? You mean that suicide is the leading cause of death for men under the age of fifty; that after divorce, you tend to not get primary custody of your children; that you are far more likely to end up in jail than women; that you are judged harshly if you are not tall, or buff, or lavish of hair, or powerful, or wealthy. And who talks about these problems, and writes books about them, or sings joyous songs about being a young man trying to change men's lives? No one.

Let me be very, very clear here—*women* haven't created these problems that you face. These things are not *feminism's* fault. Women gaining greater power and freedom hasn't *taken away* your powers and freedoms. The problems that you list are all down to feminism's greatest foe—and one I hope, today, to explain is *your* greatest foe, too: the patriarchy.

To be clear: Men—*you* are not the patriarchy. The word *patriarchy* is often risky to use, as I think many men hear it, and instantly fear that nine thousand angry women are going to come and cut their penises off and burn them in a big bonfire. Let me reassure you right now—no penises will be cut off and burned during this conversation. There are similar fears about the phrase "toxic masculinity," which is misinterpreted as women accusing *all* men of being *poisonous*. No! "The patriarchy" and "toxic masculinity" are basically the same things: they are simply a quick way of referring to old, stale, confining ideas about what it is to be a man or a woman, *which are hurting men just as much as they are hurting women.*

Consider the list: When men itemize their problems, they all have the same root. They are problems caused by rigid ideas about what "being a man is": insisting that men bottle up their worries and doubts, that child-rearing is best done by women, that men need more severe punishments than women, that men need to be SUPER-MANLY, BUFF, AND LOADED, or else have no value in the eyes of either women or other men.

Here's the quick and easy way of telling if the patriarchy's screwing you over: If your problems are based on clichéd assumptions about gender that have been around for thousands of years, that's gonna be down to the patriarchy, bro—because women weren't defining *anything* thousands of years ago. We didn't get to define *shit*.

We didn't write the Bible, or preach, or make laws, or decide society's rules. We didn't write plays, or poetry, or books, or even a fucking scroll detailing all the wells in the area. And neither did most men, either. But some of the guys who did, decided what was "male" and "female," and they both casually and rigorously enforced them for centuries. *And THAT is the patriarchy.* And, as you can see, with these gender roles, the patriarchy's bumming you as hard as it's bumming us. We *all* got patriarchy problems up the bum, dude.

Logically, then, if feminism is about equality between the sexes, we must address the inequalities that *both* sexes face—or the project is incomplete.

And, so, feminism for men.

At first, it seems oxymoronic—especially to my brother, Andrew.

"Feminism is all about hating men," he continues, eating his cauliflower. "It's gone too far. Women are winning now. Girls are doing better than boys, educationally; they go on about men objectifying women but then go *on* and *on* about *Magic Mike XXL;* all the jobs that men used to do are disappearing, and the kind of jobs that women do are taking over. And if men complain about this, they're told to 'stop whining,' or that they're sexist. So, okay, I give in. I *am* sexist. If complaining about men's problems is sexist and anti-feminist, I'm an anti-feminist—because I'm not going to pretend I don't have problems. I've got loads. Could you pass the pepper?"

Andrew is eighteen, and knowing a man who is so young, and being able to put myself in his shoes—well, my fucking slippers—allows me, for the first time, to understand male anger against women. Because anger is, as we know, just fear brought to the boil—and why wouldn't he be scared? If he looks at both sexes between the beginning of the twentieth century and now, the difference between men and women's progress is total.

One hundred and twenty years ago, women could not vote, they could not own property, their children were owned by their husbands, the range of education and employment open to them was almost nil. Their paychecks were paid into their husbands' bank accounts. If their husbands did not like their wives, they could consign them to a mental asylum.

Now, although across the world there are still women facing appalling oppression and discrimination on a daily basis, for many of us, our lives are demonstrably better than those of our mothers and grandmothers. We generally believe our daughters and grand-daughters' lives will be even better than our own. Women vote, they become politicians and heads of state, they run multinational businesses. They control their fertility, they talk openly about their sexuality, they play sports, they earn money, they are educated, they wear trousers, *they are in space.* Things have improved massively for women.

Now, by way of contrast, let us turn to men. What has improved specifically *for men*, in the last 120 years? Nothing. Broadly, the only real difference between our grandfathers and our sons is that our sons are unlikely to wear a top hat—unless they are Slash from Guns N' Roses, playing the Artful Dodger in a musical production of *Oliver!* Otherwise, men's lives look pretty much as they did at the beginning of the twentieth century. Whilst women's lives have expanded exponentially—gaining more freedom, joy, power, a sense of community, and progression—men's have remained static. When comparing the lives of men to those of women, no wonder so many men feel like they are losing. Like they are being left behind by society.

Basically, the only difference between men and women in those 120 years is simple: feminism. Feminism decided to reject the old, old rules about gender. Women got together and created a culture and network where they could first raise their problems, then discuss how to change them—one piece of bullshit at a time. We have spent a century establishing an entirely crowdsourced, informal network where we can talk to each other, ask for help, gain advice, campaign for change, and highlight injustices. We have coined new phrases to phenomena that, even a generation earlier, were simply presumed to be our own isolated faults: women's liberation, male privilege, coercive control, gaslighting, the Bechdel Test, TIME'S UP, #metoo, Queen Bee Syndrome. Whatever the problem of a woman in the twenty-first century, she can, in minutes, find a website, chat board, hashtag, book, film, TV show, local group, or political party that will be addressing these issues. Women are connected. Women have organized. Women have identified the things they wish to have changed, and then acted upon it. Women have changed the idea of what it is to "be a woman" *utterly*—and in what is, historically, the blink of an eye. They have challenged the patriarchy.

Men, meanwhile—they do not have this at all. They have no network. They have no way of talking about their problems—what saddens them, what they would like to change. They have no way to ask one another questions, and find answers. They have not found a way to challenge the patriarchy. They are, essentially, stuck with the lives of their fathers and grandfathers.

So I understand why a young man would look at his female classmates—members of the feminists' club at school; going on marches; talking about Channing Tatum dancing to "Pony"; discussing Jacinda Ardern, Little Simz, and Billie Eilish—and feel, well, anger. Fear. Women talk about what women are, or will be, *constantly*—the concept of "woman" is expanding all the time. It's where all the heat and hope and creativity are. Captain America is a woman, now; the Ghostbusters are women. *Lord of the Flies* is being remade with girls; everything's being gender-flipped, and gender-flipped one way only. Women have *velocity* now; every week, some new pop star, or TV show, or politician, comes along, and is spoken of as revolutionary: This is the world of Malala, Greta Thunberg, Alexandria Ocasio-Cortez, Phoebe Waller-Bridge, Beyoncé, and *Girls*, and girls, and girls. Girls are where the heat is; girls are where the future is. Being a girl *means* something—for it is discussed, improved, and expanded, all the time. *It's questioned.*

But no one's talking about boys.

No one's making *their* world bigger. No one's organizing boys' things. There are no revolutionary boys. People aren't excited about boys. Boys aren't inventing new things. Boys aren't being cheered for their new ways of thinking. Boys don't have devoted boy fans who champion them on social media. Boys don't write books about their brave, taboo-busting lifestyles. Boys don't question what they find difficult about being a boy. Boys aren't news—unless they're a problem. Unless they habituate chat boards, encouraging each other to become men's rights activists, incels, radicalized, or to shoot up a school. If you want to get attention as a man, by and large, it only happens by being controversial, or negative, or destructive. There's no good, generous, joyous news about being a young man. Women get in the news by being the first women to win prizes; the first to earn a certain amount of money; the first to rule a country. To be a woman is to be in a world of "firsts." Men have no firsts left. The only way they can be in the news is by becoming bad news. If I had young boys, instead of young girls, I think the world would look very different to me. I think it might look far more hopeless. If my teen-age boy had just cried because *he* was ugly, how would I have helped him? There is no framework for dealing with a man's essential belief he is unlovable. I would have no tools to help him in his loneliness and despair.

I think this world might look like Andrew's world.

I think I might ask feminists, "But what about the men?"

PONDERING THIS, I go on Twitter. Twitter's the place to ask a question! And so I ask: "Men. Men of Twitter. What are the downsides of being a man? We discuss the downsides of being a woman very frequently—but what's going on with *you* lovely guys?"

I expected there to be a few responses. What I was not expecting was for the replies to go on for *days*—scrolling frantically up my feed like a ticker tape. I get *thousands* of replies. A month later, and I'm still getting twenty or so a day. Eventually, it gets picked up as a news story in newspapers and on websites around the world, and not surprisingly—for it seems to have opened a whole new conversation that I didn't even know we needed. And the answers I get range from the amusing to the heartbreaking.

We began with the jokey, and practical: "I'm a person—not a walking jar opener, or sentient spider catcher." "As a man, I have to pretend I like the song 'Summer of '69' at parties, and barbecues. I have to punch the air and sing along, when I actually hate it." "Sometimes, if you sit down too quickly, you can accidentally sit on your own testicles."

Three things that women have, yes, never experienced, and for which we are now retrospectively grateful.

Then we moved on to a category we could loosely describe as "Men's bodies are just funny, basic objects."

"It's impossible to make yourself sexy for your wife, beyond basic personal hygiene, or working out at the gym. There's no designer or Ann Summers outfit that's gonna make your wife go 'PHWOAR.'"

"There's no equivalent of sexy nightwear for men. Women have so many options when it comes to sexy fun times. Men? A comedy-posing pouch, with a picture of an elephant on it, or the slogan, 'BEWARE OF THE BEAST.'"

Although this initially makes me laugh—Beasts! Sexy elephant knackers! HAHAHAHA! That *is* amusing!—the more I think about this, the sadder I get. Ann Summers thinks men's genitals are either terrifying or funny. Dangerous or risible. If women were being sold knickers that made their vadges look like mad beasts or screaming marmosets, feminists would *assemble*. Well, *I* wouldn't: Personally, I'd quite like the marmoset knickers. My vadge *does* look like a screaming marmoset. To paraphrase Dalí ("I don't make art—I *am* art"), "I don't *need* furry knickers—I *am* furry knickers." But the point remains. Penises are either to be feared—or laughed at. It reveals an awful truth about how we see male physicality. That's harsh.

The third category could be titled, "It's more fun to be a woman."

"You can't go out for a lovely meal with man friends. The only time eating is allowed is after alcohol, and then it's for a mediocre curry, or a kebab whilst standing next to a bin."

"Father's Day is depressing. All the cards suggest that all men are into is football, beer, golf, or cars. Our lives look really limited."

"I am *deeply* jealous of the ladies' toilet. Occasionally the door swings open on the opposite corridor, and the sweet smell of a scented candle wafts across to the uncannily accurate re-creation of the WWI trench in which I have to ablute."

"Yesterday at the gym there was a male engineer working in the ladies' changing room. So for one day, they swapped the men and the women around. It's like I've been to the moon and come back and everything on earth is just shit compared to the fucking amazing moon."

"Going on a night out and having a complete stranger become your best friend in the ladies' toilet and compliment your clothes, sounds pure and wonderful, and I want it."

But how could men compliment one another on their clothes? Men's clothes are all the same. "My wife can dress a million different ways—casual jeans, slinky dress, pretty blouse, businesslike suit. I just have trousers. Every day—trousers. In black, or brown, or navy. It's SO BORING."

I see what he means—for however much women might still struggle to find something to wear for who they need to be today, we can reinvent ourselves, over and over, a dozen times a week. To be a woman is a creative act that encompasses many moods. Men are just men, in men clothes, every day. No change. No experimentation. No expression of mood. When fashion is a multitrillion dollar industry of confidence and dreams, that fact is . . . dispiriting. That men just dress "like men" every day. They never get to try being someone, or something, else—unless it's a fancy dress party. Maybe that's why so many men are obsessed with fancy dress parties. It's their only chance to cut loose, clotheswise.

And if you can't experiment with who you are—if you cannot improve yourself with a new dress or haircut—what do you do when you feel, as all humans do, at some point, ugly? Fashion and makeup might sometimes be a double-edged sword, but the simple fact remains that, by using them, women can make themselves feel better by *looking nicer*. One recurrent complaint from young men's rights activists is that women "don't like ugly, normal guys like me." It doesn't seem to occur to them that life's pretty shitty for ugly, normal girls, too—but they just go off and talk to their mom, get their "colors done," find out that their eyes pop in a nice burgundy cardigan, and that a layered bob would be better than a perm, and they *upgrade* themselves in the eyes of a primarily visual society.

I would suggest this is part of the reason why *Queer Eye* has been such a smash hit across the world—for a light entertainment show, it is quietly revolutionary in that it shows five joyous gay men changing the lives of unhappy, often straight men, by applying what is a traditionally female solution to their problems. They sort out their facial rashes with good skincare; buy them a flattering shirt; cut their hair into something nicer; put sidelighting into their houses; put flowers on their table; talk to them about what makes them sad about their lives ("When your mom died, that must have been tough. You had to nurse your dad through Alzheimer's? Dude, I'm so sorry."); let them weep, hug them, show them what an avocado dip is—and then throw a party for all their friends, that they might see they are loved. That they are not alone.

The message is "Men who are unhappy and lonely, don't waste your time being escalatingly bitter on social media with other unhappy and lonely men! Do as the women do—have a cry with friends, get yourself some nice new trousers, then go dancing."

In other words: The patriarchy offers no cure for sadness, feeling lost, or self-loathing. How could it? The patriarchy's solution to crying is bellowing, "Man up!"—become even *more* male. But repressing your sadness never, ever cured it. The only time it's ever acceptable to cry, if you're a man, is (a) when your football team loses an important match or (b) if you're Alexander the Great, weeping because you have no new worlds to conquer. How *exhausting*—to have to be a conqueror of worlds. Surely just making your own world nicer would be far more time effective *and* save you having to invade Persia.

The next category moves us toward the heartbreaking: The idea that men are less valued in their roles of emotional support than women. That they're neither needed nor celebrated.

"Here are your children's favorite things, in order of preference: (1) Mom, (2) siblings, (3) pet cats, (4) pet dogs, (5) friends, (6) cuddly toys, (7) Dad."

"You'll always, always be second-best to mom."

"I've made my daughter playlists about being an empowered woman, and there are hundreds of songs to choose from—most by Beyoncé. Then I tried to make something similar for my son, and there's nothing. Nothing about it just being *joyous* to be a boy. Instead, it's all 'Bad boys for life,' or 'Boys are back in town.' The only songs about being a boy are about causing *trouble*. They all sound like the prelude to being arrested for taking dick pics on the bus."

This possibly segues into the next category: Men don't have a way to talk about being unhappy, or their lives going wrong. Men don't have the words to be sad.

"When women get beaten up by life, their friends gang up to support them. Men don't. Sometimes, all you need is a hug."

"I quit my PhD through unbearable stress and depression but spent all this awful period talking about the European Cup and the merits of 4-4-2 vs 4-3-3 whenever I met my friends for a drink."

"When my daughter died, there was no one to talk to. My wife had tons of support."

"You will grow up with your male role models repressing all their emotions, and then have to spend seventy pounds an hour in therapy to deal with it when you're older."

"Men aren't conditioned to talk to each other about our lives. We meet up, have a four-hour conversation about who would win in a fight between RoboCop and Inspector Gadget, but never get our worries off our chests."

Although more than 1,000 people "liked" this comment, one man had a very salient observation to make about it: "Inspector Gadget vs Robocop? *Why* would they fight? They're both in law enforcement!"

And this conversation about how men cannot *get* help turned even more distressing—for men started to talk about how they cannot *offer* help, either. How they are seen as . . . threatening. Dangerous.

"The worst thing about being a man? Being feared by women. I mean I fully recognize men caused this state of affairs, but it's sad."

"My next-door neighbor's young daughter, about fourteen or fifteen at the time, was locked out, and it was freezing. I didn't dare offer for her to come into my house, as I was home alone, and I knew it would terrify her."

"If I see a kid who's lost in the playground, I can't go and help them. I have to go and find a woman and get *them* to help, because men are scary."

"Men are scary." This sentence cuts my heart like a knife. This is not a good world we have created—where we have told children that half the population of the world is to be feared. That you cannot be helped by a man. That men are to be wary of and run away from.

As I ponder this, I think of how absolutely destructive this must be to young boys—to know that you could help a fellow child while you're still twelve, or thirteen, say, but as soon as you grow above a certain height, or your voice breaks, you have crossed a Rubicon. You are now seen as dangerous; your presence will instill fear in others, no matter how gentle you are. Add into that, race—how much more threatening young black and brown boys are seen—and that is a terrible burden for young boys to carry, for it is hardwired in humans to want to help each other. We *want* to be good. We *want* to save, and comfort, others.

Have that denied you, and you are crushing a huge part of what it is to be human. I can't imagine how damaging that is. As a woman, I might be scared—but I have never known what it is like to *scare others*. I have always enjoyed the knowledge that I can walk in anywhere and comfort people. Imagining that being taken away is unexpectedly devastating. To be thought of by society as . . . a potential *weapon*. And to be able to do nothing about it. I suddenly realize there is such a thing as "female privilege"—for whatever my troubles or fears in life, as a woman, I've always known no one is scared of me. That I can approach anyone and not have them fear me. That no one has ever looked at me and wondered: Is this person going to hurt me? Should I run?

There is a terrible loneliness and restriction to being a man it seems—unable to help, talk about how you feel, sing a song about your life, make your wife fancy you, change what being a man *is*. It is a bleakness—this confining, utilitarian aspect to being a man that, over the years, defines you as a simple beast interested only in booze, sports, or basic underwear and disinterested in the loveliness and magic we *all* loved as children, no matter our sex.

"My wife buys beautiful scented candles that smell like a church— but when she goes to bed, she blows them out. She presumes I don't like them."

"My wife turns the fairy lights out when she goes to bed. It makes me so sad."

"I wish I could give, and receive, presents that aren't 'men presents.' So much whisky and socks! I'd love flowers. I think they're beautiful. No one buys men flowers."

One man who saw this tweet—I was retweeting them all, frantically—tweeted me the next day. "I went and gave my ninety-three-year-old father flowers yesterday. Sunflowers, because I know he loves them. He'd never received flowers before. He cried."

Half the population never gets flowers. Flowers! That are every-where, for everyone. Except—not for men.

AND AS I looked at all these replies—thousands and thousands of problems, listed, in a space where they'd been requested—they all seemed to add up to one thing: that whilst women have spent a cen-tury reinventing and expanding themselves, rejecting ideas about what women are "supposed" to be, men have not had that revolution yet. In this respect—and this explains so many of the "men don't understand women/women don't understand men" arguments—we are totally out of sync with each other. The existences of men and women, although ostensibly side by side, have slipped radically apart from each other. The recent history of men and the recent history of women have very, very little in common. Were they turned into films, they would be utterly disparate—they have different icons, mile-stones, victories, anniversaries, languages, and arcs, and the current ending is very, very different. Whilst women's stories are beset by many, many obstacles, the arc looks upbeat, and would probably end with a bunch of girls strutting down the street high-fiving each other, soundtracked by Lizzo's "Juice."

Men's—currently feels like it's played in a minor key; soundtracked by a solo Thom Yorke song in a broken falsetto, before some grinding beats kick in. Like it would end with a man walking down a street, alone, to who knows where? A bookshop to buy a Jordan B. Peterson book, perhaps.

And there is a societal unfairness at the base of all this—an unfairness that, perhaps, explains why there are so many angry young men. For the ways in which women have expanded the definition of "being a woman" are, by and large, by claiming attributes that were previously deemed to be male. Guys: We stole all the men's things! We ram-raided all your exciting, powerful-looking shit and totally appropriated it! We decided all *your* cool shit didn't need to be gender-specific at all! We can now aspire to a life where we are intellectual, educated, sexual, sporting, confident, businesslike, political. We cut our hair short, we wear trousers, we drink, we drive, we organize, we agitate—the big and little things that were all deemed, a short while ago, to be entirely male. ALL YOUR BASE BELONG TO US!

But it has just been a one-way swap. For whilst women can now do the things that were thought of as "male," as well as everything that was thought of as "female," men have not come and claimed the "female" things from us. Women have gained from a raid on the world of men. Men have taken nothing from the world of women— even though we would absolutely have helped you take it, and even given you one of our many Bags for Life to carry it away in.

Talking about your problems; being honest about your emotions; having a tightly bonded peer group with whom you can discuss your hopes and fears; being able to reinvent yourself day after day; feeling united in a common, hopeful aim; being desired; rejoicing in beautiful things—these are all seen as "female things." And these are the things men say are missing from their lives.

Why do they not feel they can simply come and take them—

take them, as women have taken "wearing trousers" and saying "I'm horny?"

The answer, I'm afraid, is awful: it's because female things are, still, seen as "lesser."

It was understood why women want the men's things—they are the things of power. We took them, and we grew in stature. But if men wanted to take women's things—crying, hugging, flowers, community, emotional self-improvement, gardening, beautiful textiles, and looking sexy—they would be seen to be taking the soft things. The "losing" things. The things of the inferior gender. Things that are seen to have no power—and are, therefore, second-rate or consolation prizes. They would be judged. By who? By anyone—male *or* female—who has notions of the patriarchy buried so deep in them, that even a suicidal man weeping to his friends about how hopeless he feels, would be told "to stop being such a fucking woman/big girl's blouse and man up."

If there is this hunger amongst men—and my Twitter feed suggested there was—for a new, bigger, more varied and joyous way to be a man in the twenty-first century, then the solution isn't at all mysterious. We don't need to invent something new or wait for some huge discovery. Implicit in men asking women, "What about the men?" is, surely, a deeply buried assumption that *women have the answer to men's problems.* That talking about it is necessary. That it would need empathy. That it would require change. *That it would be better, somehow, if women were involved.* And why would you think that if you didn't, deep down, see something in women that you desire? Maybe the biggest secret men have isn't that their biggest desire is that they want to fuck women—but that, perhaps, they would like to be them? Just a little bit? Just have some of the things we have?

I'm happy to admit there are "man things" I envy: I'd like to piss standing up, I'd like to walk around at night on my own without being scared, and I'd like to be able to throw a ball properly. I can go proper King Louie in *The Jungle Book* about all the "male things" I have either craved, or simply taken and repurposed as my own. And it feels unfair that men cannot do the same with women.

Maybe this can only happen when being a woman isn't seen as "being lesser"—when "female things" come to be seen as higher in status, and, therefore, desirable. In which case, every book, film, TV show, and song about being a woman that focuses on the positive, glorious, amusing, nourishing, joyous aspects of being a woman is helping both men and women alike. Every woman who succeeds is making the idea of "being a woman" more powerful. A thing *everyone* would like to be.

Although it may not feel like it to a man who feels scared, or left behind, every time a woman succeeds, she is, ironically, making things easier for men as well. She is, ultimately, succeeding for *all* of us. This is why feminism can't go "too far." Women can't "win" *enough*. Because when "being a woman" and "doing things like a woman" are seen as equally powerful to "being a man" and "doing things like a man," then men will feel no shame in taking the things that have made *us* happier.

We will finally live in a world where there are no such things as "girl things" and "boy things"—it will all simply be seen as "humanity's massive resource box."

AND THIS IS an urgent need—for, when we see news stories that are apt to make us feel dolorous about the future of humanity, the roots of so many of them are grown in the thin, thin cultural soil we grow our young men in. There are basic skills in "being a human" that we are not equipping our boys with. Take, for instance, romantic rejection. Every human being will be rejected, multiple times, in their lives—but women are far better versed in how to deal with it. When a self-proclaimed "incel"—an involuntary celibate, who could not "make" any woman want to have sex with him—shot thirty-two people in Canada, after being rejected by a prospective girlfriend and having been celibate for *more than two years*, I went on Twitter and asked women what they do, when *they* have been celibate for more than two years.

"I knit," "I read poetry," "I took up capoeira dance classes," "I bought all the Wainwright books and started walking in the Lake

District," "I adopted a cat," "I wrote a book," "I took up pottery," "I learned to cook," "I had a wank." There are hundreds of thousands of disaffected, sexually rejected women, and not one of them is shooting up a nightclub or mall. *A woman has never shot multiple people because she feels rejected by society*, despite women being, I would suggest, romantically rejected at least as equally often as men.

We see it as a low-status, low-value thing to be able to cope with disappointment, disaffection, and rejection—but life will, absolutely, deal you your share of disappointment, disaffection, and rejection. If we are not giving half the population a constructive way to deal with this—if we are not making heartbroken pottery an option for them— that's not fair to them, and it's really not fair to the people some of them are shooting. We shouldn't be telling boys that rejection is so awful and final that people must *die* for you to cope with it. What a terrifying thing to tell a young boy. What a terrifying deal to present to the world—that men *cannot* fail.

I am minded of the words of Hannah Gadsby, who—as one of the most truthful and philosophical comedians of the last decade— talks both about the unexpected bonus of being the gender that is still disadvantaged, and the unlikely power that being a lesbian has given her emotionally: "We've got a generation of young men who believe that they are victimized, because they've been promised the world, and not received it. That's a poisoned chalice—because now there's a gap between what the cultural narrative is, and what their actual experience is. Looking back, I think it's done me more good than harm to be promised *absolutely nothing*. That's why I haven't responded to the more brutal aspects of my life with violence or bitterness."

If we see how vastly, game-changingly improved women's lives are from adopting The Things of Men, imagine how rapidly the world would be transformed if men now adopted The Things of Women. The hardest work has already been done.

The answer to "What about the men?" is already here. It's "Be more like a woman."

CHAPTER TWELVE

The Hour We Remember—Don't Eat Your Sisters

6:00 P.M.

AT 6 P.M., I DECIDE TO HAVE A BREAK FROM WORK. I GO ON THE INternet to see how it's going for all the women.

I'd say it's a . . . "mixed grill?"

On the one hand, there are more non-wired bras available than ever before; there's four or five petitions about feminist causes that are picking up traction; there's a funny and clever blog about "emotional labor" that's going viral; and someone's found a clip of Chaka Khan playing drums in a golden ball gown, which is an absolute tonic for the soul. Plus, there's a meme of an angry owl in a cardboard box, which is speaking to a *lot* of women I know, as its furious, yellow owl eye glares out of a tiny hole it's ripped in the side. *Je suis* angry owl in a box, internet. *Je suis.*

On the other hand, when I look at my DMs, I can see that four of the first ten are from women in the public eye who are currently going through either being publicly shamed on social media, or dealing with its aftereffects. One has been #cancelled over a job she took that many people think she shouldn't have. The second is being criticized for "letting transwomen down" by not speaking out enough about her experiences as a trans woman on a daily basis. A third woke up to find three furious blogs had been published, overnight, picking holes in a book she's written *that hasn't even been published yet.* And the fourth is being roundly trolled for her friendship with another woman who is currently in the center of a separate Twitter-storm—my friend is being told she should announce, publicly, that she disowns *her* friend and *also* apologize on her behalf.

All are incredibly distressed—they're talking about how it's affecting their sleep, and their mental health. Until you've been in the center of one of these flurries, it's hard to convey just how unexpectedly destabilizing they are. Those who've never experienced it might find themselves saying, "Dude, why are you so upset about finding out that lots of people hate you enough to talk about it publicly?"—before realizsing they have, perhaps, just answered their own question. It's the sense of *being in trouble;* of having done something so categorically wrong that people are now spending time they could have otherwise spent having a bath, or putting a wig on a dog, shouting "NO! JUST NO! YOU'RE CANCELED!" at you, instead.

Imagine opening your laptop, or turning on your phone, and suddenly finding that what seems like *the whole world*—but, in reality, probably only a few hundred people—is staring directly at you, whilst discussing with others how hateful you are, and actively believing that you have acted from the worst possible intentions. It's a bit like the scene in *Superman II* where the Council of Krypton holds the trial of General Zod—and dozens of gigantic faces, including that of Marlon Brando, all boom "GUILTY!" before condemning Zod and his gang to the Phantom Zone. Except, in this case, you're not an intergalactic fascist who's tried to stage a violent coup on Krypton, killing millions—but just a woman who has said or done something, usually quite minor within the scheme of wars, and famines, and death that others disagree with.

And although we know that social media can be a brutal place, what's notable about all these women in my DMs is that they aren't getting abuse from anonymous, misogynist male trolls, threatening to kill or rape them, as we would expect when someone is talking about "abuse on the internet." No. I mean, they're obviously getting these *as well*—every woman does. But the abuse women are *particularly* upset about is from *other women.* And women who are broadly aligned with their own sensibilities: progressive, liberal, left leaning, and feminist. For the abuse they're getting is that they're not being progressive and feminist *enough*.

WHEN I WROTE about female role models in *How to Be a Woman*, ten years ago, the problems faced by women in the public eye were very different. Then, I noted that the primary problems for our female role models—big and small—were (1) it was hard to gain prominence, back then, if you weren't *either* a delightful, fragrant woman in a beautiful silk blouse with flawless skin who was never photographed in a bad outfit, *or* a glamour model—this was the era of Katie Price being voted one of the most powerful women in Britain. And (2) once they became famous, so much of their narrative was congruent with *either* managing to hold down a successful relationship—lest they become like "poor, tragic, single Jennifer Aniston," *or* submit to endless questioning about when, and if, they were planning to have a baby.

As we can see, a whole heap of feminist water has passed under the bridge since then. The *good* news is that we are in an unprecedentedly fertile era of producing many, and wildly varied, female role models compared to 2011: days of yore. This is a stelliferous age, boasting the previously unimaginable stars Greta Thunberg, Malala, AOC, Baroness Lady Hale, Simone Biles. . . . I could go on—saying each of those names is like a party in my mouth.

The *bad* news is that there is now a recognizable career arc for so many feminist women who have gained a public platform. They come along—with a show, film, book, or campaign that catches the imagination. Everyone is like "Hurrah! A new lady hero! Let the memes and the bunting abound!" There may be six months, or a year, of this time of celebration. It's like some manner of Lady Christmas—for there is little more lovely than seeing someone from your team hitting a home run and creating a little moment of communal joy.

Then, at some point in all this happiness, something will happen that throws this all into reverse. The new lady hero will tweet something thoughtless; they'll make an ill-advised comment in an interview; they'll create a piece of art that is seen as "uninclusive" or "problematic"; or perhaps, something supercilious or "off" that they said off the cuff, drunk, in 2012, will be discovered and blogged about.

Of course, fair enough to point out if someone's done something wrong—a response along the lines of "Eh?" or "Nah," or "This looks a bit off," or "Maybe don't do this again, you asshat!" would not be out of place.

But, so often, that's not how social media works. This incident will be retweeted and reposted—gathering a little more heat and anger each time—until, suddenly, in the space of a few hours, this singe incident will be seen as this woman's *defining attribute*; the moment we saw her *true* nature.

There's no point in trying to suggest a bit of perspective— pointing out that there are very few single incidents that *genuinely* invalidate a woman's whole life, or career; that reverse *all* the good she has done—for the storm will be at full force. It seems like everything she has done—maybe over decades—has now been undone, in a single moment.

In the coming weeks, she might be disinvited from events, or, worse, lose work. Any value in her current project risks being overturned by all the *shouting*. Disconcertingly, *anyone* who publicly springs to her defense—or even suggests there might be some manner of overreaction at work—will *also* be dragged into the controversy and examined with the same rigor, giving the woman the appearance of being someone so shameful that even being seen to associate with her is in some way contaminating. Suddenly, this woman is someone you can't trust—someone who'd *tricked* people into thinking she was a feminist, but has now revealed her true colors. There's a sense that people were almost *waiting* to be disappointed, or betrayed, by someone they'd previously cheered on.

And all by other women.

Now, feminism's ability to turn on other feminists has long been chronicled, and there are plenty of case studies on it that you can terrify yourself with, if you want to spend a couple of the more unhappy hours of your life googling them. And of course, it's worth repeating that feminism doesn't mean *never criticizing other women*. If a woman has done something actively hateful, she deserves all the criticism coming to her. Feminism isn't Buddhism. You don't have to love every woman. You are high on the concept of equality—not Ecstasy. There are just as many awful women as men out there, and if we can't have a fruity discussion about their wrongs, then obviously, that's sexist, too.

But I'd like to, if I may—having witnessed this sequence of events happen over and over—bring a little perspective to the whole matter, and point out how whenever we pile on a woman who hasn't been feminist *enough,* or has been found to be imperfect, we don't improve feminism or strengthen it—but, instead, make it more difficult for *all* of us.

For, as always, when we make demands on women, it's always best to check there's no sexism afoot by asking, "What's happening with the men? Are the famous men having to deal with this? Is this something we're insisting *men* handle, too? Are men presumed to have trampled on, or belittled, other men if they do not make statements, or art, that includes every race, socioeconomic bracket, sexual orientation, or religion that other men identify with? Are men told that *everything* they make must be for *everybody*? Are men ever accused of letting other men down, and not uplifting their gender enough? Are men ever told they've betrayed *half the world* with something they've said, or done? Do men "cancel" other men over their views about men?"

We're not telling famous *men* they have to speak up, on behalf of everyone, and being furiously disappointed with them when they don't. Jimmy Fallon isn't expected to give thoughtful quotes about what causes men to become rapists. Ed Sheeran's not being asked to speak at a march on the intersection between feminism and disability. Dustin Hoffman isn't being questioned on his views on transphobia—even though he dressed up as a woman in *Tootsie.* Famous men are just allowed to get on with their paid jobs; their social media timelines are full of pictures of them goofing around backstage, or enjoying their holidays, and they're not expected to suddenly appear on *Newsnight* talking about hijabs, female genital mutilation, or how STEM subjects are dominated by men—then be torn apart on Twitter by other men, if they get it wrong in some way.

These days, women with any kind of public profile have two jobs: The first is their career, and the second is Professional Being A Woman and Representing All Women. And if they slip up in this second, unpaid job—in which they are eager but also, unmistakably, amateur—the punishment on social media, and toll on their *real* job, can be brutal.

Of course, if this all, in the end, resulted in proper debates and understanding—the strengthening of feminism, and the welcoming to the ranks of more eager, young, and old, feminists—perhaps it would all be worthwhile. Every struggle, sadly, has its casualties—the suffragettes had *bombs*—and a whole load of hurt feelings, a couple of little nervous breakdowns, and a few stalled careers are but small fry if the payoff were true equality, for all women, across the world.

Sadly, however, it doesn't have that effect.

Firstly, the internet is the worst place to have these debates. Twitter's ability to allow calm, nuanced debate is virtually nonexistent— huge subjects have to be crunched down to 280 characters, and what starts as a "conversation" between two people can suddenly have hundreds of other onlookers taking part and chipping in. Both sides feel wronged and wounded—and wronged, wounded people tend to heat their fear up into anger. More often than not, this ends up with two factions of scared people furiously shouting at each other ("YOU GOT THIS WRONG!" or "WHY ARE YOU SHOUTING AT ME???")—an occurrence I would say that, broadly speaking, makes up around half of social media on any given day.

And the problem with this—other than the sheer volume—is that everyone is responding to the *emotions* of the conversation, *rather than what people are actually saying.* What *could* have been a genuinely useful exchange ends up as loads of women shouting at each other— burning bridges that would have been useful for future coalitions and campaigns.

Meanwhile, the patriarchy's just sitting in the corner, smoking a cigar, with an erection, murmuring, "You keep fighting each other, ladies. I find it sexy. Would one of you—the thinner, younger one, perhaps—like to wear a leotard?"

And secondly—and most importantly—it's all an anger *directed at the wrong people*. Someone accusing another woman of getting feminism "wrong," or not doing "enough," is usually saying this because the subject *they* are passionately interested in is underrepresented: if this famous feminist isn't talking about it, then *no one* will—so applying pressure on her to do what *you'd* do, if you had her platform, is the only way you can, obliquely, get your voice heard.

However, although these "wrong" women might be pressurized into, or taught to, talk about what *you* wish to talk about, they don't have any actual power to change the structure of things. They can't commission TV shows, or debates, or movies, or books. They can't get more women elected. They can't change the makeup of the industry, or politics, or business.

When you get angry, you need to get angry with the *machinery*. You need to get angry with the *people in power*. The ones who choose who gets the money, the platforms, and the jobs. It's simple to compile a list of the most powerful people in the entertainment industry—the commissioning editors at TV companies, the heads of A&R at record companies, and the heads of studios in Hollywood. The people in charge of short-listing MPs. The bosses of the women you're criticizing.

Tweet about *them*. Blog about *them*. Cancel *them*. What you're seeing is based on *their* decisions.

If you dislike something a woman is doing—if you disagree with her book, or research, or song, or opinion, or campaign—I, personally, believe that it's pointless to attack it. Over many years, I've come to believe that expending your time and energy trying to destroy something that someone else has created is a waste of time. What's the best you can hope to achieve? If you're fully successful, and end up reducing what she has said or done to rubble, you're still in the position where there now needs something better to take its place.

Why not simply forgo the destruction phase—and *start* with the "now we need something better" part, instead? Be the alternative. Be the change you wish to see. Allow people on the internet to be "wrong"—and focus all your effort on doing the new, cool, improved thing, instead.

For starters, it's more fun to be a creator than a destroyer, and secondly, it prevents what we see so often with women in the public eye: A rapid turnover of hot, new, bright things, who aren't allowed the kind of long-term, comfortable development that men in the public eye—who are so much less likely to have a massive public downfall or backlash—enjoy. We're all aware of that saying, "Men fail up." Here's Michelle Obama on the phenomenon: "I wish that girls could fail as bad as men do and be OK," she said. "Because let me tell you, watching men fail up—it is frustrating. It's frustrating to see a lot of men blow it and win. And we hold ourselves to these crazy, crazy standards."

Let's make sure that *women* aren't part of the reason that women can't fail up. Let's let women make their mistakes—but still continue. A woman who has made mistakes but is still given the chance to carry on to learn in public, to correct herself, and to still proceed—*without* having been psychologically battered and canceled in the process—will have far, far more useful things to bring to society than the current informal system we have: that the majority of women who still have a public platform are the ones who just haven't made a mistake *yet*.

And if you are not a creator—if you have no story to tell, or song to sing, or campaign to run—but are merely a disappointed and furious audience, then find the things *others* have created that you love and pour all your energy into raising those up, instead.

Feminism's current hypervigilance—always looking to point out imperfections in other women, and then dragging them in public until they correct their mistakes—is a fundamental misunderstanding of the Darwinian theory. We've all been raised to believe, to a greater or lesser extent, in survival of the fittest. This is what animals are like, and we are animals still—so this is simply nature's process: If a woman spots a flaw in another woman, and feels *she* would have been better placed to talk about a subject, then taking the flawed woman down is the correct thing. It's a healthy marketplace of ideas, and if your ideas are better than the ideas of Jan, with her shitty blog, song, or film, taking her down is the right thing to do. It will, eventually, lead to the betterment of our species.

However. This isn't what Darwin argued. Recently, I read *On the Origin of Species* and was amazed to discover that when Darwin coined the term *survival of the fittest*, he didn't mean the fittest animal would triumph over the other, less fit animals. No. He meant the animals with the greatest chance of survival were *those who were fittest to survive their climate, landscape, or environment*.

The battle isn't between one another, then—it's with *the world we live in*. And when you know this, everything changes: for the climate we are unwittingly making for women, is one where we are hypercritical of one another, and every hero must fall, and every flaw must be exposed, and the bar is set approximately twenty feet higher for women than it is for their male peers—who get on with whatever *their* ideas are, never considering a "duty" to speak for everyone, or address every issue.

We all specialize in *something*—usually the things we know most about. So as long as your cultural and political diet is varied enough, you shouldn't be relying on one artist, or source, to provide *everything*—just munch on all of humanity's lavish buffet, dude.

Women are—as they become more powerful, taking up platforms previously denied to them, telling stories that have never been told before, and campaigning for things previously considered unimportant or unchangeable—making an environment in which *all women* live in. We are each other's environment. We need to make one all women can survive in——and one where the motto is "No one can do everything. Everyone can do *something*," is the one where most women will feel unafraid to step forward, and show us what beautiful, tiny thing she can do. Rather than—as is so often the case at the moment—always worry that the next thing she says, writes, or tweets might be the thing that sees her exiled for months.

Forever. That unleashes all the bots and trolls, and stops her—and all those fearfully watching her subsequent public shaming and trashing—from opening up her laptop, logging in, and saying the words that are at the beginning of everything good: "I just thought of something . . ."

CHAPTER THIRTEEN

The Hour of Aging

⤚

7:00 P.M.

ANYWAY, ENOUGH ABOUT EVERYONE AND EVERYTHING ELSE, FOR THE time being. Amidst all these problems and crises and issues and profound thoughts about how the patriarchy basically needs a good night out with the girls, I am still *me*.

I'm still here, under all these things—I am still managing to be "an actual person," sometimes for up to twenty minutes a day. Things are still happening in *my* life, and, when I go upstairs to the toilet, to enjoy some luxurious "me time," and look at myself in the mirror, I cannot deny a very obvious thing: I am aging. Possibly because of all the crises, issues, and profound thoughts, but more likely because once you get to thirty-five, it feels like the world slams its foot down on the accelerator, and you go through three hundred sixty-five days in what seems like three weeks, screaming like you're on a roller coaster, and saying, repeatedly, "But it feels like I only took the Christmas decorations down last month—and now I'm putting them up again! WHAT THE FUCK!"

I look in the mirror and assess what "aging" means, visually. We are led to presume that *everything* to do with aging is negative, but there are so many aspects to it that it seems statistically unlikely you will hate *every single one*. Personally, I find I am fine with most of it.

Yes, I am losing skin elasticity—but I find it quite amusing, and oddly comforting, to bunch up all the loose skin on my arm, or thigh, and turn it into a little ruched skin pelmet. As a child of the 1980s, brought up on endless pleated bed valances, to my eyes, it looks kind of . . . "fancy." And besides, whilst you lose skin elasticity, you also lose the amount of fucks you give. Perhaps that's *why* the skin is so loose now—from all my fucks leaving. If so, I'm happy enjoying the space they have left. Byeeeee.

Encroaching loss of skin elasticity is all about a *state of mind.* Yeah, you *could* look at it like you're losing something—all your collagen—but you could also look at it like you're *gaining* something. It's all about *abundance.* For, as I wave goodbye to my thirties, I say hello to an entirely new development—my wattle. As foretold in the prologue of this book, it has started to assemble, on my neck.

I should probably slap some moisturizer on that, I think, on Monday, spotting its wobbly beginnings—and then immediately forget about it.

And by Friday, it's too late—some final, tremulous outposts of muscle and collagen have, seemingly, collapsed, and I now have, overnight, what looks like a dangly neck bollock garlanding my above-the-collar area. *Now* I know what it is: It's a wattle. Such as turkeys have. I have a wattle. This is what Nora Ephron meant when she penned the essay "I Feel Bad About My Neck," in which she wrote the most famous—and, indeed, only—description of the female neck over forty.

"Sometimes I go out to lunch with my girlfriends, and I look around the table and realize we're all wearing turtleneck sweaters," she said. "Sometimes, instead, we're all wearing scarves—like Katharine Hepburn in *On Golden Pond.* . . . We all look good for our age. Except for our necks. Oh, the necks. There are chicken necks. There are turkey-gobbler necks. There are elephant necks. . . . There are scrawny necks and fat necks, loose necks, crepey necks, banded necks, wrinkled necks, stringy necks, saggy necks, flabby necks, mottled necks. . . . One of my biggest regrets . . . is that I didn't spend my youth staring lovingly at my neck."

Having also not spent my youth looking lovingly at my neck—as far as I recall, I spent most of my youth looking lovingly at the works of Nora Ephron—I now, for the first time, look at my neck. I vaguely remember that, before, it looked like a thigh or a piece of bum. Now—now, it looks entertainingly more *prehistoric*. Like those delightful ruffs on dinosaurs, which puff up when under threat, before reverting back to a deflated dino-flesh cravat, suspended from their jaw.

I have to admit—I like it. I like to move my jaw from side to side, and watch it ripple—like the sail on a galleon, catching the breeze. I like to pinch it together and make a little neck-buttock. Most of all, I like to wobble it with my index finger—like an executive stress toy I will always have with me. I find it soothes me. I've always wanted to have a long, gray beard that I could stroke, whilst pondering things—to give me the air of a distinguished professor. However hard my chin has tried—and it really has, to give it its due—to grow face fur like Brian Blessed, it's always fallen short. Now, I have a *beard made of skin*. I am *proud* of it.

Away from the neck and on to the hair, and I find I also super don't mind my hair going gray—which is just as well, as my original gray streak on top has now been joined by a second one, over my left ear. I am, it seems, very slowly turning into a badger—perhaps the actual Badger from *Wind in the Willows:* authoritative; a bit grumpy when dealing with foolish, young toads; but always willing, in the end, to help them out. Again, I like this vibe.

Personally, I can't wait until I have so much gray that I can bleach my entire head white, like a swooshy glacier. I'd like to pretend that this is because I am *so* feminist that I will be able to loftily dispense with dyeing my hair, unlike my weaker and less feminist contemporaries—but it's actually because white hair will really suit my skin tone, and make my eyes pop. When it comes to the politics of graying and hair dye, this is, really, the only criteria by which to make a judgment. If feminism is to mean anything, it is, surely, for women to have the hair that looks most awesome? If you look best dyeing your hair jet black until you're ninety, you keep dyeing your hair jet black until you're ninety. If you're lucky enough to have the genes that give you the gift of great hair *for free,* enjoy the cash savings—but don't pretend you're Malala for doing it. (Who knows what Malala will do with her hair when she's in her forties? I'd like to think the least we could do for her, given what she's done, is let her keep her options open re: Clairol Nice'n Easy.)

And still the benefits of aging go on—for I'm even enjoying my dwindling party stamina. I entered my thirties still able to rave all night long, but in my middle age, I find myself not only unable to do that but also newly horrified by the mere thought of it. Ever since I got so drunk I twerked on my brother Eddie on Christmas Eve, and, therefore, spent Christmas Day in some manner of Shame Booth, going to bed at 9 p.m. and reading a book has seemed like some blessed reward for giving up wine. No one ever woke up regretful that they'd had ten hours sleep and read six chapters of *The Language of Trees*.

But there *are* ways in which I am aging that I (a) didn't expect and (b) am not enjoying. Take, for instance, the Day of the Great Wardrobe Betrayal.

I have spoken to many middle-aged women about this, and it appears to be a common, although undocumented, phenomenon. One spends one's twenties and thirties doing what we are societally encouraged to do: building up a perfect capsule wardrobe of items that can be relied on, no matter what the occasion. Eschewing the madder fashions of our youth, we invest in a couple of nice cashmere things, a posh coat, three nice frocks, a selection of the most cheering trousers, some trustworthy blouses, jolly T-shirts that make your tits look great whilst not overly troubling your belly, and the only holiday shorts in the world that don't make you want to throw yourself out of the window. At the end of this process, you are covered for *everything*. Your wardrobe stands as a moving testament to learning what colors, shapes, and cuts suit you. You feel as if you can, finally, tick "Attain perfect capsule wardrobe" off The List. You've *done* it. You've *nailed* the fucker. Well done you.

And then, at some point between thirty-eight to forty-five, overnight, and for no reason anyone has been able to ascertain, *all your clothes turn evil*. Inescapably, there always comes a day in a middle-aged woman's life when she opens her wardrobe and realizes that all of her clothes have decided, suddenly, overnight, THAT THEY HATE HER.

My Day of Wardrobe Evil came when I was forty-one. I woke, as my normal self, got up, took off my nightie, and opened the wardrobe door—wondering which fabulous, friendly outfit I was going to wear that day.

Forty-five minutes later, I was on the verge of panic. Most of my clothes were on the floor. Somehow, whilst I slept just three feet away from them, all my clothes had gone to shit. Every single thing. Everything I'd tried on was too tight, too short, too floral, too weird, too slutty, not slutty enough, or just, somehow, conspired to make me look like Su Pollard—and not like how hot, young hipsters look like Six from *Blossom*—and not how hot young hipsters look like Six from *Blossom*, but in a *bad* way. My clothes, clearly, hated me. When I put them on, they hung, sulkily, off my tits, with a palpable "I didn't *ask* to be here" expression.

Of course, as a woman, when you've been round the block a few times, you're used to days where many of your outfits seem momentarily "on a break" from your relationship. You've woken up a bit water-retention-y, perhaps, and learned to deal with half your clothes becoming temporarily unwearable. You know, in a few days—maybe just after a particularly pivotal poo—you'll be back to rocking that badass fleece with a motif of a wolf howling at the moon and those burgundy leggings like a pro.

This was *different*. Over the next month, and during every single varied phase of my uterine "specialness," my clothes remained sullen. The condition appeared to be terminal—I had Clothes Disease. Everything was infected with crappiness. My wardrobe was now a Bad Narnia.

Thinking about it now, I understand most of the reasons behind this terrible development. Most women, when they enter middle age, experience at least two of the following three "situations": (1) They develop an inability to/intolerance for wearing anything but the most comfortable shoes and sneakers; (2) they put on a reassuring stone in weight—nature's way of making sure the female tribal elders will survive a bad winter, and be able to continue leading the group, as is to the benefit of humanity; and (3) they get the Middle-Age Lop, wherein thinning hair and general impatience means you get a mid-length bob, which you ask for by saying, "Something like Alexa Chung, but old."

Whilst I have always favored the kind of clothing that is what I would call "Big-Bum Proof"—so the delivery of, essentially, four new buttocks was neither here nor there—the addition of short hair and limited "shoeage" seemed finally to torpedo my strong yet limited wardrobe. *Nothing* worked anymore.

For two weeks, I walked around in the one outfit that had stayed loyal to me—a baggy pair of jeans and an outsized checked shirt. Man, I wore those fucking things to death—waiting for my other clothes to fall back in love with me. Every poo I did, I did hopefully— like some kind of Sam Beckett in *Quantum Leap,* hoping this poo would be the poo that took me home to Awesome Outfitsville. But it never happened. Everything in my wardrobe remained too sassy, not sassy enough, or just indefinably tragic.

I found myself engaging in a very common middle-aged pastime—looking through old photos and not noticing old friends I missed, but old *clothes* I missed, instead.

"God—I remember that blue jumper. It was brilliant! Where did it go? Shit—that dress! That dress went with everything! If only I hadn't spilled turmeric down the front, it would still be with me now—and maybe everything would be different."

Sadly, and finally, I surrendered to my fate: I sent everything to the charity shop and started again from scratch. Here is what I have learned so far about dressing in middle age:

1. The Toast catalog will call to you—but with a deceptive siren cry. *These are the simple, classic, elegant, expensive "pieces" one should wear in middle age!* you will think. *Surely, a woolen smock and padded Chinese-style jacket are the things that will make me feel distinguished and elegant! I'm going to wait until the sales and then clear those fuckers out!* Unfortunately, the truth is that the only people who look good in Toast clothes are wiry, five-foot-

eleven, bohemian intellectuals with strong cheekbones, who would naturally find themselves wearing a floor-length corduroy smock whilst holding a basket, and walking amongst fishermen on a Hebridean wharf. *You* just look like a small, round, old lady wearing her dead grandmother's clothes.

2. The wide-legged trouser *is* your friend. You were born in an era of skinny jeans—you instinctively fear turning your legs into what are essentially sails and being blown away in a high wind, but these trousers can be a valuable ally. Wear them with a tight T-shirt, or tucked-in white shirt, and pretend to be Gene Kelly in 1947. The only problem with these trousers is that none of your existing shoes work with them. Your entire cache of ankle boots is now useless. Be bold—buy wide-legged trousers, wear them with a pair of white leather sneakers, but do make sure you check your weather app before you leave the house. If the wind's over ten miles per hour, stay at home.

3. When Meryl Streep put on her overalls and shabby white blouse in *Mamma Mia!*, she invented 90 percent of what you can wear once you're over forty. Overalls are so your new friend now. They're like an all-in-one head to toe clothing solution that you can "ring in the changes" with, using a variety of polos or shirts underneath. When you think about it, it's obvious overalls would always be faithful and loving to women—for their huge pockets on the front turn us into lady kangaroos, carrying our most precious cargo—a joey, our iPhone, and a pot of lip balm—in our pouch. Likewise, jumpsuits.

4. Hit anyone who tries to make maxi dresses go back out of fashion. Strike them violently. There's something so calming about donning a maxi dress, and essentially becoming just a five-foot-six column of pretty fabric. All the separate and disparate worries every other piece of clothing gives you—"Do my tits look 'fall-y out-y' in this?" "Does my arse look lopsided in this?" "Be honest—do my legs look like two Porkinson's Bangers?"—disappear when you turn yourself into a tube of pretty polka dot or chinoiserie. Plus, you can wear any shoes

you like underneath a floor-length dress, because no one can see them. You can turn up at a wedding in a pair of Crocs, and no one will know. All thanks to your fabulous "dress booth," which conceals everything. Defend the continuing stylishness of the maxi dress, as you would defend the future of liberal democracy. Consider marching, if necessary.

5. Stop wearing calf-length socks. Think about it: They make you sad. Whenever you sit down, your trouser leg shoots up, and reveals the top half of a calf you haven't shaved for two weeks. And when you stand up, you're aware the elastic is cutting into the fattest part of your calf, and essentially strangling your leg. Why the fuck are you letting these bastards on your leg, when they fail in every job they're given? Get a lovely knee-length sock, enjoy its elastic resting on the thinnest part of your lower leg, and revel in the leg coverage and warmth they provide. You deserve it.

6. Ask yourself: What are the men doing? Why do *they* not have these cyclical wardrobe panics? It's because 90 percent of the time, they're wearing a suit. Copy them. Steal this power move. Buy the best suit you can afford, in the most non-creasable fabric, buy a spare pair of trousers for it—they wear out quicker than the jacket—and then wear it with a variety of T-shirts, blouses, shirts, thin hoodies, and polo-necks. You might think you can't afford it, but if you look at the amount of secondhand cocktail dresses you keep buying on eBay when you're drunk, for attending fabulous parties you never go to, you will realize you've actually spent far, far more than the cost of a suit already. Let the abused become the abuser—now *you* sell those secondhand dresses on eBay to *other* drunk ladies, and use the money to buy the sexy tuxedo Tina Fey wore to the Golden Globes.

7. Do you habitually not wear your nicest dresses/blouses because you're worried about "sweating up" the armpits, and you can't be bothered to handwash them after, as the label piously demands? Stick a sanitary towel in the armpit, sweat like the perimenopausal boss you are, and then—at the end of

the night—peel off your arm-juice pad, and chuck it in the bin. No need to thank me. I love you.

8. Forget about handbags and get a rucksack. A lovely, colorful backpack with loads of pockets. Not only is your spine going to love you—enjoy spreading the load, rather than victimizing one shoulder over the other—but most backpacks have a special outside pocket specifically designed to fit a small Thermos. If you can leave the house with half a liter of hot tea in your luggage at all times, you will feel *a god*. There is *nothing* the day can throw at you that can't be remedied by suddenly remembering you've got a brew in your bag, and that you can sit down in the middle of a full-scale riot and just have a reflective sip, whilst the police work on clearing the streets again.

And this is what I have learned so far about middle-aged dressing. A few useful work-arounds, but also a deeper knowledge: "Get Capsule Wardrobe" is a recurring task throughout your life. It is never actually completed. Truly, The To-Do List never ends.

AND WHILST BATTLING with some manner of Fashion Black Death—looking on the Boden website, and thinking, *Although everything in my life until now told me it wasn't, maybe a hotchpotch skirt is now the answer to my problems?*—a second aging problem manifested: I was fine with all the wrinkles, wattles, and gray, but what I *couldn't* reconcile myself to was looking permanently sad and defeated.

Years of scowling at a laptop, and watching the news whilst shouting, "YOU ASSHATS!" seemed to have left me looking as if I was about to lie facedown on the ground and start crying. I had been absolutely prepared for looking older. I was *fine* with "looking *older.*" I even respected the thinning of my lips—as if my face was already partially preloading a disapproving hard stare at teenage boys throwing chips around on the top deck of the bus, and shouting, "You bummer." I don't think it's entirely un-useful for a middle-aged woman to look like she's ten seconds away from raining down hellfire and fury on any and all bumptious asshats in the locale.

I was, simply, happy about my encroaching Hag Years. Hey—if life has been hard, I'm totally down with that showing on my face. I *want* people to know I've gone through shit. I *want* to scare the more foolish and jejune away from me. THE MORE LIKE A WIZARD I LOOK, THE SOONER I CAN START WEARING A CLOAK AND BRANDISHING AN OAKEN STAFF AT SOCIAL EVENTS. Intolerance and fury, I could handle.

But the one thing I hadn't reckoned with was . . . looking so *sad* all the time. Because—I didn't feel sad all the time. In order to look how I felt on the inside, I would have to stare in the mirror and make a conscious effort to undo the sadness. If I consciously unpinched my mouth, relaxed my forehead, and held my head high again, a happier person would emerge, once again. But as soon as I forgot to relax, everything bunched up again into what I can only describe as a "deflated Lady Gruffalo."

Some people have a Resting Bitch Face. I appeared to have its cousin—Sad Widow Surveying Her War-Ravaged-Village Face. I appeared to have Inherited Woe. This wasn't an *aging* thing. This was . . . a *trauma* thing.

As a can-do person, I decided to do something about this. A huge part of my "facial bunchiness" was, I knew, down to spending most of my life hunched over a laptop—so my first stop was buying one of those facial exercise gadgets. You know the ones. From QVC.

Once I received it, I would spend a solid month dutifully gurning away on it, trying to fortify my facial abs, like some kind of Facial Athlete. I would strengthen my face the natural way! With exercise!

Of course, as a huge part of my "facial sadness" was down to working hard, and being very busy, we can all guess the outcome: I simply didn't have *time* to do the things that would make me look less busy. And I never used the stupid thing.

Undeterred, I moved on to Phase Two of Operation Looking Less Like Eeyore: buying stuff. I bought *all* the serums; I consumed oily fish and healthy seeds, as if I were a supermodel puffin; I even bought one of those expensive silk pillows to prevent facial creasing—which

I obviously and immediately shrunk down to dollhouse size the first time I washed it.

I read one article that suggested the best way to prevent "facial wear and tear" was by setting an alarm on your iPhone—so that, every half hour, when working, you could "check in" with your face, and see if it had collapsed into a scrunchy frown, and then consciously "relax" it. Every time the alarm went off, and I checked my facial expression when "thinking," I was amused to see that its natural state is "Looking like Henry VIII deciding which wife to kill."

As neither a monarch nor a murderer, I desired this not to be the case, so I stepped it up into third gear. I got help. As I now have the income of a middle-class woman, I went and got a couple of those posh facials you read about in the magazines—the ones they go on about in *Tatler* and *Vogue,* when detailing how "facialists to the stars" are responsible for keeping our royalty and A-list so glowy. Ones where they do mad things, like "massage the inside of your mouth," or "electrocute you a *tiny* bit."

I got on the waiting lists, trekked across London to various clinics, paid the money—and, big reveal, either looked "plumped" for twenty-four hours, then reverted back to normal, or walked out looking exactly the same as when I went in. In both cases, the most notable difference was that I was considerably poorer.

In short, I spent nearly two years doing all the things that are seen as natural and allowable to look better, if you're a strident feminist, and it just fannied away hours I could have been working, or watching *RuPaul's Drag Race* with the kids; it cost a bomb, and—crucially—made no real difference at all.

"Do I just have the *wrong kind of face?*" I finally asked a friend in the beauty industry. "I've had literally every single famous facial it's possible to have, and yet I still look sad. I don't understand—[redacted Hollywood actress] is ten years older than me, yet I look like her aged Victorian housekeeper. Are me and [redacted] experiencing time differently? Am I living in dog years? Am I going to 'go to the farm' by the time I'm fifty, whilst [redacted] continues to swan around looking like she's made of face cream until she's 109?"

"Oh, mate!" my friend replied. "No facial can make you look like that. There's no point in wasting your time and money. She has Botox. They *all* have Botox."

"All?"

"Yep. You know [redacted actress, famous for looking hot 'despite' being sixty]? Botox. Luminous national treasure? Botox. [Pop goddess] has Botox. There isn't one of these bitches who isn't using Botox."

"But, in interviews, they all say it's just down to drinking water, and never using face wipes!" I cried. "And maybe a slick o' Vaseline on the lips."

My friend was laughing so merrily, she could barely speak.

"I *know*," she said, in the end. "It's hilarious. Anyone who knows the slightest thing about beauty knows it can't be the case. It's literally written all over their faces."

"But, to me, they don't *look* like they've had anything done! They all just look . . . *well*."

"Well, yes," she agreed. "That's because, if you go to the right people, you *don't* look like you've had anything done. You just look well slept and happy."

"Wouldn't it just be better to actually *be* well slept and happy?" I asked. "Isn't *that* the answer?"

She looked at me. "As a matter of interest, how much time and money do you think it would currently cost you, right now, to organize your life so that you got a minimum of eight hours sleep a night, and had no problems at all?"

I started to do the mental math. I find mental mathematics very hard. I could feel my facial aging accelerating as I frowned and gurned through the calculations. My friend, distressed by what she was seeing, quickly added: "Because, just so you know—Botox is two hundred pounds and takes ten minutes."

OBVIOUSLY, A WEEK later, I was on the Tube to see the best Botox specialist in London.

When I got there, the Botox lady made me look in the mirror, and said, "What do you want?"

I consciously and effortfully relaxed my face, pointed at it, and said: "Like this?"

"Easy."

She did nine tiny injections—three around the eyebrows, two on each side of the mouth, and two on the underside of my jaw. It took seven minutes in total.

"I've just put in a tiny bit—come back in a couple of weeks, and we'll see if you need more. I'd rather do too little than too much. You'll see the difference in a fortnight. Bye!"

The whole thing, door to door, took an hour and ten minutes. It was the easiest beauty treatment I've ever had. For starters, there was no time for small talk. On this basis alone, I was sold. As you get older, you tend to count all your experiences in terms of the Small Talk Toll. This one had been as minimal as my relationship with the dentist, but without the precondition of having his hand in my mouth. It was win-win.

On the way home, I felt the Botox start to take effect—my face felt like it had just had two Nurofen Plus: a pleasant, relaxing, codeine warmth. This had an unexpected side effect: As I'd been told during birth visualization classes, when we tend to hold tension in our faces, it causes other parts of the body to become rigid, too. TL;DR, if your mouth is in a tiny moue of pain, your vadge's going to close up, and that baby's gonna get *jammed.*

As the weeks went by, I noticed that because my face was acting like it was on holiday in Antigua, the rest of my body relaxed, too. It was like being in the company of a non-annoying Buddhist friend who takes everything in their stride. I'd be like "Face—something stressful is happening. Should I freak out?" My face: "Nah, mate—the universe continues in its elegant expansion. Everything is as everything should be. Have a piña colada. It's all gravy."

And visually? What did I look like? Well, you can see on the cover of this book. I don't look younger, or hotter, or more perfect. It's not an *actual enchantment.* I just don't look like I'm going to lie on the floor in the fetal position and start wailing, "You can run as fast as you like—*but you can't outpace eternal sorrow*" in the middle of

Morrisons, which is the bare minimum I need from my face, on a
day-to-day basis.

As I observed, looking in the mirror, two weeks later, I just looked
. . . like I did when I was making a *massive effort* to look relaxed. But
without making an effort at all. Botox is the working woman's facial
minibreak. Botox just does your relaxing for you. It takes a job off
The List.

OF COURSE, IT'S terrifying for a feminist to admit they have had Botox. Not least if, in their 2011 international bestseller *How to Be a
Woman*, they merrily denounced anyone who gets Botox.

"When we live in fear of aging and pull painful and expensive
tricks to hide it, it makes us look like losers. It makes us look like
cowards. It makes us look *scared*," I said, in what was the first—but
I'm sure won't be the last—case of my Younger Self judging my Future Self without walking a mile in her shoes (orthopedic sneakers,
sixty-nine ninety-nine, Asics).

What I have realized since then is that women can easily believe
we need some manner of . . . Botox Police. I know, because I, clearly,
had the Botox Police hat.

Whilst, in the twenty-first century, we would be unlikely to
launch a fusillade against someone for dyeing their hair, microblad-
ing sparse eyebrows, or getting veneers for their teeth, Botox—along
with fillers—is seen as a level of artifice and vanity *so* extreme, women
who get it must undergo a small, public punishment-beating from
the Botox Police, ostensibly on behalf of other women, presumably
to discourage others from seeking it.

Consequently, a great many of the women who have Botox never
admit it—as very few women would willingly put themselves in a
position where their face would become the center of a conversation
about how it's generally letting the sisterhood down, as badly as Eva
Braun's vagina did in 1939. This leads to the catch-22 illustrated in
the earlier conversation with my friend—where most famous women
of our age have to pretend they look better than "normal" people
simply from an expensive serum and lots of water, or crystals, or put-

ting a jade egg up their vulva—leading to "normal" women who genuinely *are* only using serums and water to despair that they appear simply to have a great deal more "tired-gnome DNA" than people on the cover of magazines.

If we *really* wish to make women feel better about themselves, living in a world where all the hot people feel able to cheerfully share the realities of their beauty regimes would mark a considerable improvement. Now I know both how common Botox is, and how simple and effective it can be—better, quicker, and more effective than any cream, serum, or facial—it seems genuinely odd to me that there is this febrile exceptionalism to this beauty treatment, above all others. So long as you're going to a qualified practitioner who, vitally, also has a good aesthetic sense, both adverse reactions and glassy, frozen LA faces from the '80s are extremely rare. It's not as if you're drinking the potion that makes the Little Mermaid grow legs—changing your essential nature forever at the cost of terrible pain. It's just a general "face chiller," used by millions of women, which you can use as and when you wish. Botox isn't a gigantic moral maze—the use of which places you in one feminism camp or another. It's just . . . one of many options.

"BUT IT'S NOT natural!" people say. No. It's not. And, these days, I passionately hymn all the "unnatural" things I have seen improve lives: Using contraceptives is unnatural; my emergency C-section was unnatural. The orthopedic insoles in my shoes, for my naturally flat feet, are unnatural; as are my acne medications, my eyebrow threading, and my Clairol "Dark Chocolate" hair dye.

Fuck it, I'll keep going—my washing machine is unnatural, my Wi-Fi is unnatural, and this individual chocolate mousse I am eating right now did not grow on a mousse bush. Progress is full of everyday wonders.

Let us be honest: A "natural" life is, often, an actively dangerous one for a woman. In my "natural" state, I would have lived a life as a waddling, spotty woman with mousy hair and a monobrow, who was pregnant at seventeen and died during a difficult labor at the age of twenty-four. Whilst there are many natural things that we can love and enjoy, as I have gotten older, I have realized that un-natural things have been—time and time again—my best friends, as a woman. The idea that a woman is born a fixed and unchangeable thing is dispiriting. I *don't* accept my fate! I'm *absolutely* the kind of person who wants lifesaving surgery, and/or a face that isn't hunched in misery! I mean, why not? Give me all the good things that science can provide, during my short span on this earth! Show me your in-ventions, that I might use them! I am unashamed to say that I am interested in partaking of all things that are awesome! Why ration the good things, because they are "unnatural?"

Don't insist I must die as I was born! That was not my hottest day! *Let me change!* Let me be a thing I dreamed up myself!

There is a further twist to the idea of "natural beauty"—one I could probably argue in favor of myself, at various points in my life, to wit: Why *shouldn't* having a sad face be acceptable for a woman? Why *shouldn't* you be able to walk down the street looking utterly sorrowful—but with pride? You should be *militant* about this! Don't give in to societal constructs! Fight!

And in many ways, of course, this is a valid argument. I can-not argue that were we to live in a world where it was deemed not only acceptable but even desirable for women to walk around looking very, very sad or "a bit rough," we would be living in a more truthful world. I used to be a Goth. A scruffy Goth—*of course* I would like that. For, in that world, I would be as a god.

However, the simple truth is that if I have only twenty minutes before I leave the house for a work engagement, not only do I *not* want to look sad but *I simply don't have time to change all of society.*

Indeed, as a rule of thumb, I'm incredibly wary of situations where women, or girls, have a small, urgent, specific problem, and the solution to it is "boldly fly in the face of convention, then devote the rest of your life to effortfully and exhaustingly effecting the revo-lution." That kind of feels like you're lumping someone already deal-ing with quite a lot with a pretty chunky chore—changing the hearts and minds of seven billion people—and one, let's face it, they're un-likely to achieve before catching the 3:35 p.m. bus.

So if you really, really want to try some Botox, but are worried that's it's not feminist, give yourself a break. If you don't want Botox, enjoy spending the money you've saved on shoes or rent. It's all gravy.

And whatever you choose to do, it's important to remember the biggest, and most crucial thing about aging: Every so often, you will look at pictures of yourself from ten years ago—when you were convinced you looked shit and were going downhill—and exclaim, "My God, I was so young and hot back then! I was at my *peak!* Look at my fucking *legs*! They're like those of a *sexy horse*! Why did I not *appreciate* it at the time? I should have just walked around *naked* all the time insisting people take pictures of my face! I will never be that beautiful *again!*"

And this will happen *every* ten years until you die.

Whatever age you are, and whatever's happening in your life right now, one thing is constant: older you is *totally* perving on you right now. Enjoy it.

CHAPTER FOURTEEN

The Hour of Demons

⁓

8:00 P.M.

So much can happen in a year. A month. A day. A minute.
Something gigantic can happen in a second, but you are not ready to
see it, so—you don't.

You have an unhappy girl, who doesn't like the way she looks—
but you just think, *Well, these are the teenage years. It will pass.*

You keep finding packed lunches left on the kitchen table, but
you think, *She probably just doesn't want sandwiches. There's a cafeteria
at school. She'll be eating chips, instead.*

Pictures of Amy Winehouse start covering her bedroom wall, but
you're like *Well,* Back to Black *is one of the bestselling albums ever, it would
be odd if she did* not *like this classic album, and her eyeliner is, to be fair,
amazing. That's why she loves her. There's nothing sinister going on here.*

She gives up red meat first—"It gives me a bellyache"; and then
all meat—"It's just kind of boring"; and then fish—"It's kind of
spooky"; and then becomes vegan—"Dairy products are cruel to animals, and there are so many other things to eat."

And you can't argue with her choice because this is a popular
trend amongst young people, and you're happy to buy oat milk, and
cook with lentils more, and to research and purchase the best sup-
plements to make sure she has everything she needs. It's just a little
cooking challenge—nothing more.

In the mornings, she comes down later and later—so late she has to rush past the breakfast things on the table, shouting, "The bus is coming, got to go, bye!" And you know it takes teenage girls a long time to get ready in the morning, so you start pressing smoothies and breakfast bars into her hand, saying, "Eat them on the bus!"

"I will! Thank you!" she says, smiling, looking you right in the eye.

And then, at the end of the month, you find ten uneaten bars in her bag.

But all you can go on is how she looks, and she doesn't *look* unhealthy, and she always tells you everything—you are close, so close!—and it can't be an eating disorder, because you are her mother, and she is your baby, and you are a body-positive, cheese-sandwich-eating feminist who walks around the house naked saying, "Look at my lovely, wobbly tum-tum," and telling your daughters that they are brilliant and strong and beautiful, and so how *could* your baby have an eating disorder? She doesn't have the *genes* for it.

"I don't want to medicalize something that might just be a fad," you say, in bed with your husband. It's 1 a.m., and you've been talking about this since teatime, when she took her plate to her room—"just want to chill for a bit!"—and then you found it on the floor, outside her door, afterwards: salad eaten, but all the brown rice, Quorn, and bread left untouched.

"I'm just into raw stuff now," she said. "It's the most delicious!"

Because the thing is—she's so cheerful now! So happy! So—*progressive*! So organized! Every piece of homework done on time; a neat schedule pinned up on her wall; her clothes laid out the night before; her bag packed, just so.

She has lists of what she needs to do; lists of places she wants to go; lists of songs she wants to learn on the piano. She seems totally on top of her life. The unhappiness of a few months ago seems to have burned up—she is now full of energy: a bright, shining energy. It's as if there is something inside her spinning faster and faster. In almost every way, you would think this is a good thing—she is being a hardworking, happy, model girl.

But you can't shake this recurring mental image—that, in the center of this shining light, there is a darkness. And the faster the light spins, the bigger the darkness gets.

PETE IS THE first to say it.

"It's manic behavior," he says, as we lie there. "I saw it in a friend, at college. This is like manic depression. Or some kind of mental illness."

I, too, have seen manic-depressive behavior—the revelatory, joyous, Icarus-like flying toward the sun, before your wings suddenly melt and you plummet. And I foolishly believe we can parent our way out of this—*of course* we can.

"I have a plan," I say. "It starts tomorrow. We can sort this out. It'll be over in a couple of weeks."

I WILL JUST . . . *parent her better.* If she is worried about her body, I will show her a better, more stable way. I will take her swimming, after school—me and her, playing together—and she will work up a healthy, childlike hunger she can't deny. And then I will make her something delicious—that fits in with her dietary preferences, but still gives her all the nutrition she needs—and I will positively affirm her eating it, and everything will be better.

That is how you parent a child. That is how you keep them healthy and well fed. That's how I taught her to eat as a toddler, and how I will rectify this little blip now. It's not an eating disorder. It's just an eating . . . *blip.*

I PICK HER up from school, and she's happy but a little tired, and she is delighted we will go swimming together.

"Yes!"

Looking back now, the idea of putting a teenager with a developing eating disorder in a swimsuit, in a place where lots of other teenage girls are also wearing swimsuits, is, obviously, incredibly stupid. Just because I am happy to wander around semi-naked with my battle-scarred, imperfect, happy, old body, I presume she—unscarred, long-legged, glowingly teenage—would be *even more* at ease. That she has absorbed the family motto—"Whatever other people think is *none of your business*"—and feels it in her bones. That she still sees "going swimming" as a joyful treat—like she did as a child.

The fact that she keeps her towel around her until we reach the water's edge suggests that's not the case, but I just think, unjudgmentally, *Oh. She's just a bit* modest. *Fair enough.*

All the other teenage girls are in bikinis. She has a sensible black Speedo swimsuit. I see her eying the other girls and mistake what she's thinking.

"Do you want to get a jolly bikini, like them?" I say. "There's some nice ones on ASOS."

"*No!*" she says, horrified, sliding into the water.

We swim together for ten minutes or so—racing each other—and then I find her, at the end of a length, clinging to the edge of the pool.

"Can we go home?" she says, in a small voice. "I feel a bit tired."

"Of course!" I say. She seems reluctant to get out of the water, until I realize why and fetch her towel.

She shivers all the way home, even though I hug her tight. "You can have my body warmth," I say. "And when we get back, I've got tea ready, and we can eat it on the sofa, and you'll have that lovely, tired-but-happy feeling in your legs. It'll be *cozy.*"

"I'm not that hungry," she says, in an odd, distant voice.

"That's because you've gotten *too* hungry," I say. "Wait until you see your tea. You'll get hungry then. It's a special one."

I've made one of her favorites—lentil soup with a toasted-seed salad and homemade bread. These are all things that she loves.

But when we get back, she looks at it, and says, "Sorry, but I just feel a bit sick. Maybe I'll eat it later."

"You probably feel sick because you're so hungry," I say.

"Maybe," she says—in the same distant voice that feels like something I can't get a purchase on, or find a way into. It's a curious trick. How can a voice do that?

She goes to her room.

I wait an hour, then bring the soup up at 6 p.m.

"Maybe later," she says.

I bring it back at 7 p.m.

"I still feel *so sick*."

At 8 p.m., I go into her room and leave it on her desk. The delicious smell will, surely, compel her to go over and try it.

At 9 p.m., I find the tray outside her room, untouched.

"Maybe the chlorine in the pool made her feel sick," I say to Pete, in bed, at midnight. We've been talking for two hours now. "I'm a fucking idiot. But she'll wake up tomorrow *starving*, and it'll be okay. It'll be better tomorrow."

IT IS NOT better tomorrow. This is the weekend the storm breaks.

She does not eat breakfast—"I still feel sick"; or lunch—"Stop going on about it!"; or tea—"Mom, you're freaking me *out*. Leave me *alone*."

By 6 p.m., I am determined to sort this out. There will be a reason—a worry, a thing, a single thought—that is making her not eat, and I will make her tell me it, and then I will solve the problem, and then she will eat. This is, surely, the simple logic. She knows why she is too unhappy to eat, and I will make the unhappiness go away. This is what we have done with every other problem in her life.

I go to her room. Her hood is up. She's just sitting on her bed, rammed into the corner.

"Baby, what's wrong? You're not eating."

She shrugs.

"Just tell me! Whatever it is, we can sort it out."

I sit on the bed. She shrinks away from me. I hug her—if I hug her long enough, she'll melt, and then she'll cry, and then she'll tell me. That's how it always works.

That's not how it works anymore. She becomes stiff, and hard, in my arms.

I let her go.

"Tell me!"

"You know what's wrong with me." That distant, cold voice.

"I don't!"

Maybe I do, but I don't want to say it, because that might put the idea in her head if she *hasn't* thought of it yet—saying it might make it happen.

"You need to eat, or you'll become ill. If you feel terrible now, it's because you're starving. Just eat something—I promise you'll feel better."

"You control my life."

Oh! I didn't expect this! It's so wrong I become angry.

"Control your *life*? That's *balls*. You have more freedom than *any* teenager I know. You can do whatever you *want*."

Slyly, furiously: "You're trying to make me eat, when I've told you I don't want to."

"That's because I know how sad being hungry can make you. I promise you'll feel better if you eat."

She's silent. Then: "Why don't you know the right things to say?"

"What *are* the right things to say?"

"You know."

I don't know. I really don't know. I promise you, I don't know. Or: I'm too scared to say them. I don't want to say it. I am in charge of this silence.

THE SCREAMING STARTS an hour later. I've never heard her scream before. It's ungodly—it sounds like something trapped, even though she roams around the house, locking herself in the basement, then the bathroom, as Pete shouts, in panic, "What are you *doing* in there?" and tries to kick the door down. We're both, suddenly, very frightened. When she finally comes out of the bathroom, she bolts down the stairs and tries to run away into the street. Pete grabs her, and she roars, "YOU'RE HURTING ME! HELP! HELP!" as we drag her back into the house.

She finally collapses, sobbing, in bed, at 2 a.m.—repeating, "I'm sorry, I'm sorry," over and over, crying, as we watch *Absolutely Fabulous* on my laptop, and I wince every time Edina Monsoon says, "I'm so *fat*."

"I love you," I say. *I love you means a million different things. Here, today, it means: Please don't be unhappy. Please don't be ill. Please tell me what's wrong. Please don't leave us. Does she know this? Does she know that this is what "I love you" means, here in this bed, as I hold her?*

"I love you too," she says, and falls asleep, holding my hand.

I wake next to her, on Sunday morning, and stare at her face. Asleep, she looks—perfect. Serene. Everything in her body looks right. The problem is in her beautiful head—where one tiny synapse misfires, one neuron sparks too hard. Something the size of a grain of sand, in some tiny electrical root, buried deep in her head, is causing all of this. I imagine being able to put my hand inside her head and remove this tiny thing—just as I have splinters of wood or glass from her feet. One tiny thing wrong. But it's somewhere I cannot reach. *The calls are coming from inside the house.*

SHE DOES NOT eat today, either. She walks around the house with dark smudges under her eyes—eyes which look different today. They seem oddly glittering, snakelike. She looks like she's seen a vision or is hearing other voices. I am more scared than I have ever been in my life.

At 7 p.m., we google "eating disorder specialist."

God bless the NHS—at 8 p.m. a doctor rings us back, and says, "Bring her in as soon as possible."

WE ARE SEEING a doctor now, which means we will be safe, and this whole thing will end soon. Maybe it will take a couple of weeks, but she will be well by Christmas—*at the latest*—and we will look back at these bad couple of months and laugh.

"Remember when you didn't eat for three days!" I will chuckle, as she eats her turkey, and she replies, "Yeah—that was so *weird*. Not like me at all! Soz! Another sausage, please!"

In my mind, the biggest, hardest thing has happened—we have admitted she has an eating disorder, and we have sought professional, official, medical help. They'll know exactly what to do, and they'll fix her fast—because we're us, and she's her—and things will go back to how they were.

In reality, we go to a hospital that seems like a huge gray Soviet Bloc with clusters of cancer patients smoking in the rain by the doors. Why would you place a children's mental health unit inside a building that seems designed to inspire terror, and hopelessness, in a child? Does benign architecture cost *that* much more? Over time, it would cost less, surely, than the cost of missed appointments—for, the first two times we go there, My Girl balks, weeping at the idea of entering somewhere so sinister and grim. I cannot blame her—it terrifies me, too. It feels like, once we cross the threshold, everything will change. We will, officially, be a problem.

On the third attempt—after another week of weeping—we finally make it into the building and see a serious doctor, who tells My Girl that it sounds like she has a problem. He then passes us on to a nurse, who is very kind and helps My Girl write a list of all the food she should eat in a day: three meals and three snacks. We are to come and see this nurse every week—to "check in"—and we are on the waiting list for therapy.

I wait, throughout the appointment, for a prognosis, a schedule, a plan, some firm advice—the bit where they go, "And, ta-*da:* here is the cure!"—but . . . it all seems so *vague.*

"But what do we *do?*" I ask, in the end. "What *happens?*"

"Well, we don't know her story yet," the nurse replies, kindly. "We have to wait, and find out."

On the way home, My Girl stares at the piece of paper they have given her, with her "Eating Plan" written on it: porridge, toast, or cereal for breakfast; a sandwich and a yogurt for lunch; sausage, mash, and broccoli for tea; pudding, biscuits, or cheese for snacks.

We all know she will not eat this. This is Chamberlain's piece of paper held by a hungry, sad girl. We all know *what* she should eat. But neither she nor we know *how* she should.

Now, years later, I know how mental health services work. To be brutal, wherever you are in the world, they are swamped. Child and adolescent mental health is a booming, dark phenomenon in the uncertain twenty-first century, and in the building we walk into, there are children who look like skeletons, or who have made multiple attempts on their lives, or who live in chaos with parents who are also mentally ill. In the tiny, cramped waiting room, we sit with children with NG tubes; children with bandaged arms and scarred faces; children who fight and run away; or else just sit there, quietly crying. Several are on their own—I can't begin to imagine what their stories are.

In this Pandora's box of unhappy, pained children, My Girl—who is eating less than 600 calories a day, or else nothing at all; My Girl who is screaming; My Girl who is not sleeping; My Girl who is ringing from school at 11 a.m. in the midst of a panic attack, begging to come home—is not at the top of the list for help. I can see how desperate the situation is—on three separate occasions, during appointments, our doctors have to excuse themselves for an emergency in the Eating Disorder Ward. The looks on their faces tell you something the seriousness of these emergencies—these are the children who will not drink water in case it makes them fat, or who have smuggled blades into the unit, crept into the bathrooms, and quietly shredded their arms.

The mental health unit is like a tiny rescue boat in a sea filled with drowning children. It is the ones who are repeatedly slipping under the waves—the ones who are minutes from death—whom they must attend to first.

In this world, My Girl—who turns up to every appointment so politely and quietly; who says "please" and "thank you"; who listens attentively, and never argues back; who is still able to walk—is a low priority.

She needs—I find out by ringing the eating disorder charity Beat, by talking to a friend who is a child psychologist, and by reading every book I can get my hands on—a dietician and cognitive behavioral therapy (CBT). The hospital has just lost their only dietician, and the waiting list for CBT is more than a year long.

In the meantime, what we are left with are the weekly "check-ins" and a list of foods she will not eat. For three meals a day, seven days a week, we are on our own with this illness.

We have help, but yet we must wait for help.

"Why won't they help?" she sobs at 2 a.m. "Help me. Help me. Help me. Help me."

HERE ARE ALL the things you can do while you are waiting for the professional psychiatric help that will stop your daughter from being scared of food and, by association, life. Here are all the ideas you will come up with to make the days better!

- Buy new plates, bowls, and cups—thinking that they might make eating "nicer."
- Redecorate her room—thinking a different-colored wall could "lift her mood."
- Buy her specially engraved spoons with "I choose joy" and "Joey doesn't share food"—the motto of the sandwich-obsessed Joey Tribbiani in *Friends,* whom she loves—written on them to make eating "happier."
- Drive six miles at ten o'clock at night to find a shop that is open and sells the particular (and only) brand of tofu she will eat.
- Enroll her for "equine therapy."
- Eat more than you would usually eat—*Look! I'm eating! You can, too! There's nothing to be scared of!*
- Plan outings and holidays with the clinical rigor of a war strategist: emailing cafés, restaurants, and hotels in advance to see if they serve any of the tiny range of foods she will eat and bringing your own supplies in Tupperware, if they don't. Explain to friends that you'll be coming to their house, and this is what you must say around the dinner table. This is what must be on the plates.
- Fill a whole drawer in the fridge with chocolate—for you know, sometimes, in the night, desperate with hunger, she will come down and take a small piece—like a hummingbird, sipping a tiny bit of nectar. The idea that she might, one day, find none fills you with a level of horror you had never thought possible.

- Scout every hotel and house you go to—lest there are scales there that you must hide.
- Have sudden, violent visions of hurting anyone in her earshot who says, "I'm so fat!" or "I've eaten too much!" or "I mustn't have that—*it's naughty!*"
- Dream of shutting down Netflix when they broadcast teen dramas like *13 Reasons Why* and films like *Close to the Bone* about eating disorders, mental illness, and self-harm.
- Go into her room in a fury one day, when she is out, and take every picture of Amy Winehouse down off the wall, and put them in the bin—crushing them down into all the mashed potato and Quorn sausages she has not eaten. Fuck you, Amy Winehouse. Stay away from my child.
- Try to fill her room with life, instead: a tank of tropical fish, flowers, two pet rats. *Look! Here is the world! It is your world! There is so much beauty and joy!*

Then there are the different phases of tactics you employ, to make this sad, angry girl eat.

We began with a simple logic: She is not eating because she is unhappy. Therefore, we must make, and keep, her happy. *Then,* she will eat.

We began by being parodically cheerful—greeting her with an overly lighthearted "Oh my God you're *home!*" as soon as she came through the door, then bombarding her with the evening's schedule of carefully planned joy: "I've run you a lovely bubble bath, then you're going to put on your snuggliest pajamas, and I've set up an *obstacle course* for the rats, and we'll teach them tricks! How cool! I've made your *absolute favorite* dinner, and we'll watch *High School Musical* on the laptop while you eat, and then I'll give you a *relaxing* foot massage while we look online for pretty dresses."

This was all done with the best possible intentions, of course— but when a girl trying to step into adulthood whilst in the throes of a mental illness sees her parents suddenly acting like they're on *The Truman Show*, she will, obviously, find it all quite unsettling.

Sometimes, the enforced jollity helped—she would meekly bathe, dress, and be snuggled, exhausted by the day. But, more often than not, she would understandably retreat to her room—issuing forbidding "I just want to be alone, thanks" to the cartwheeling, fucking clown knocking on her door and saying, "Daddy's got Buckaroo! out, darling—you *love* Buckaroo!"

Buckaroo! with two jazz handsing parents is *not*—I can tell you now—*the* cure to an eating disorder.

WITH HER RETREATED to her room, we embarked on Phase Two: Intellectual Reasoning. She's a clever, clever, girl, and we're reasonable, modern people—we could simply *bombard* this illness with explanations and chase it out that way!

I am still haunted by the look on her face when we would both knock on the door and come in, like the fucking Logic Squad, to explain to her *why* she shouldn't be ill anymore. Sitting on the end of the bed, wearing the faces of Enlightenment philosophers, we would TED Talk our sad thirteen-year-old girl: "This could turn into a really serious problem, love—so we need to nip it in the bud. You need food for energy; you need food so you don't get depressed. When you're starving, your brain function drops, and your cortisol levels rise, leading to this anxiety we can see is so bad for you, sweetheart, so—*eat!* It's very simple!"

Oh, those explanations! Pete and I, sitting on her bed, lecturing her for hours—lovingly, rationally, firmly—on the logical solution to her problem. The more sullen and unhappy she would look, the longer our illustrative anecdotes, colorful metaphors, histories, and reference points. We called on the history of nuns who fasted and hallucinated and experiments that were conducted on prisoners and dogs. We talked at her for *hours*—as she shrank, smaller and smaller on the bed. Oh, we believed in common sense! Oh, we believed in our power as communicators! Oh, how we crushed her—steamrolled her with all our thoughts and beliefs! Oh, how hurt we were when she nodded, in the end—"Yes. I see"—but then still. Refused. To eat. Her message: Fuck you, Wikipedia. I am sad.

A WEEK LATER, I am in the chemist. I've spent five minutes pretending to buy deodorant. I finally walk up to the counter.

"I need—my daughter has cut her arms," I say. "I need dressing for razor cuts to her arm. What should I get?"

I can't believe I'm saying these words out loud. I expect the whole room to fall silent. This feels like an aberrant, and awful, admission—something outside the normality of this small, local pharmacy. I'm not sure the chemist will know what to do. I'm worried I'll upset him. Or that he'll throw me out of his shop, or call Social Services to report me for being so bad a mother my daughter has self-harmed.

Instead, the chemist calmly walks over to a shelf, and says, "Here—you need medical tape, sterilizing spray, and sterile dressing pads. We've sold out of the small ones—we've only got the large ones left."

He gives me the things.

"There's a lot of it about," he says, matter-of-factly, shrugging.

THE BIGGEST PROBLEM when you have a child with an eating disorder is this: Every tactic you have ever used in parenting is useless. Worse than that: It's *wrong.* You can't get through it on instinct, or logic, or emotional appeals, or punishments, or anecdotes, or rewards—everything you've used since the day they were born. What you need, urgently, to do is forget about being a parent and become a mental health professional instead.

There are very specific things you should and shouldn't do—specific words and phrases you must employ, accurately, without deviation or improvisation.

There is a script you must follow that, over time, and if adhered to, can effect what feels like a miraculous change: Each word, said in the right tone, undoing some small patch of anxiety and horror in your child's head. There are things you can say before a meal, during a meal, after a meal, on the way to a hospital appointment, and when they cannot sleep, which do the thing you so desperately want: to make you seem, to your child, as if you are a calm, wise, endlessly loving person who is gently leading them somewhere safe—where all this will, one day, be over.

Unfortunately, at this time, I do not know these words. I have not yet found the books, or received the advice, in which they reside.

Instead, my head is full of what I read last week, in one of the books I was searching through, for this spell: "Eating disorders have the highest mortality rate of any illness. The average length of an eating disorder is between five and seven years."

Five and seven years. Her whole adolescence up in flames, like that. What you had fondly imagined to be full of parties, proms, carefully prepared-for exams, bicycles, sleepovers, driving lessons, and a slow unfolding into adulthood will, instead, be this: the hospital, twice a week. Bandages. Hiding all the knives. Weighing every meal. Sitting with her until 2 a.m. Searching her sleeves for hidden food. Casually folding sheets on the landing when she goes to the toilet, in case she's making herself sick. A new to-do list—but this one the most important, the most crucial of all: a list of things that will keep her alive.

A week later, we are in the hospital for one of our appointments—my child now bandaged, like so many others. We have come, finally, to ask for Sertraline—"It might help her get her head above the waves for a bit," a psychiatrist friend advised, when I rang her, weeping at 11 p.m. "It sounds like she's going under."

On one of the tattered magazines on the table, someone has written in the margin in a shaky, childish hand: "Nobody gets better here."

I cover it, with my bag, before she can see it.

And still, I do not say the simple, simple thing I should: "I can see how unhappy you are. It's okay to be unhappy. I'm not scared of it. I'll stay with you until it passes."

Instead, we keep trying to make *her* make it go away. And she can't. She's *ill*.

CHAPTER FIFTEEN

The Hour of Self-Help

❧

9:00 P.M.

I AM SITTING ON THE PATIO, IN MY GARDEN, TREMBLING, AND SMOK-
ing a cigarette. I have an all-day hangover. I have my bathrobe on,
hood up—like Obi-Wan Kenobi, when he's trying to walk amongst
enemies unnoticed. I feel I might be among enemies. This is an unkind hangover. It is making the birds, gargling in the trees, sound
malign. It is unnerving me. I feel . . . The Fear.

I have never felt The Fear before. All my life, drinking has been
fun, and the subsequent recovery, unexpectedly pleasant. A hangover
is, after all, a bit like having a mild cold—thus, allowing one to legit-
imately abandon the to-do list for a day and instead coddle oneself
in comfortable clothing, eat reassuring carbs, and watch soothing
television programs. If you're a busy woman, a hangover is a secret
mini-holiday—your "illness" excusing your comparative sloth.

In the same vein, I've spent years wondering if we might, actually, secretly enjoy being on our periods, too—for the modern
woman needs a reason to spend a few days being a little bit "fragile,"
and being allowed to cry off otherwise onerous things because "I'm
cramping up to *here,* and off my tits on codeine. I'm gonna have to
swerve the team-bonding zorbing session, Mark—you don't want to
return one of the orbs all covered in my Rhesus Positive."

The ultimate manifestation of needing a *reason* to have a break

comes with a fantasy I have heard many, many of my most industri-
ous friends admit to, after a few drinks: "Sometimes," they say, "I
think how nice it would be if I was hospitalized for a few days. Not
with anything *serious*, mind—just a classic broken leg, say. I could
lie there and just watch telly, without anyone hassling me, and having food brought on a tray. I wouldn't even care that the food was
shit—at least I wouldn't have had to cook it."

I would say roughly 80 percent of my middle-aged female friends
have admitted to this dream at some point or another. The stats are
quite high.

So this is the vibe I've always had with my hangovers—I drink
to have a joyous night of release, and then a subsequent day of quiet,
pleasantly trembling self-care. This is what women *do*, to relieve the
pressure—we use booze medicinally, as our foremothers did. Medieval
nursemaids were given porter rations, all housewives had a "tincture"
in their cupboards, and the Second World War was *won* on everyone
singing "Roll Out the Barrel" in an East End pub. Boozing is our *heri-
tage*. Having a drink is a key part of being a hardworking, independent
modern woman—we say, "gin" when we mean "I will not be working
for the next few hours." We say, "wine o'clock" when we mean "I am
still a fun person!!!!!" We say, "get drunk" when we mean "I still exist
outside my duties! I still want adventures! I am not dead yet!"

But: It's not working anymore. It doesn't make me feel better. I
do not feel recharged.

Instead, I can feel anxiety as a definite substance inside me. It
never goes away. It cramps my guts—I have the shits, constantly. It
makes my joints brittle and dry. I grind my teeth in my sleep. Every
fleshy part of me is hard with tension. I think alcohol will soothe
these pains—disinfect, lubricate, or heat them—but it doesn't, not
anymore. I am immune to my old medicine. It has turned against
me. It makes me worse. And the hangovers are *existential*. They are
the kind of hangovers that are two hundred miles high—towering,
terrifying—and that seem impossible to climb back down from.

At forty, my hangovers have turned into something else—in the
same way Mogwais turn into Gremlins.

"You just ain't got the enzymes anymore," my sister Caz says, when I ring her from the patio, and tell her in a sad, noble voice that my stomach is full of demons. "It's part of the bitch of being a middle-aged woman. As women age, our guts stop producing the digestive enzymes that process alcohol—so it just sits there, like the poison it is. So, no—it's not demons, which you would know if you'd ever read a single medical paper, you ignoramus. It's undigested alcohol."

"Is there some pill, or woozy-making cordial, I can take that will make it better?" I ask. "Something I can do that will make me be able to get drunk again?"

She laughs.

"Mate, if you find it, tell me—we'll become billionaires overnight."

I admit—this information has me discombobulated.

"So, is there some kind of . . . alcohol substitute, that I could move on to, instead?" I ask, hopefully. "Something invented by hipsters, perhaps? In East London?"

I can feel my hand moving toward my purse. I am *ready* to make an online purchase. Whatever it is, I'll buy it.

"Something you can have a couple of times a month that chills you out, and makes everything seem great?" I continue.

"You weren't so good smoking weed, were you?" Caz says, tactfully.

We both know what my stoner phase was like: a dedicated and all-encompassing two-year skunkweed binge, which ended when I had a psychotic episode watching *Stand by Me* and became convinced that because I fancied Kiefer Sutherland, I was a pedophile.

"He was *twenty* when he made that film," she says, again, wearily. "This is ground we've gone over many, many times. He was *already married to his first wife.*"

"But he was *playing* a sixteen-year-old," I say. "This issue is a whole episode of the *Moral Maze.* I still worry. Does it mean I have *tendencies?*"

"I'm not rehashing this again," Caz says, tetchily. "You're *not* a lady pedophile, and you are also *absolutely* unsuited to psychotropic drugs. Weed is *not* the answer for you."

"So, what else is there? What takes the pain of existence away?"

"All right, Lou Reed," Caz sighs. "There's Valium, or heroin, but my understanding is that a smack hangover will make you wish you were simply back to dealing with gin demons."

"So—what can I put inside me that will make me happy?" I ask. I feel as lost as a child. "What will make things better?"

"Dude, you know where you're heading?" Caz says, thoughtfully. "The Big G. God. I really think you're very vulnerable right now to finding Jesus."

Jesus? Jesus! This is so unfair. *Why* doesn't booze work for me anymore? It was so cost effective and sociable! When will they invent booze that doesn't hurt? Also, sidebar: when will they also invent fags that don't kill you? WHY CAN'T THEY INVENT FUN THAT IS GOOD FOR YOU?????? HOW AM I SUPPOSED TO BE HAPPY? I CAN'T FIND A WAY TO BE HAPPY ANYMORE.

Why does fun make me want to die?

I HAVE TO find a new way to be happy. I have to find a new fun that doesn't make me want to die. There can't be two unhappy people in this house: Unhappiness is not an option when you are a mother. Your role is to provide food, shelter, love, happiness. You must be the emergency cache of joy people dip into, when their stocks are low.

I just want something—one thing!—to keep me going. Something that is, simply, *good*. Something that makes things better. Something for me. I can't run away to a forest in Wales, or spend a week buying secondhand books in Hay-on-Wye, or learn how to Eat, Pray, Love in India: I need something that is cheap, nearby, and can fit in around work and home. Something that drains the anxiety out of me and stops my body hurting—even if just for a short while. And if it could, possibly, make me a bit high, that would be marvelous. Because I can't—I really can't—feel this bad for much longer. I'm a phone on 4 percent; 3 percent; blank screen.

So, look. Everyone knows that yoga makes you feel better. *Every-one*. It's not hung around for two thousand years for no reason.

But the problem with yoga is, when people who do yoga talk to people who don't do yoga about yoga, it makes the not-yoga people *very tense*. It's a terrible paradox.

"You're tense? Man, you should do some yoga."

This is a sentence that invariably inspires no other reaction than, "Fuck OFF with your yoga. FUCK OFF! I actually *was* going to start doing it—*tomorrow*, in fact—but now you've piously *told* me to do it, I'm going to delay it, *for at least three years*, JUST because you've made me INSTANTLY AND IRRATIONALLY ANGRY."

I think the word *yoga* itself must actually work as some manner of evil spell. The muscles the face uses to say "yoga" seem to make it, unfortunately, go into what I would term *a smug shape*. I would say *yoga* is a problematic a word—it says, "Hey—I'm feeling some bad energy over here, bud," whilst trying to massage your neck in an intrusive way.

The problem is that yoga has a point. We *do* have some bad energy. We *are* quite tense—*of course* we are. Have you seen the world? *Everyone is tense. Everyone.* "Tension" isn't just a character trait that only "uptight" people have—it is a basic description of the reality of 99 percent of all bodies on earth.

Indeed, I would say the more pleasant a person you are, the more tense you are likely to be. "Politeness," "reasonableness," and "kindness"—indeed, the whole concept of a civil society—is based on you regularly clenching your bum cheeks tight like a carpentry clamp, and then shallow breathing to prevent yourself from screaming out loud at the awfulness of this colleague/child/work/news report.

And so, over the years, your body gets stiffer and sorer. You go into your thirties able to talk for two hours about which bras give the most tit support, and when you get into your forties, you can talk for two hours about which chairs give the most back support. Some days, your lower vertebrae are so locked that, if you dropped, say, a quid on the floor, you'd just . . . walk away from it. That's just an Old

Tax you've paid to not have to bend over. You're happy to wave that money goodbye if you don't have to fold your creaky, old, wooden back in half.

THINGS CAME TO a head for me two days after I'd talked to Caz, and she'd suggested my only salvation might lie in Our Lord Jesus Christ. When I woke up, got out of bed, and walked downstairs, the whole operation took more than five minutes, and I made an *OOOOF!* sound *every time I moved a body part*. The soles of my feet, my jaw, my hands—everything felt like tight, rusty wire. I clutched and pressed down on the bannister so hard it actually came off the wall. There was something so deeply wrong in my lower spine—something so dense and crushed—that all I could think of, obsessively, was being picked up by a giant, who would hold me in his hands and just pull the vertebrae apart: *pop! pop! pop!* I would give *everything I own* to have the Hulk come over and push his big, green thumbs into either side of my pelvis. Or roll me into a hot ball, in his hands, and gently crush all the torque out of me. Crush me so hard, physically, that my brain emptied of all this hot electric soup.

Being an aggressive problem-solving person, I concluded that what all this tension and anxiety needed was for me to work tirelessly and remorselessly at becoming relaxed again—so I booked a Pilates lesson. Pilates is good for the body, right? And I'm middleclass now—so I needed, clearly, Pilates. I just needed to be *fit*. *Fit* means your body stops hurting, right? Your body only hurts if you're unfit and *weak*.

"Put me onto your machines, and let's ruthlessly *grind* me into tranquility!" I cried, hobbling into the instructor's studio in my new leggings and disgustingly old T-shirt. "I am ready to PUMP this body!"

And she looked at me—a rigid, knotted item—and said, "Mate, you don't need to strengthen your muscles—you need to *stretch* them. I can see it from here: You are severely hypertonic. Your whole *body* is in constant spasm. Come on—I'm going to take you through some stretches, instead."

And because she didn't *say* "yoga"—just "stretches"—I meekly complied.

I was, finally, in the end, after years of resistance, *tricked* into yoga.

She stretched me to the left, and to the right—she made me curl up in a ball, holding my knees, and rock on my back, like a bug. She made me stand up tall, and then touch my toes—"Hang like a rag doll," she said, as sheets of muscles in my back and arse slid, shifted, and finally settled into the right place. There were crunching sounds. There were *pings!* as vertebrae unglued from each other, and spinal fluid rushed into the newly created spaces. One ear popped—I realized I'd been semi-deaf for months, if not years.

And, after ten minutes, I felt a physical ease, for the first time in possibly *decades*, that hadn't involved drugs, sex, or booze. Here, in the middle of the day, sober and dressed, moving around was a thing that was simple again, and didn't necessitate going *OOOOF!* and *AGH!* and *GNAH!*

After twenty minutes, it felt like all the cranky poison in my muscles was being blasted out with a hose. I could feel it leaving, in vapors, through my feet—the fascia turning from brown and black to pink and white.

And, half an hour in, I just got very, very high—superlatively calm and floaty, and full *of thrill* about having arms and legs. When I stood up, I felt an inch taller, and as if the whole world had shifted into a panorama view. My eyes felt like they were the size of my whole head, and I felt like I could do *anything and everything* and—more importantly—I *wanted* to. My body felt *gleeful*—like it wanted to just . . . arse about, being silly. Being *joyous*. Scientifically, I would say my status was that of a "giddy goat." I tried to remember when I last felt this way. I concluded it was probably when I was five.

And this was when I realized what people mean when they say, "You need to do some yoga." What they *really* mean is "You need to move around like a child again."

For becoming an adult means "moving like an adult." It means you stop impulsively running into a room and hurling yourself upside down on a sofa. It means you stop doing cartwheels and headstands, or sitting with your legs wide open on the floor like a mad toddler ballerina. It means not swinging your arms around, or reaching up to the sky, or standing with your legs stretched wide like Peter Hook playing bass in New Order.

It means "not fidgeting," which means "not moving at all"— not sighing, or shouting, or grunting when you feel unhappy, but simply holding your breath, and counting to ten, and burying those emotions deep in your belly, your arse, your thighs. It means sitting hunched over for hours—over a laptop, over a sleeping baby—and not moving a muscle.

This is what you are told to do, over and over, by teachers, parents, carers, lecturers—stop messing around, sit up straight, stop grunting, stop sighing, don't loll. Even when I was giving birth, a midwife said, "Could you be quieter?," as I mooed, mid-contraction. There is no point in adulthood, it seems, where it is acceptable to be loud. For the rest of my labor, I sat quietly in my birthing pool, using all my energy to not "make a fuss." To be adult is, mainly, to be silent and still.

And so, gradually, over the decades, you build—and get locked into—this aching, tense, adult body; you have built the cage of your own destruction. This is what we are trained to do. This is what is "proper" to do. And we do it.

And then, at some point—when we are finally rigid with anxiety and repressed energy and emotion—we have to put on some leggings, find an empty bit of carpet, and start the slow process of undoing all those knots and bolts, and letting out all those sighs that have sat in your chest since 1997.

So the first time you do yoga, you aren't "doing yoga"—but just "relearning what your body knew when you were a child," instead. After my first lesson—looking at the world through my new, huge eyes—I watched children playing and saw how often they naturally went into yoga poses: hands and feet on the floor; in Triangle; staring at the world in Downward Dog; pushing their bellies up to the sky, in Bridge and Plough. I saw how they had not yet learned all the awful, mannerly tricks of adult physicality.

And when I finally got down on the carpet, in my own front room, and basically copied their moves, I saw how this makes time go backward—how yoga screws with the clocks.

Because, previously, I feared getting older: I knew my body would get stiffer, and more painful, each year, until I was quite lost and locked inside it, and all that would be left was my face, and my voice, and the walking sticks—and the same limping and painkillers of my parents.

But now—now I do yoga—the clock is thrown absolutely into reverse. The older I am, the more yoga I will have done—and so the *younger* my body will feel. I am losing hours, weeks, *years*, every time I get on the mat and let my sockets open, my bones melt, and my breath make a pleasing *Huuuuuuurgh* sound, as I go upside down. That is a crazy, time-warping magic—the *only* crazy, time-warping magic of physically aging. So as long as you do yoga every day, you will get better and better at it—the day you will be best at it will be the day before you die.

This simple new fact, brought about by a simple new hobby, disrupts your view of the future. You have stepped outside your mortal, declining monkey fate, and now you slowly turn into an earthbound god, with nothing but welcome for your fifties, your sixties, your seventies. I might, finally, be able to stand on my head by the time I'm ninety! *That* is what my old age will be: a supple, giggling hag, standing on her head, watching everyone else walk by, upside down— finally seeing the world the right way.

EVERY TIME I get on my rubber mat, I feel like I'm doing housework on myself. My body is a loft, or basement, that I've been piling rubbish into for years, and that now, every day, I am gradually emptying.

For the first year, every time I stretched out my legs—in a lunge or some wobbly, half-completed split—and unlocked my hips, I could *feel* exactly when each square centimeter of them had first become jammed. It was like archaeology. *Here* was the hard, tight pebble of tension, right in the hip socket, from that bad first birth—three days in the labor bed, the baby's head grinding against the bone—and then turned diamond hard with the compression of a subsequent year in a chair breastfeeding.

There was a brittle, brown sheet—the thoracicolumbar fascia—right across my lower back that had gradually gone into a long, endless spasm between 2010–2015, as I wrote every day, on a garden chair, chain-smoking, and shivering in a coat and fingerless gloves. The first time I stretched into that, it felt like a Velcro hook and eye tearing open, in a good way—dust and mud crumbling off, and the sunshine pouring in for the first time in a decade.

Before yoga, I carried this around with me like an ever-increasing bag of pain on my back. Sometimes, it used to panic me—I could feel myself filling up with cortisol, drowning from the inside.

Now, though, I know that however awful a day or night is, I can get down on the floor in something comfortable, breathe slow, fold my body into various shapes—a pigeon, a plough, an archer—and the stress will pour out of every opened joint. We talk so much about achieving—getting things, sorting things, improving things, *doing things*—but the very opposite of this, *undoing*, is an astonishing trick to learn, as you get older. The philosophy of looking at the things that cause you pain—either physically or mentally—and rewinding, to the start, and beginning again.

This, I think, is the business of your older years—your middle age. Finding the weak spots in your programming, undoing them, and starting again.

I know, now, that over the years, I had learned to sit, stand, and walk incorrectly; that my breathing had collapsed into short, shallow licks. And I know *why* all those things had happened—at the time, they were a solution to a problem. I had weak muscles, so it hurt less to slouch. I was stressed, so my breath became tight. My pelvis was destroyed by childbirth—so I threw all my weight out of my hips and into my quads instead.

And now—these things don't work anymore. Now, it's time for this older woman to find a quiet place in the house, for twenty minutes a day, and undo the knots. Release the hounds. Allow the bones to, finally, slide into their proper lines. And as the body undoes, the mind does too—for anxiety finds it harder to spawn when you have no dark corners, or tangled muscles, anymore: when you are limp and full of light, lying on the floor, staring up at the ceiling, and feeling very, very high.

I had always thought the only way to be happy, or high, was to put something in me. To drink, or smoke, or have sex. But the best way to get high is to take something *out* of you. To drain away a lifetime of hunching, cringing, tongue biting, and fist clenching. You're too old to carry those things around with you anymore. And that's what yoga is.

Every evening now, I roll out the mat and make things, just in my own bones, better.

CHAPTER SIXTEEN

The Hour of the Bad Marriage

⤟

10:00 P.M.

I AM ON THE BUS, ON MY WAY TO A DINNER PARTY, EATING A BANANA, when I get your phone call.

Ten p.m. is the usual times these come, although it can be 11 p.m., or 3:30 p.m., or noon. I am always ready.

The picture that flashes up is of you laughing at a party—bottle in the air, dancing. It was taken an hour before the crying started: The phenomenon of Dance Floor Collapse, where one song will come on that is so sharp, and so perfect, unhappy women start crying on the dance floor. Oh, there are always women crying on the dance floor, after 11 p.m. There is always a song that will end them. In the twentieth century, this song was "I Will Survive." In the twenty-first century, it's Robyn's "Dancing on My Own"—a disco-knife that cuts down the secretly unhappy on the dance floor like a scythe. I have seen whole rooms of women broken by it. All sad women need to find a song they can cry in.

Everyone you know talks about your relationship—all your friends know what it is like. Because we are older, and wiser, we do not cheerfully slag your man off, as we would in our teens and twenties: We have learned the hard way that the ex-boyfriend we call "the worst person we have ever, ever met" can be your groom at a wedding six months later. As, indeed, he was. Perhaps this is why brides, traditionally, wear veils—so they cannot see all the knowing faces of friends who hate their partner, as they walk down the aisle.

It's me. Hahaha, I know you know it's me. Oh, today has been . . .

You start crying—the kind of crying where there are few words; it's just sad-sounds soup with the occasional crouton of "he said!" or "I can't!"

I am going to start as I always start: "Oh love, don't cry. Don't cry!" Actually, *do* cry—it always makes things feel better, in the end. Crying is like your heart pooing out bad feelings. You cry babe.

I know I've said all this before—please don't judge me. It's just a bad patch. He's a good man really.

We all know that love can be tough—that every couple goes through bad phases. I can tell you, with 100 percent scientific truth, that even a good marriage goes through days, sometimes *weeks,* when one person spends their idle time imagining how they could move into the house next door to get some *space.* That's *totally* normal. That *absolutely* happens. We are a multiplicity of people throughout our lives, and sometimes, the person *you* are this month will not get on with the guy *he* is this month. There are, e.g., some dry, hacking coughs that can make your love close shut like a clam—until the soothing honey lozenges kick in, you will feel murderous.

Hahah yes—I just need a Love Lozenge. Where can you buy them? I'm near a Boots.

But you, I think, ultimately, are *not* in a good marriage. I can say that, without fear I am wrong. There are no lozenges that will kick in for you. For when *you* describe love—the love that you have—you talk about it being something painful, and dark, and unknowable: something that leaves you feeling uncertain. Love as something that comes and goes at will, leaving you turned inside out—or else hungry and alone. You quote lyrics about love being a wild beast, or a force that possesses you, or an addiction, or poison, or drug.

There are so many poems that describe how I feel! So, this must be love, right? This is totally normal—I should not be worried about what I am feeling, because this is love, as described throughout time.

But there is a very important thing you must know: All those descriptions of painful love are descriptions of *unrequited* and bad love. These songs and poems are *bad information,* from lyricists and poets just as confused as you—perhaps because they learned about love from *other* confused poets and lyricists. They have passed on this bad instruction, throughout time, in deceptively lovely poems and songs. There are generations of tortured artists confidently talking about love when they have never actually experienced the *real* feast of love: instead, they are chronicling its famine cousin—love malfunctioning, unreturned, unrequited—and this is poor advice, for you.

You, in your marriage, see love as something to endure—like a marathon or a fight. Something that only the strong—and stubbornly determined—will triumph in.

Love is a test! You must show courage during the dark times! I will not quit!

But if love has become a test—this long and this hard—love has already quit *you.* These aren't emotional GCSEs; there's no certificate that will testify that you were a good spouse; that you completed all your modules, no matter what the odds. No one appears on the day that you die and praises you for having dutifully and dedicatedly withstood so much unhappiness. There are no Unwavering Wife Medals. *No one is keeping count. There is no reward at the end.*

Love—true, real love—is the reward *now.* That's the simplest and most honest answer I can give you—that love is *now.* Love is today. Love is the last thing he said, and how you feel when you hear the key in the door, and whether or not you can sit in a car together, in the rain, listening to the radio, and thinking, *This is happiness. If there is an afterlife, I'd be happy if this was it.* Love is a thing you have—not a thing you will, eventually, earn; it is not something that appears only occasionally like a check or a rainbow. If it's not in your house now, and most of the time, it never will be.

But he does love me. I know this. He absolutely loves me.

You will notice I will not talk specifically about *him*—I am not talking about anything he does, or says. This is because, ultimately, no one—not even your best friends or family—*really* knows what happens in a marriage. There are invisible strings and chemistries between people that cannot be observed—a marriage is like Schrödinger's cat: What it looks like when it's looked at *is what it looks like when it's looked at*. It's not the actual cat. So I cannot say with 100 percent reliability what he actually is, or what your marriage consists of—even though I dislike his taste in shoes and distrust the sour face he pulls when you sing, when you're drunk. Like I said, *no one* is keeping count. No one will ever be able to tell you what your relationship is. There is no receipt. And I believe you when you say he loves you.

But there are two kinds of love I have noticed, over the years, and I will describe them to you—to see if you recognize which love he gives you. What *love* means when *he* says, "I love you."

Go on . . .

The first is where two people create a big pile of love, together, and then use it as and when they need. Sometimes, you need more love. At other times, he does. But it's your love, together, and, in the end, the amount stays constant—you're just swapping love between each other. It's an equal, communal effort.

Okay. And the second kind?

I have heard *this* love described many times, as if it is just as good as the first kind. I remember first reading it in Bob Geldof's autobiography, when he talked about his late wife Paula Yates: "In every relationship, there is one person who loves, and one who is loved."

At the time, I just accepted it: I believed it to be true. I thought it a fact. Perhaps that *is* the way of love? A yin and a yang, a nut and a bolt, a lover and a loved. I wondered, *Which would I be? Which would be best? Which one would work for me?*

I believed it right up until the other kind of love came along and swallowed me up whole, and I marveled that anyone would settle for anything else.

No. It is not a good love, when one is loved, and the other loves. For—how can it work? Who loves the lover? How do they get *their* energy? Who tends to them, when their love is all spent and they feel they can't go on?

That love treats love as a commodity, in a marketplace, where there are buyers and sellers. It presumes some people simply produce so much love they *have* to give it away; that you are doing them a *favor* to take all this adoration and care off their hands. No. No. Love, in the most elemental analysis, is your time and thought: your *days*. You cannot give your days away without anything in return. They are all you have. You can get no more when they are gone.

Oh, I don't mind—I'm a carer! I love to look after people! I'm a nurturer!

Although I have met men who have said this, they are few and far between. This is generally a speech given by a woman—women respond to being needed. Women are raised in cultures where they take pride in being needed.

Need seems such a similar word to *want*—we often use them interchangeably. But there is a whole lifetime in the difference between the words *want* and *need*—and both are, fatally, often used to describe love.

Beware of the person who says "I love you" but means "I *need* you." Not "need" as in "I need you around to be happy, or amused, or comforted"—the luxurious extras of life.

No—*needs* you. Needs you for something they cannot do.

I'm not going to talk specifically about your husband, but—here is a very common thing: a man whose emotions have been crushed and suppressed. It is a sad and common fact that there are men who have been taught, from day one, not to cry, not to be scared, not to be anxious—the kind of boys who were told to "man up!" from an early age, and teased, or perhaps beaten, for their sadness.

The only negative emotions they were allowed to express, growing up, were anger—"Oooh, he's going to be trouble! A little bruiser!"—although, of course, all those other emotions were still inside them.

And so, by the time they start dating, what they are looking for, desperately, in a woman, is their "other half"—the missing, needed part of them that can feel all the sadness, and anxiety, and fear. They need the desperate release of being part of something that can be heartbroken, or terrified, or on edge. And that something is *you*.

If you were in the business of neologism, you would call this kind of man *iraphagus*—a man who eats fear.

Do you know these men? I have known them. The men who absolutely break you—and then hug you, crying, at the end, as they apologize, over and over, and tell you they love you—men who seem now *relieved* by this outburst, even as you stand there, shivering and crying. It's been a *release* for them. This is the only way they know to experience these cauterized, suppressed emotions—through *you.*

But that just makes me feel sad for him! If I can't help him, who will?

While he's using you for his emotions, you're not having yours. You're not an emotion donor. You're not there to cry for the man who cannot.

But it must mean something that I love him so much! There must be something in him that is good for me; that I need. There must be some magic in him—magic that you just cannot see.

Here is the one truth I can tell you about your bad marriage: You don't love him this much because he's amazing. You love him this much *because you are capable of loving very hard.*

I cannot say this enough. It's not him—it's *you.*

But—what do I do now? He needs me.

Oh, my love: It is, I think, one of the most poisonous things in the world for a woman to be raised desiring to be *needed.* Every woman deserves to be *wanted. I* want you.

I want you to leave him.

And I know you won't for such a long, long time.

I have to go.

I know. Talk to you tomorrow? I will talk to you tomorrow. But here is one thing I know for a fact: One day, you will stop feeling confused, or sad, or angry, or scared, and you will become, instead, just . . . *tired.* Too tired to do this anymore. Your stores of love will have become empty, there will be no more thoughts, or reasoning, to be had—there will be nothing left—and you will feel a simple *weariness* with all of this. It will become undoable for a single min-

ute longer. You will be spent. It will be impossible to do this anymore.

That's the day you'll finally leave him.

And when that day comes, my absolute love, my spare bedroom
is waiting for you.

CHAPTER SEVENTEEN

The Hour of Counting All the Things a Woman Will Have by the Age of Forty

~⦇~

That Show What She *Wanted* to Be but Hasn't Been—Yet

11:00 P.M.

EVERYONE IS IN BED, WHEN I GET HOME. AURALLY, IT'S QUIET, BUT visually, it's loud—loud with the hundreds and hundreds of things, big and small, that aren't in their place, or have never had a place, and so fill every countertop, cupboard, and chair. Each thing makes a tiny, high-frequency noise that you feel in an untidy room—some barely noticeable squeak, or sigh, that when taken collectively, turn into a dissonant orchestra of clutter sound, which make the spirits vexed when you return. Women, it seems, can hear this sound. Others cannot.

To run a household is to feel like a tidal wave of *stuff* enters the house, every day, that you, Canute-like, are constantly trying to repel, or order, or throw away—only to be buffeted by the next new wave. Socks, magazines, games, unopened post, mugs, shoes, single gloves, a pair of tights, a box of curtain rings, waiting to be opened and used for, what—three years, now? As the curtains sit in the bedroom, waiting to be hemmed, and put up, and finally used.

I MOVE FROM room to room, made newly listless by the shambles; sometimes picking something up, and meaning to do something with it—only to realize another four things would need to be done before I could do *this,* which is why it's sat on top of the cupboard for so long. The door without a handle, the coat that needs relining, the record player that needs a new needle. All these things that *need* to be done, before I can do what I *want.* To be a middle-aged woman is to count the times you've waited to do the things you *want* in months or *years.* Sometimes, *decades.*

These piles work by way of archaeology: I keep finding things, buried in the strata, that show some excited idea I had, once, that got put to one side. Some plan that got shelved; some little vision that remains furloughed. This is how *every* middle-aged woman's life looks, I think. Buried within the house are both all the clues of the woman she *wanted* to be, and the very things that prevented it.

If a teenage girl's bedroom wall shows the woman she *wants* to be, a woman's house shows you what stopped her. For now.

One day, someday, I'll be able to take up all these stalled future lives, and finally live them. Is that what your sixties are for? Your seventies? If so, I don't understand why the phrase *old lady* is so often pejorative. "Old lady—finally free to do all the things she likes" sounds like a *fine* thing, to me. "Old lady" is what I'm holding out for.

"Old lady" me will move to a totally empty house, and take with her only the things she actually loves. I will shed this whole house like a cocoon—every Tupperware without a lid; every pair of trousers that needs mending, broken bowl, and unread book about investments—and live in a wooden hut with a view of a mountain, with only things that fulfill William Morris's dictum: "Have nothing in your house that you do not know to be useful, or believe to be beautiful."

I start to take an inventory, as I wander from room to room, of

"All the Things I Have That Are Useless to Me Right Now, But Which One Day Might Form My Future Life":

A box of cables from old printers, computers, video cameras, and phones long since stored in the loft. They are tangled together like a rat king—to try and separate one from the pile would be to have to separate them all—and so you cannot find, say, the charger that would allow you to, finally, rewatch the footage of your child's first birthday, which is currently trapped in the amber of a defunct mini-DVD recorder from 2003. You presume the first chance you will have to do this will be in your seventy-seventh year. Or, maybe, your child's. You are not a reliable chronicler of family life. You are not Nancy Mitford.

This is the adjunct to the "box of special photographs" that you meant to have framed and mounted down the hallway and up the stairs, so your family sees its glorious history of fabulous holidays, parties, and hugs, and is, therefore, reminded, on a daily basis, how wonderful it is. Perhaps, it is because they still sit in this box—without any new additions since 2013, when you started taking all your photos on your smartphone, instead—that your teenage children can so passionately shout "THIS FAMILY IS SHIT" during family arguments. You have failed to provide them with the correct visual data that proves you were a good parent, after all. It's all on you. You are not Annie Leibovitz.

A folder of "lovely walks"—torn out of newspapers and magazines—that you've never gone on.

Ditto, holidays. You are not Judith Chalmers.

Ditto, "spa retreats." You are not "regularly recharging your batteries."

A collection of single earrings—the partners of which were all lost whilst, you know. Having a good time. Or just walking down the street. You will convince yourself you might, one day, make them into "chic brooches." You will, absolutely, die with a tin full of single earrings, and no chic brooches. You are not "uniquely stylish."

A daring red lipstick—the "dare" of which you repeatedly decline in favor of a trusty, old lip tint. You are not a sexy lady.

A collection of dusty, dead houseplants, still in pots, that you've hidden around the back of the shed. In your mind, they have the descriptor of "Hedgehogs might use?????" You are not in tune with nature.

A lovely, eco-friendly compost bin you don't use, since you opened it and found a rat staring up at you. You are not saving the environment.

A scented candle so eye-wateringly expensive you never found an occasion "special" enough to light it, which has now lost all its scent—and so is essentially just a worthless turret of fat sitting on your mantelpiece. You do not live a well-scented life.

Very expensive face mask you're saving for "a special occasion," such as if you were invited at the last minute to a royal wedding, or the Oscars, and needed a face that's ten years younger. Its sell-by date was 2013. You are not "radiant."

A pair of smart, navy high-waisted shorts you've never worn but are convinced you will need if invited to a yacht at Cannes. You are not "chic and jaunty."

A book on meditation. Never had time! Too stressed! You are not calm.

A pair of linen trousers that you bought to go on holiday—little realizing the collateral crease-damage that can happen around the crotch by midday on the first day of wearing. Although you can never wear them again—not wishing to make your genital area look like a picture of Miffy—you also can't throw them away, as they were ninety pounds from Boden. You are not elegant.

A collection of more than one hundred pairs of suspenders, hold-up stockings, fishnets, and brightly colored tights of every denier and pattern—all stored for "a sexy weekend away." You will never wear any of them, because you never had that sexy weekend away. Instead, all your lingerie needs have been handsomely met by four pairs of "menopause friendly" pants, and the same six faithful pairs of black sixty-denier opaque "Bottom Control" M&S tights that you use, on rotation, until their feet go all gray and crispy. You are not a sultry temptress.

The pasta maker. Oh, how you imagined the whole family making ravioli together—learning new skills and bonding like on a Ronzoni advert! Oh, how you have never even read the instructions, and just wanged a bag of dried shit in the pan and covered it with cheap pasta sauce! Another generation of your family will grow to adulthood without being able to make their own spaghetti—and that feels like a bitter failure. You are not Nigella Lawson.

A "posh coat" that you were going to wear to have cocktails with the girls. Every time you went for cocktails (cider) with the girls (three cackling hags of your age) it was raining, so you left the posh coat on the hook and just wore your anorak instead. You have never worn your posh coat. You're beginning to suspect now that you never will. It's always raining. You are not Carrie in *Sex and the City*.

Ditto, that hat. What hat? *Any* hat. You have never worn a hat, despite having three. They just blow off! How does *anyone* wear a hat? Do they use a stapler? You are not Isabella Blow.

The abdominal exerciser. Hahahahaha. No. You are not toned.

The pelvic-floor exerciser. You used it once. It went wrong. You don't wish to talk about it. Now it's just a weird, dusty plastic egg in your bedside cabinet—like some odd hen laid it there in secret. You are not fully continent.

A music instrument. Perhaps it's something small scale like a recorder—you always enjoyed playing it at school, and nursed fantasies of taking it back up and playing the forbidden, funky tunes you wished you were learning in 1986, instead of "London's Burning." Or perhaps you went bigger—a guitar or a piano. Yours was going to be one of those houses where, when everyone had had a few drinks, there would be singsongs: With you, in the center, playing any requests by ear, whilst people murmured—in between harmonizing perfectly with each other—"God, she's *amazing*. Totally self-taught. Like Prince. But *better*." You casually play a honky-tonk solo. At the end of the solo, you would hear, from outside, the entire street applauding you. You would open your front door and bow. Maybe you were wearing a hat.

In reality, you learned how to play a D chord, and then your hands really hurt, and then you got pregnant again, and now the guitar is in the spare room next to the abdominal exerciser, and the piano is just the place where people dump old vases and library books, and no one knows you're secretly Prince. And never will. You are not the life and soul of the party.

An untouched "Craftwork Box," filled with glitter, glue, paints, wooden pegs, ribbons, and old birthday and Christmas cards. On rainy days, you were going to gather everyone around the kitchen table and spend a delightful afternoon making tiny dollies or collages, whilst listening to Frank Sinatra. In reality, on rainy days, you all just had an argument, two people went to sulk, and you ended up watching *The Incredibles* again. You don't really regret that—Mr. Incredible is hot and can never be looked at too much—but if you'd known, in advance, that you'd never actually need thirty empty cotton reels and lollipop sticks, you could have just chucked them all away and used the shelf space to display fabulous *objets* you'd bought from flea markets instead. You are now keeping the Craftwork Box because you've made a decade-long emotional investment in it and are now telling yourself that "the grandchildren" will love it. You are not Martha Stewart.

Marked as absent: fabulous *objets* bought from flea markets. You never actually bought any of these. The one time you went to a flea market the smallest child got its finger stuck in an antique French birdcage in the first five minutes and nearly lost a fingernail, and you had to go and find ice cream to make it stop crying. By the time you got back, the flea market was closing—you initially arrived at 4 p.m. because the oldest child was busy watching *The Incredibles* for the ninth time. And you sat down and joined her. You are not the posh woman from *Antiques Roadshow*.

A favorite mug. If someone makes you a cup of tea in a mug that is *not* your favorite, all your happiness and gratitude is somehow crushed by a disappointment and fury that it's not in the favorite mug. You have to go into the kitchen and secretly decant it into "the good one," and then spend the rest of the day thinking, mournfully, *No one knows the* real *me. No one at* all. *The real me is a phantom, never realized, that haunts this house from a parallel universe where all these things got used.*

You are not half the women you thought you would be by now.

CHAPTER EIGHTEEN

The Hour of Crisis

❧

4:00 A.M.
CHILDREN'S WARD, ROYAL FREE HOSPITAL, HAMPSTEAD

IT IS NEVER DARK IN A HOSPITAL WARD. THERE IS A WEIRD, GREENISH half-light that glows from the corridors; the white lamp at the nurse's desk.

It is never silent, either: there is always a hushed conversation between the staff; a child crying; someone coughing; something bleeping.

It is not day, and not night; you are not awake, you are not asleep. The sealed windows and central heating make you feel sticky. This is the world—but not the world. You are you—but not you.

I remember what the writer Russell T. Davies said, in the years he was nursing his husband through a brain tumor: "There are two worlds—the world of the well, and the world of the ill. No one in the world of the well can imagine the world of the ill. And no one in the world of the ill can remember what the world of the well is like anymore. They marvel that it ever existed. They feel they will never go back there."

My Girl has taken an overdose.

It is her third this year.

Today is the worst day. The very worst day.

I climb into the tiny bed with her and say: "My poor baby. This is so hard for you. I am so sorry. I'm so sorry. I love you."

She turns her head into my chest and cries like a little girl.

"I love you, too," she says.

"Did you do this wanting to die?" the on-call psychiatrist asks.

On the last two occasions, she has answered this question, blankly, "Yes."

On this occasion, she says, firmly, "No."

The psychiatrist leaves. We sit, awhile, on the bed. I tuck the blankets around her, tight.

"Mom—I don't want to do this anymore."

For a terrifying moment, I think that she means *live*. I have never felt a horror like it. The moment seems to go on forever.

"I don't want to come *here* again," she continues, as I breathe again. "I am never going to do this again. I am going to get better. I am going to do *all* the work, and listen to *everything* the therapist says, and I am going to try, so hard, and I'm not going to give up. I've never said this to you, because I couldn't, but I'm saying it now: I *promise* you I won't do this again. I *promise*."

I've been told, with these kinds of illnesses, that—once it has taken hold—there is very little you can do, save wait for the moment where the sufferer hits rock bottom, and their coping method causes more problems than it gives short-term relief. It's the moment of *un*-revelation: The moment they lose faith in the malign voice in their head. It's where they break up with their illness—because they realize they have been betrayed, and broken, by it.

I wonder—is this it? *Is* this the worst day? Is it, finally, passing?

She falls asleep, still holding my hand.

Her face is serene and childlike—even though the bandages on her arms speak of a girl who is dealing with problems that would make a wrestler buckle.

In this moment right now, there is nothing I can do for her. I cannot mother her. Nothing to say, nothing to get. I have time to think.

I can see her, not in close-up—but as one of millions of teenage girls in the twenty-first century. The product of her times. The receipt on the world my generation has made.

There are so many girls out there like her. In my social circle, fully a third of the teenage girls I know are on medication; they self-harm; they starve themselves; they have panic attacks so intense they must leave school, or else be taught at home. This epidemic can't be by chance: In screenwriting, when you are having problems with your third and final act, it's usually because of problems in your first act. Your children are your third act. If they are troubled, what did you screw up in the first act? Why are our children so depressed and anxious they hurt themselves, in so many ways?

I think, reluctantly, of the conversations she would have grown up hearing. These are anxious times—the debates around the kitchen table, with my friends, whilst she played on the floor with her dolls: "Politics is fucked!"; "Racial-hate crimes are rising!"; "We've returned to Victorian levels of inequality!"; "Climate warming will put ten major cities underwater by 2070—Big Ben will look like a lighthouse."

Those are the conversations of left-wing liberals—a panicky mourning for a future that looks thinner, shallower, and more unpleasant as the years go on.

Had she been raised in another kind of house—right-wing, conservative—she would have heard similar unhappiness about the present: about moral values going to waste; about civilization going backward; "PC going mad"; freedoms being destroyed; a fury that the golden age of the past was ruined by foolish schemes.

Very few twenty-first-century children, I think, will have been raised in a house full of dizzying hope for the future; a house that felt the right people have made the right decisions; that humanity is currently at its best, and things will, slowly but surely, get better. All sides of the political debate are in a state of furious pessimism. All have a sense that there is a fight for simple things: law and order, housing, employment, clean air. By 2020, this is joined, brutally, by "being able to leave the home without contracting a terrifying virus," and "having a global economy not teetering on the brink of a Depression." All houses have a dissatisfaction with how they are. All houses have anxiety flowing through them in the twenty-first century. We are a cortisol age. We have made cortisol children. Have we ever raised a generation of peacetime children so anxious?

Then I think of how we would often conclude these conversations—perhaps when we become aware of the little pair of eyes sitting in the dog's basket, with its Polly Pockets, looking worried: "But it doesn't matter that *our* generation has screwed things up—because the next generation is *amazing*," we will say, suddenly, with forced jollity and optimism. "You kids are so much kinder, and cleverer, and more connected, than we were. You'll have your school strikes and your extinction rebellion marches; you'll find some new center ground between the left and the right, based on a whole new set of ideals. You'll invent new economies and medicines! You, and your Greta Thunbergs, and your Emma Gonzálezes. You'll form new political parties and write new manifestos—you kids are incredible. The kids will save the earth!"

And we will toast our children, in the belief we have shown our faith in them, and that is a good thing. They will feel a capable pride in being better than us. That we have assuaged their panic about the future by telling them they will have control of it.

But of course—they have no control over it. They're children. They can't even vote. So what we're essentially saying is the most terrifying thing a child can hear: *Save Mommy and Daddy. We don't know what to do.*

If we want to know why we are raising an anxious, depressed, panicking generation who assume all the bad diversions of animals in psychological pain—self-harming, not eating—the answers to much of it might be here. We have charged them with saving the world.

When we ask our children's therapists, confused, "But their symptoms are like that of a child raised in a chaotic household, with ill or absent parents. But we are not ill, or absent! We are there! We love and care for them!" This, I think, might be part of the answer.

We have absented ourselves from coming up with solutions to our adult social, economic, and political problems. The generation above these children does not look calm, rational, reasonable, forward thinking, and moving toward a solution. It does not look cooperative and compassionate. It does not talk about how we might live normal lives with dignity, hope, and provision—it talks of battles, and struggle, and revolution, and fortresses, and how there is a fight ahead—whatever side you're on.

And then, what is the kicker we—loving, modern parents—put in at the end of every conversation with our children? "All we want is for you to be *happy*, darling. That's the most important thing. That's all me and Daddy care about. It kills us to think of you as sad. Just be happy!"

Again, we think this is a loving, kind thing to say. But an overburdened, worried teenager hears this, simply, as another duty. Another thing on their list, along with exams, and homework, and relationships, and saving the world: That we, their parents, *need* them to be blithe, carefree, roller-skating, and joyous—dealing with everything with a cheery, "No problem! I will be optimistic, untroubled, and happy with my life at all times! For I know my sadness will hurt you."

Obviously, this is not a hard-and-fast rule, but if you are not allowed day-to-day sadness—if your wholly natural bouts of pessimism and hopelessness are something you feel your parents try, immediately, to jolly you out of—or else, you must conceal from them completely—then is it any wonder that small amounts of suppressed, daily sadness and anxiety start to metastasize into something darker, and harder to shift? That it starts to mutate into symptoms, a syndrome, an illness? In the same way adult women enjoy their *Fleabag*-like boozing, and hangovers, and periods, and dreams of going to the hospital for a break, is this now darkly echoed in our young girls?

For once an existential unease becomes "an illness"—diagnosable, treatable, discussed at seminars by medical professionals—then you can turn and point at it, with relief, and say, "Look: My unhappiness and anxiety were *not my fault*. I tried, but I am *wired wrong*. It's not that I am weak—that I didn't try hard enough to be happy—but that I am *ill*. And, now I am a patient, an ill child, you will be told ways to help me."

No one starts self-harming or starving themselves thinking they will do it forever. It's just to get through *this* tricky bit. To distract you from worrying. It's like a dreadful mindfulness app, really. Aside from the scars and the hunger, there's no harm done—save teaching yourself, very early on, that you are a person it's fine to hurt. That women are meant to feel pain. It's just part of being a normal woman—like morning sickness and cramps.

PETE'S HERE NOW. My other daughter is at school, so he sits with me by My Girl's bedside; both of us watching over her like loving hawks.

We hold hands. We are hopeful. We have been silent a long, long time. Eventually, Pete asks:

"What are you thinking?"

What am I thinking?

I am thinking: We just do not make being a grown woman look like an appealing job. We do not sell the idea that being a woman is, yes, difficult—but also amazing, and joyous, and powerful, and freeing. We do not show them a world where we value the skills of women or seek out their knowledge. We do not show them that however hard they might cry, they will almost certainly end up laughing three times as much; that they will, in the end, come to peace and pride within their bodies; that they will remake themselves over and over—better and stronger each time—and that, at the end of their lives, they will be able to look back at their life's work and think, "Yes. Yes—I loved my life. I made things just a tiny bit easier and happier. I loved and was loved."

Currently, what eleven-year-old girl would volunteer for growing into a woman? Because we don't tell them all those things, at all. We are not selling that role we're all living now. Perhaps, because we know that, however amazing feminism has been, it's still just an informal network of millions of unpaid women, trying to squeeze "make the world better for our children" in between the other six thousand things on our To-Do List. It is a fragile and precarious system.

I am thinking: Things have to change. But how?

CHAPTER NINETEEN

The Hour of Wanting to Change the World

⤳

5:00 A.M.

WE LOVE TO THINK WE CAN SOLVE ALL OUR PROBLEMS OURSELVES.

That we're one self-help book away from becoming our true and powerful selves. We just need to learn some housekeeping life hacks, get the right clothes, Kondo our clutter, get a promotion, lose some weight and meditate—and then *everything* will be all right. There is no problem that can't be solved by hard work, and a cheerful attitude! Go us! Yay!

Humans are oddly reassured by being told that all their problems are down to them—and them alone.

And it's easy to believe this when you're young and only responsible for yourself. Let's be honest: if your main problems are having sex with the wrong people, being hungover, living somewhere with poorly utilized storage solutions, saying inappropriate things at parties, and twisting your ankle in a pair of wedges, quite possibly, a few of your "bad pickles" *are* down to you.

However, as you get older, the chances are that the problems in your life *aren't* just down to you anymore. Your problems become other people. Other people's problems. Other people who are either harming you—abusive partners, sexist employers, destructive peers—or other people who need care, and for whom the only person likely to give that care is *you*.

Margaret Thatcher might have said that there's no such thing as society, but there *is*—there always has been. *Women* are society. It's *us*. We are registered as disproportionately in the excess here, as we are disproportionately missing from every other arena—politics, business, banking, land ownership, the military. Society is the one realm women dominate. Middle-aged women, informally and without any official support, providing the resources and care that one would more usually expect to come from an economically successful first world state.

And there is a problem with this informal provision of care for those who are ill, or troubled, in that it only works if you are *someone who is loved*. If you have family and friends around you who love you, and can step in to help you, and—additionally—have the resources, space, and time that these problems need.

If you have fallen out with your family; if your family is abusive, or troubled; if there are already so many troubled or ill people in your social circle that there is simply no time or resources left for *your* bad fortune, then what are your options? What is your fate?

Under this current informal system, the working classes are disproportionately screwed. As you go down the socioeconomic scale, the instances of mental and physical ill-health rise. In these circumstances, those who are fit enough to be carers often find themselves caring for *multiple* people—by way of a life raft being swamped by those around them who are struggling.

The fatal blindness of our current system is that we can't see these carers. We can't see the women who support others—for there is no metric yet invented by which we can see care. Love. The comfort, ease, and relief given by those who help others is registered nowhere.

Love, we believe, is the most powerful force on earth—we are told it is what every human being craves, above everything else. It is to the massive benefit of our economies that it exists—for unpaid domestic work and care, allows paid workers to work. It's the unseen third element of our economy.

And it is never talked about with the seriousness it deserves.

Care, love, and *help* are the only words we have—tiny, basic, childlike words that go nowhere near describing the reality of spending a decade with a parent with dementia; guiding a schizophrenic through a paranoid episode; sterilizing the wounds of someone who self-harms; supporting a partner through a hypermanic episode, or recurrent depression. Raising children. These are genuine skills; these are things that take immense strength, ingenuity, and patience to deal with, day after day.

But the problem with living in a meritocracy comes if your merits don't register on the spectrum. So many of the key merits we think of as female don't register on the spectrum. *You cannot see what we are doing because it happens in the home, and the home is a place that is silent. No stories come out of it.*

I WONDER, NOW, if this is where some of the pressure for women to have children comes from: The presumption that your children will care for you and your husband, in your old age—meaning you are less likely to need an expensive nursing home, or will have a child who will pay for it. Perhaps *this* is why women who choose not to have children are called "selfish"—I can think of no other reason. You must, brutally, breed your own carers.

I want to look to politics for the answer to all this—but, in the current climate, it seems . . . unwise. The major political parties— all founded in earlier centuries—are all struggling with who they are, what they believe, and who they represent. Every major party has a fissure—or multiple fissures—at their center. It feels like, over the next few years, the old parties will break under these divisions, and new parties will form—but, for now, how could politics find the space and time to talk about a new way of seeing things? And— the continuing, big question—how can women be in the room, and make up half the people suggesting a different way to do things, when the structure of our lives still, notoriously, makes it so difficult to take part in traditional politics? How can women—millions of women—be heard?

CHAPTER TWENTY

The Hour of Imagining a Women's Union

❧

6:00 A.M.

HALF AWAKE, AND HALF ASLEEP, I START A NEW TO-DO LIST, IN THE waiting room of the hospital.

This is what women do, to make things better. We make to-do lists.

But *this* to-do list—this to-do list isn't for me, or the house, or the kids. This is a To-Do List for All Women.

For if every individual woman needs a to-do list in her life, just to get things done—then women as a whole must, too.

As THERE ARE still not enough women in the rooms where the power is, we must be represented in another way.

We must be represented as a collective.

Oh, if I weren't stuck in this hospital, on this chair, right now, waiting for breakfast, and was a brilliant organizer, and had years to spare, and had any kind of talent for this kind of thing in the first place, I would form a union. A union for women. The Women's Union! Now I think of it, I want a Women's Union so badly! I don't want for women's progression to still be down to either brilliant but disparate organizations, *or* thousands of individuals busily campaigning and tweeting—for both can be either ignored or suffer massive online backlashes, on their own, which cause so many to become more timid, or paranoid, or else give up communicating completely. In the twenty-first century, women's problems are resolutely not to do with consciousness-raising, or coming up with ideas—for women have been talking about how they would change things for years, decades, *centuries now*. We have spilled our guts and come up with a million solutions—and yet, still, actual action and progress move so slowly.

What we need now is collective action—a general union we can join, whose sole purpose is to look at all the evidence and statistics on problems that affect our lives, jobs, safety, and sanity and campaign to make its members' lives better.

I think the most wearying thing about becoming middle-aged, it's that *you* are the only one who can fix things—there is no one you can complain to, or seek comfort from; for *you* are the grown-ups, now, and if you can't fix it, it will remain broken. Deep down inside, I am a tired middle-aged woman who wishes there were powerful mother figures and matriarchs, who we could turn to—female tribal elders who we could appeal to when things are too difficult or unfair. Women who have been through the same shit as us and are determined that the *next* generation not go through the same joy-sapping, potential-wasting rigmarole. When I think about how we venerate Michelle Obama or Beyoncé—posting quotes and memes of them, and sighing with love for their wisdom, or calm, or reasonableness, or work ethic—it seems to come from this same deep need: to have champions of women, who speak out for us when we are too exhausted, or confused, or unmotivated to do it, for the millionth time, ourselves.

This is why the idea of being able to join a Women's Union makes me want to shout out with joy: Guys, take my membership dues and represent the hell out of me! Make me, and so many others, feel like we're not alone anymore! Finally install some Queen of Women, who is looking out for us all—who can take all these stories, ideas, and research we have done and run with it for all of us. For we alone cannot run with them—with the time and energy they deserve—as we're too tired, too busy, and our pelvic floors are shot to shit.

A Women's Union should be seen as an *asset* to any country that has one—for it would recognize that the problems women still face affect all of us, in one way or another—and usually economically. Financial inequality—disproportionately felt by women and people of color—is put at thirty-nine billion pounds a year in the UK, through its impact on health, well-being, and crime rates. Domestic violence—£66b. The gender pay gap—still running at 8.9 percent means women just aren't spending as much as men. Man, we'd boost those High Street retail figures if we got equal pay. Women's inequality disadvantages *everyone*—not just the female 52 percent we presume.

The argument against state involvement—legislation, increased funding to support services, prosecutions for companies breaking the 1970 Equal Pay Act is always that it is costly. But as we can see, we're spending those billions *anyway* in bills that will never disappear and which don't *solve* the problem: it merely patches up the survivors, using costly emergency services, and sends them back out again into the same old, bad world; or leaves them in the same bad position for decades to come.

Once we acknowledged how much money we're wasting by ignoring women's problems, who would not want to start saving those billions—by preventing what almost always starts as a small problem, from escalating up into a crisis? Perhaps it takes those who have mending kits—and a *practical* experience of how "a stitch in time really does save nine," to put the saying into practice.

For *everyone* has one idea for how things could be better. *Everyone* has one solution to a problem: whether it be something relatively small—like mentoring children raised around domestic violence, so they don't repeat the pattern—to a huge scheme, like building whole new family-friendly garden cities with carefully planned childcare centers and public transport, so that women can work like men.

Women have done enough confessing and consciousness-raising. We have improved our own lives as much as we can, in single campaigns. The only next stage, logically, is to do something *together*.

We would have professed aims. Care work would be top of the list. Paid or unpaid. Care work is disproportionately done by women—as a job, 82 percent in personal caring services are women, and 94 percent of those are in childcare. In unpaid care work, women carry 75 percent of the burden. It is seen as low-status and unskilled. It's seen as, somehow, something women should just do out of duty, or privilege—women are born to care! Women have an *excess* of love, which they must vent, or else burst! Women *need* to care!—and in which payment is a secondary concern and slightly unseemly to complain about.

And, of course, it *is* both a duty and a privilege to care for the young, the sick, and elderly friends and family. To serve our loved ones. But it is also, surely, a duty and a privilege to be prime minister and serve your people. I can see no logical reason for paying someone handsomely for one duty and privilege, but not the other—save for that it has been, until now, *just the way we do things*.

Indeed, there is surely *more* reason to pay carers, and well, than politicians. Once you leave politics, you can secure a lifetime's worth of well-paid consultancy jobs, book deals, and speaker's fees—your years of assiduous duty have left you with a high social standing and greater earning power.

Once you finish caring, however—once your sick are well, your children grown, or your elderly dead—you have a lower social standing and lower earning power. All your work is not seen as a benefit on your CV. A Women's Union would run ad campaigns showing how unpaid care work should be seen as equally valid on a CV as "normal" employment. Perhaps, even greater: After all, what takes more guile, forward-planning, patience, and people skills than wrangling twins or someone with dementia? It's definitely harder work than chairing a sales conference in Staines.

Arguments fretting over the cost of paying carers for their work—with either benefits or tax credits—fail to see the bigger picture: They need to be reminded that any state money given to citizens doesn't *disappear*. People don't *set fire* to it, chuckling, "Thanks, Nanny State!" It immediately boosts the country's economy in payments to utility companies and purchases of food, holidays, shoes. It goes into making houses more livable, morale-raising treats, helping your children, having free time. It goes into quality of life. It gives people happiness, and dignity.

And, most importantly, it acknowledges your effort and worth. It says, "We know people like you exist, and we have chosen to not let you struggle on your own anymore."

And as for paid care work—well, if there's one thing the global pandemic has shown us, it's that the people who do these jobs do something so necessary, and so vital to the functioning of society, that we eulogize them, and applaud them, and are moved to tears by their dedication, even when their lives are at risk. If this is not the time to discuss how minimum wage is simply, morally, incorrect, then when is? When will "the things women do"—and care work is overwhelmingly a female occupation—be commensurately rewarded for how tough and essential they are?

THE WOMEN'S UNION would become the place that scrutinized all new plans and legislations for their effect on women, then it would issue statements and inform its members, accordingly. It would be aligned to no party—it would simply be an impartial, expert eye constantly monitoring whether women's lives and needs were being taken into account when decisions were being made. It would be both a powerful campaigning body and representative of a massive voting block of women. It would give women—in their thousands or millions—a voice dedicated to them.

And it would protect women's voices when they first speak out: For it could compile reports on the hostility and threats of violence meted out to women on social media, suggest technical and safeguarding solutions, and—if social media companies still did not improve—the Union could act. It could suggest to all its members that they strike: that on days of action they could post, on their accounts, a statement from the Union—explaining why social media is a hostile environment for women, and how tech companies have still not acted—and then go offline for twenty-four, forty-eight, seventy-two hours. It could remove half of the free content social media companies rely on in a heartbeat.

And if social media *still* did not improve—if these platforms still continued to host rape and death threats—then, in my dream, the Women's Union would do what I secretly hoped that e.g., the Kardashian sisters would have done years ago: work with alternative tech companies to finally build social media platforms that were safe for women. That didn't allow for bots or trolls and made everyone traceable, if they broke the rules. We would take our unpaid labor—our attention economy, 52 percent of the audience— elsewhere, that took our safety, and voices, and amusing cat memes seriously.

And the thing I would love most about a union would be that, just as industrial unions worked to recognize those who worked in shipyards, mines, and factories, the Womens' Unions would work to recognize those who work in homes. For millions of women, so much of the work we do is *in the home*—ours and other people's. *That* is our workplace. It is where we put in the same hours others put in at the office, in a factory, in a school. Often, *after* we come home from an office, factory, or school. In homes across the country, we contribute just as much to the economy as those who commute. We prop up the economy—we allow all these other sectors to survive, with our unpaid work. But the home does not have a union.

A Women's Union would have, at its core, a simple but vital aim: to reward those still female things of "love" and "care" in the same way we reward all the other, similar things like "loyalty," "teamwork," "innovation," and "entrepreneurship." It would show the true value of women—both to the world and to women themselves. Sometimes I think it is the latter that would, in the end, be the most valuable—for whilst popular culture has been successful in writing songs and telling stories about how great it is to be a young, hot, dollar-savvy lady adventurer, there is still nothing about being an older, stoic, domestic hero quietly mending and remending the world every day. We have not yet found a way to value and honor these qualities. These kinds of women who are doing these kinds of things still put themselves down: "I'm just a boring mom"; "I'm just doing the right thing"; "If I don't do it, who will?" The foster moms, the hospital cleaners, the mentors, the volunteers, the community leaders, the outreach workers, the social workers, the ones who tend to the dying. A few dozen will be honored at *The Pride of Britain* awards, or *Hello's* "Mom of the Year," or on breakfast TV, when someone writes in and gets Michael Bublé to sing a song to them. But that's not enough. That's not enough to show our daughters, when they wonder what will become of them if they spend their later years trying, simply, to be good, useful people. That's not enough to keep making women endure.

If we really want to stop our young girls fearing becoming full-grown women, we have to be able to look them in the eye and say, "It's hard work, but life *does* get better"—and mean it. We have to be truthful when we say, "There is both respect and worth in the work of women." We have to be able to say, "You will never feel like it's just down to you, on your own, to make the world better. You will be walking with *millions*."

We need to be able to say, "Women are cared for, as they care for others"—and then point to an organization that is actually doing it.

So yes—this is my dream, sitting here in this hospital, at dawn, half awake and half asleep, trying to imagine how things could be better. Trying to imagine how I can still say what I always say, "Be kind, and don't give up, and things *will* be okay, in the end. The world *is* progressing"—and mean it.

I don't dream of big houses, or millions, or jewels. I dream of a Women's Union.

I hold My Girl's hand, as she sleeps. Right now, that's the best, and only, thing I can do.

CHAPTER TWENTY-ONE

The Hour of Happiness

❧

7:00 A.M.

WE HAVE A DOG. A PUPPY. SHE IS THE SIZE OF, AND LOOKS LIKE, A white fur mitten, and is sitting in the center of the rug in the front room making the most ridiculous sound. It's clearly *supposed* to be a "woof," but, because she is so tiny and ridiculous, all she can manage is a wobbly "*Ifffff! Ifffff!*" instead. Her tail is a furry finger, furiously wagging, and, when she moves, she's so clumsy—it's as if she has eight paws all attached by strings that she is not quite in charge of. She is a puppet of a puppy. But real.

She is exactly twelve weeks old—we drove to Norwich to fetch her the very day she was old enough to leave her mother.

This is Luna.

WE ARE SUPPOSED to be eating breakfast, around the kitchen table, and we are—but we are mainly watching Luna.

"Look! She's trying to jump over a sock!"

"She's eating the sock! She loves socks! Get her more socks!"

The dirty washing basket is brought downstairs and scattered over the floor, so this tiny, fluffy beast may have all the soiled laundry it wants. She snuffles through the pile, selects an old pair of knickers, and starts contentedly chewing the gusset.

"Look how much she loves my pants!"

Her tiny blue eyes stare out from a mop of white fluff. She is dim as a bag of toes. She doesn't even know how her legs work yet. She can't even woof. She's an idiot.

She is the cleverest thing in this house. Because all she wants to do is eat, leap, sleep, and be happy—things we have all forgotten how to do in the last few years. We are going to watch this dog and learn from her. She will make us unlearn all the sadness, and hunger, and shouting, and distrust. She's like a friendly bacteria we have introduced to our stripped guts. She is simple, happy *life*.

WE FIRST VISIT Luna when she is a week old. There is a basket of puppies, and My Girl is to choose the one she loves most. There is a big, bold one that tramples on all the others; there are jolly, yapping ones that look like they want to go on adventures. And then, underneath all of them, is the runt of the litter—the tiniest, prettiest, sleepiest one, who keeps being trodden on by the others.

"Can I pick her up?" My Girl asks the breeder.

She nods.

My Girl scoops her up—the puppy smaller than her palm— and strokes her tiny, silky skull with her finger. The puppy gives a tiny yawn—mouselike mouth and tiny, pink tongue like a velvet fingernail—and My Girl looks up.

"Can I—can I have her?" she asks, like she can't believe it.

"Yes," I say.

She beams like a teenage girl should—like picking a puppy from a litter is all it takes for her to be happy. Like the world is, right now, perfect.

When My Girl first became ill, I read every report, book, and blog on eating disorders—and so I knew what our chances were of a full recovery. I found I was part of an impromptu society of dozens of other parents, all dealing with the same problems. For four years, we were part of an unhappy community of mothers and fathers discussing medications, weight gain and loss, therapists, and theories like unwilling, civilian experts in a war raging in our children's lives. Even now, most gatherings will have friends whose facial expressions and demeanors I can instantly translate into what is going on back at home—they are the ones who leave early, and whom I will text, "I'm so sorry. I know how hard it is. You're being amazing. I'm here for you," as they apprehensively ride the night bus home, to the next battle.

So, I know how lucky we have been with our girl. We have had the kind of luck you would throw a parade, in thankfulness, to have received. I take none of it for granted. Every meal is a miracle, every full night's sleep borders on magic. Each piece of wood is touched; each wish is "Please—let this continue." Every morning we wake and lie in bed in the still unfamiliar peace, and whisper, "I can't believe it's all . . . okay. Just 'okay' is . . . *heaven*." It is an unfortunate truth that, sometimes, it takes true horror to make you realize something you should have known all along: That a normal, ordinary life is the most covetable thing on earth. A day in which nothing happens but breakfast, and school, and peeling potatoes, and Monopoly, and sudden laughter over nothing really, before a sleepy movie and bed, is like paradise, relocated to a house in the suburbs. We feel beyond royal. We smile at each other like emperors ruling a whole continent of joy.

For My Girl's progress has been dizzying. Following that awful last night in the hospital, something fundamental has shifted. Her last overdose was in January; by February, she is eating normally again. In April, she eats cake on my birthday; in July, in Corfu, on holiday with friends—having been vegan for four years—she comes up to me at the seaside taverna and whispers, nervously, "Will everyone think I'm a hypocrite if I eat fish? Will everyone be horrible to me?"

"Darling, in the best possible way, no one will care remotely."

I expect her to eat a tiny piece of calamari quietly and unobtrusively. Instead, ten seconds later, down the other end of the table, she's brandishing a whole squid ring on her fork and shouting, "This is fucking *delicious! I LOVE FISH!*"

She spends the rest of the holiday consuming fish—calamari, octopus, grilled bream, fried sardines—as if she's a mermaid who has been trapped on land for years, making up for lost time. She *is* a mermaid who has been trapped on land for years, making up for lost time. She is fit, and well, and eats whatever she wants, when she wants. She makes pleasingly dark jokes about her illness. She has Sertraline, and Cognitive Behavioral Therapy, and a road map for how to stay healthy, which she studies with the diligence of a scholar. She is, in every way, *better*.

Better: For I observe that so often in people who have been through great illness, or torment, and come out the other side, there is *something extra* to them. Although it is never the method you would wish for them, there is kindness, a steadiness, a strength, an ability to find everyday life absolutely joyous. A certain steadfastness, and unbreakability. There are so many metaphors for people like this— Japanese Kintsugi pottery, where broken items are mended with liquid gold, so that the whole-again piece is a thousand times more brilliant. The way that rubies and diamonds are formed by pressure or explosions. Not everyone can do this, but if you are one of the lucky ones, it's important to know: if you end up scarred, Ovid's motto—"One day, all this pain will be useful to you"—is now invisibly tattooed beside those marks.

As I write now, I can hear My Girl playing the piano in a way that makes the whole house ring. It's just hands, on keys—but there is something else in there, which she found in the dark place and brought back here, which reminds you: no suffering is wasted. Once you find the knack of rendering it down and turning it into armor, or jewelry, or song.

SHE IS, AS a teenager, experiencing what is usually a middle-aged discovery: the knowledge that all woes end, eventually. All tasks become complete, one way or the other. Illnesses pass. Sadnesses break. Things change. Relief comes, goes, then comes again. Because we focus so much on the negative side of aging—the knees, and the neck, and the tiredness—we never dwell on the ultimate benefit of getting older and older and older: you outlive the bad times. Happiness comes again, eventually. Even for a short while. But it will come. Just by staying alive. That's all you have to do. A year can pass so quickly. Your foot is on the accelerator now.

As the children clear away the breakfast things, and leave for school, I think how utterly this last decade has changed me. When I look at what my life consisted of before middle age, I see almost everything has altered. Then, it was all babies, wine, and a certain fearless, idiot blitheness that I enjoyed at the time but am glad has now passed. As you get older, you just are a little more *traumatized* by life, to a greater or lesser degree. You are aware how precious and perilous life and happiness is—you know everything can change in a second, with a fall, or a phone call, or a news flash—but because you have survived these things, and had your fluffy blitheness rubbed off by life, you are also ready to deal with them.

The strength of young blitheness comes from an ignorance that things *will*, absolutely, go wrong. At some point, the very worst thing *will* happen—but you do not know that, yet. You enjoy feeling unbreakable.

By way of contrast, the fearlessness you have now, in your older years, is the knowledge that, whatever happens, and however hard you inevitably break, you *will* live through it—one step at a time. And as you become tougher, you simultaneously realize how fragile other people are. You are gentler. You are kinder. You automatically presume everyone you speak to has a secret soreness or sorrow. Because, almost always, they do.

But once a crisis has passed—once you enter into a period of peacefulness—what are you to do? You are like a demobbed soldier; a retired assassin on a beach holiday. A former prime minister on the bus. You have all these new powers—and nothing now to do with them. The cogs are whirring, the adrenaline is still up—but what are you to do without yourself? This is the moment in your life where there is a sudden space, and silence, where you have to ask yourself: What is my purpose now? I have spent the last decade entirely in service to others—my heart has been blown open wide, I am programmed to love, tirelessly—but this is now redundant. Look—my children dressed themselves, fed themselves, cleared everything away, and left the house, cheerfully shouting about what they will cook for the family tonight. They are taking over the The List, now.

They are sixteen and nineteen. They don't need me anymore. *What do I do now?*

I PUT THE lead on the dog and take her to the park. I stand, in my anorak, watching her try to have a poo. Sometimes, this is what a small existential crisis is like—just watching a dog that's trying to have a poo.

Our dog suffers from occasional, mild constipation. I sympathize with her greatly.

"Mate—go for it," I say, encouragingly. Then I remember a motivational chant from Wimbledon, years ago: "COME ON, TIM!" I shout.

It appears to have no effect on the dog—but I like to believe that, somewhere, British tennis champion Tim Henman is suddenly having a much easier time on the toilet.

Once I have put the poo in the bin, as is my civic duty, and the dog has gone off to sniff at a squirrel, I look up, around the park, and see that I appear to be in the middle of a wholly impromptu flash mob gathering of women at exactly the same stage of life as me: women in their mid-forties/early fifties, wearing a Uniqlo thermal coat over jeans, and holding a lead as they watch a dog, in the distance, sniffing around.

It seems to be "a thing"—families getting a dog when their children reach their teenage years. I've talked to a lot of the women here, over the last few months, and the story is always the same: Her children begged her for a dog. *Begged. Promised* they would look after it, take it for walks, train it.

But, of course, school and life get in the way—and so the dog is, now, with glacial inevitability, "Mom's dog." She's here, twice a day, walking it, training it, bemusedly watching it bark at nothing. Cracking on with this task in the same way she's cracked on with everything else—diligently, exhaustedly. And slightly surprised to find she loves this stupid dog, which she never wanted and has been foisted on her, *to bits*.

And I've heard this story so many times now—there are, genuinely, thirty women within ten streets of my house who have re-counted this tale, word for word—that I am starting to think: This isn't just teenage kids being feckless, and moms diligently clearing up their mess afterward. This isn't an *accident*. In reality, this is one of humanity's great, unconscious schemes.

For those teenage kids—they're chafing at the still ardent moth-ering: "Have you got a coat? Here's a sandwich to take with you! Those shoes look too tight!" They're half adult, now. They don't *want* to be helicoptered over. They don't *want* all this mother love. They don't *need* you anymore. It's *annoying*. Your love and attention have become a problem.

And so, they cleverly throw in a decoy: a dog. Give Mom a dog, and you will divert all her problem-solving/nurturing instincts—still running at one hundred miles per hour from those recent childhoods—into the hound, instead. Which allows *you* to slink out of the house, unobserved, to drink vodka in the park with your friends. You are *not* the obsessional love object of the house anymore. Something *else* has supplanted you. And it feels *good*.

And Mom isn't a passive patsy here. Because, let's face it, there's something quite *healing* about loving a dog, in your middle age. It doesn't argue, it doesn't freak out, or cry; it eats anything, and doesn't know Topshop exists. It just *loves* you—like the baby, who has recently disappeared. It catches your too full heart. It gives your gigantic love somewhere to go.

Yes—being given a dog by your teenage children is an inevitable stage for women in their mid-forties/early fifties. It is . . . the "meno-paws."

Thank you. Thank you for listening to my joke.

TELLING THE DOG it's the most beautiful and wondrous thing in the world—"You're a big, fluffy idiot, aren't you? I love you!"—I walk home, still pondering this bigger question: What *is* there, now? Now I have, for the time being, moved from a period of crisis to a period of peace. You think, when your troubles and duties are over, that you will just go back to being that younger self again—but that now feels like a smaller, thinner, dumber chrysalis it would be impossible to fold your middle-aged wings back into. What next?

The answer is: the world. The whole world! Middle-aged women, you are just about to be born again—for the second, or fifth, or ninth time so far in your constantly inventive life—and what I have realized is that, this time around, you're going to walk the earth as a hag. These are your Hag Years, and they are glorious.

We think of "hag" as a bad word like so many words associated with women—"fat," or "slut," or "bossy"—but hags are cool, man.

Consider the Hag archetype throughout history: when life expectancy barely reached fifty, and once a woman was no longer a bride nor a mother, she entered her Hag Years until she died.

Hags lived slightly apart from the villages and towns—in a cave, or some witchy cottage in the woods. They tended their herb gardens, and mixed up their medicines, and were surrounded by their animals—dogs, cats, particularly clever and charismatic crows. They wore a cape, and had a stick to poke things with, and they'd roam around and engage in mysterious hag activities like talking to trees or doing weird rituals by streams and lakes. They'd be the only women callow, young youths would be scared of—fostering a useful irascibleness that prevented all but the boldest from getting up in their grill and wasting their time. When trouble struck the wider community, in the end, the villagers would always end up having to bravely go and consult the hag, who would then provide them with a medicine, or provide wise counsel, or tell a story from days of yore that provided a solution to the current problem. And, every so often, they'd meet up with their coven of fellow hags and spend all night cackling in a way that terrified everyone else.

This, I note, in the twenty-first century, is exactly the life I am living now. I have Gone Hag. Observe my day, now, in my Hag Years. I'm living a Hag Life.

Dog walk over, I return to my metaphorical cottage in the woods—my Hag House—which I have spent the last decade finally turning into a comfortable and beautiful fortress of books, food, art, and bright rugs, to which very few are invited. In my Hag House, I have no fear of FOMO—it is where I return to with a sigh of relief, glad I no longer have to gad about meeting people, when I could be having a bath and reading a book instead.

Like a hag, I have an herb garden—I have a *whole* garden that I dote on, in that cliché of middle age. Making a cup of tea, I go out, into the early morning sunshine, and quietly say, "Hello" to the birds and the trees. In the last few years, this garden has become my dear love—a plain square of grass I have slowly turned into a green bower of birches, ivy, and as many roses as I could fit against each fence, pillar, and wall.

It is only in middle age that you have gained enough mastery of time to plan a garden for all seasons: that you can plant a tree knowing it won't start to enter its full glory for a decade or more—but that's fine, because the decades pass so quickly now, so that's an easy commitment for you to make. An older woman can look at a garden in February— all mud and twigs—and lay over it, in her mind's eye, the tulips in April, the roses in June, the maples in October, the frost on the hydrangea heads at Christmas. Mentally cueing in the apple blossom in three weeks' time; knowing that now is the time to stake the peonies—for, by next month, they will have toppled, fat, into the roses.

A gardener can lose herself in a whole day of digging and planting—surrounded by her dog, her cat, the robins, and the wrens—talking to them as she goes: "There's a worm, mate. Fill your boots." She'll be on the side of the blue tits gathering dried grass for nests and carefully leave out seeds, so they can feed their babies. She's on the side of *all* mothers—however tiny and feathered they are.

At the end of an hour's work, she can stand—back aching slightly—and feels she has made the world, this tiny part of the world at least, almost perfect.

I am dressed like a hag, these days. My wardrobe is full of Hagosity. I have long swishy coats with big pockets, and a stick to poke things with, as I walk. The clothes of middle age are, I find, the modern versions of Hagdom: comfortable, enveloping, all-weather, brilliantly unappealing to the young.

And my stick-poking walks are full of hag activities. I leave the house again at 10 a.m. ready to be fully pagan in my yomp. I am unashamed to go to the woods and lean against a tree to feel the unusual comfort of putting your arms around something a hundred years older than you—connected to every other tree in the wood—disparately engaged in much the same activities I am.

My mind was blown when I learned that every wood has a mother tree, which tends to the others. They send sap, through their root systems, to ailing trees; they send electrical impulses to the whole community when they're under attack by insects, so they pump toxins into their leaves to kill off the predators. As a middle-aged woman generally unserved by stories in modern popular culture, and short on viable role models, I find I have more in common with the big beech in Highgate Woods than I do with, say, a sexy, kung fu lady scientist in a Bond film. We're kind of engaged in the same things.

Also, as a middle-aged woman, a tree will be one of the few living things I will encounter in my day that doesn't want me to feed it, worm it, listen to its problems, or give it a tenner. It's good to hold on to something that just radiates a treeish, comradely vibe of "I get you, mate. *Me too.*"

I pass a group of teenagers, smoking fags on a bench, and their body language is not what it was when I passed similar groups when *I* was a teenager—these days, they are deferential. Callow youths are wary of me, now: my thin lips and orthopedic foot stomp make them instantly stop pissing around at a bus stop. No one shouts "Oi! Tits McGee!" at me now, as I walk down the street, which is the Hag Bonus, and prevents my wise thoughts from otherwise being interrupted by constant low-level sexual harassment. This means that when I *am* finally consulted for help in urgent matters of the village, I can pull fully formed solutions out of my head and cheerfully present them, for the good of the community, or the weeping toddler, as is appropriate.

And as for my mysterious Hag Activities out in nature, well, from May to October, I daily pilgrimage here, to my final destination, to the huge, cold, muddy ponds of Hampstead, where I have a single, wild determination: to jump in.

Previously, as a young woman, I was always too scared of swimming in the sea or lakes. The dirt, and the mud, and the things that might swim up inside you. Eels. I feared eels.

Now, of course—now I have known *real* fear; now I have looked the end of the world in the eye—eels seem laughably inconsequential. You could fill my whole house with cold, muddy water and I'd be like, "Oh. Eels. Odd choice," before calmly brooming them out of the house. Long-term terror and misery do not bring many gifts, but the wholesale destruction of all lesser fears is one of them.

I notice that—like all the women in the park, with the dogs— the Kenwood Ladies' Pond is another territory for the older woman. There are not many places where they are widespread and triumphant—but they are here.

There is a sprinkling of skinny, *jejune* young things in bright bikinis, of course—but they do not last long. Screaming at the cold, taking ages to descend the ladder into the water as the older women shout, "It's just a bit of cold water, dear!," they are in and out in minutes. Almost everywhere else is, but this is *not* a place for soft, young, sexy things.

Instead, the ponds are ruled by doughty matriarchs. Janets, every single last one. Veined thighs; stretch-marked bellies; bosoms like the prow of a ship; grey or white hair up in a bun, or else a jolly swimming cap—these are women who have raised children and grandchildren, seen houses burn down, prosecuted fraudsters, scrubbed front doorsteps, and scared off bastards.

I watch one, in a navy one-piece, briskly descend the ladder.

"Now I don't care about my *children*," she says, on the first rung. She takes the next step down, shivering joyfully as the cold water reaches her thighs.

"And now I don't care about my *job*," she says, gasping.

On the third—up to her waist—she yells, "And now I don't care about my *fucking husband*," and launches herself into the water, sculling off into the willows with a determined breaststroke.

I twist my hair into a bun and jump in.

Hitting the water, all I can see is golden, golden brown—the soupy water shot through with sunshine. The cold is the kind that makes your teeth crackle.

Uttering a single "Oh!"—which bursts out of me with my last warm breath—I swim, hard, for a minute, feeling my chest shudder and my throat close. And then—after exactly a minute—hot, sweet syrup fills my belly and radiates up through my heart, out through my fingertips, and pours from the top of my head like steam. I keep swimming. I have never felt like this before. I feel *perfect*. Utterly perfect.

When I get out, I lie on the hot meadow grass—turning to hay in the sun—absolutely naked and overwhelmed with how *astonishingly lovely* I am. I am an absolute *god*. I briefly saw my reflection in the lifeguards' hut window, and it showed a middle-aged woman with straggly, wet hair with green mud across her breastbone, walking awkwardly, barefoot. Like I say—*astonishingly lovely*. I am smiling like I am in the photos after I had just given birth. I think I might have just given birth to happiness. Or: of who I am going to be next.

WHEN I GET home, still muddy, but still glowing, I sit at the kitchen table and look at my house. My little queendom. My Hag Pod. Girls—now women—looking for their car keys, or else cooking tea; a dog on the sofa; a husband putting away the shopping.

This isn't the only happy ending for a woman—there are millions, equally satisfying, that don't involve children, or husbands, or what appear to be seventeen tubes of Pringles—but this is definitely one of them, and preferable, I think, to having perfect tits, six billion dollars, or colonizing the moon.

What goes on in a house—behind a billion doors, on a billion streets—is still seen as, primarily, the work of women. The laundry and the broken hearts and the boiled cabbage and the teaching of manners to toddlers; the plans for the future and the way you face adversity and the tone you use on the phone, to customer services.

I remember, a few years ago, walking home from a fundraiser

for domestic abuse. The stories I had heard were the kind that make your bones sick; women and children, in everyday clothes with everyday faces, telling everyday horror stories. The monster in the house. The war in the bedroom. The fear in just sitting in a chair, ears still ringing from the last explosion.

For months afterward, I found every street I walked down inescapably *sinister*—for who could know what was going on behind each door I passed? Once a door closes, *anything* could happen behind it: It is amazing how much atrocity you can fit into a small, semi-detached house. How many bones you can bury under a patio.

For a while, I became uncharacteristically negative, and dolorous, about humanity—I could not get over this image of how, behind every front door, there is a world that no one save those behind it *really* knows about. How every street, suburb, village, and city holds thousands upon thousands of microuniverses—all with different rules, vocabularies, and ideas of normality. This is where the women are, and their worlds are utterly secret to us. Women's domestic lives are secret to us.

But then, a second, comforting thought: the majority of untold stories, happening behind every door, are *good*. They are breakfasts, birthdays, Christmases, and the whole family being excited to use the new fluffy towels; they are handles being glued back onto cups, and weeping friends being consoled, and the money being found, somehow, for a holiday with Nan. The laundry and the broken hearts, and the boiled cabbage, and the teaching of manners to toddlers; the singing of songs, and painting the walls, and running what is essentially a small company from which you don't expect profits, or goods, but merely the endless production of calm and love. Adventures still happen, inside these homes. Quests are embarked on. Transformations happen.

But we do not hear of these adventures because we do not tell stories about middle-aged women and their lives. Their triumphs and woes. What we do is either seen as just boring, or else ignored entirely. The lifestyle choices of younger women—the wine drinking, the years of sexual buccaneering, the intense friendships, life lessons, and messy explosions—have, thrillingly, in recent years, taken on a cultural significance and weight. We acknowledge them in their sometimes swaggering, sometimes tearful stories—*we see these girls*. We know they are a new, established archetype; you can now buy cushions for twenty-five pounds embroidered with the legend "Hot Mess."

We have been these girls, and now, older, we cheer them on, as they racket through the cities we once racketed through. I hear them laughing in the street at 2 a.m.—returning drunk in cabs—and I fall back to sleep, smiling. They are the shiny ball bearings tumbling through the pinball machine. They are the buzz of electric trainlines being hit by the rain. They are out there, conquering the world, as they should, scattering single earrings as they go.

I feel like I'm on my sofa, quietly content, and texting them, "Just so you know, guys—there is something even more marvelous waiting for you, when you finally land."

As NIGHT FALLS, I sally forth into the world to engage in the final activity of Hagdom—meeting my other hag friends in our coven.

When you are middle aged, you find other middle-aged women inescapably more glorious than any other kind of person. You may love the men, and the younger people, *passionately*—but it is only with the rest of your kind that you feel you can assume your true form: sharing stories and laughing hysterically about things in a way that could, yes, be described by others, passing fearfully by, as "cackling."

We like to meet away from other people—were it warm enough, we probably *would* meet in the woods, and dance, naked, around a fire; but as this is Britain in September, we all go to my shed at the bottom of the garden, where we gather around a single bottle of wine that will last us all night. No one in this shed has the enzymes for alcohol anymore. But we don't need them—for you can get drunk on the right people, when you're older, and these are the right people.

Sal, Loz, and Nadia—oh, these are the right people, who have sustained me through these years. When I was younger, I believed

Christopher Hitchens when he said that women just weren't as funny as men. I grew up in a generation where "comediennes" were rare and regarded as a freak of nature—once-in-a-generation one-offs, like Joan Rivers, Roseanne Barr, and Victoria Wood. Some kind of genetic accident, mutated to make this rare "female humor."

What I realize now is that Hitchens and I were, respectively, too male or too young to have ever been invited into a coven—of which there are millions, across the world. You are probably a member of one. If you are not, I truly hope you meet yours soon. Covens are where middle-aged women withdraw from the world to be with those who have, like them, gone through abortion, death, miscarriage, nervous breakdowns, funerals, unemployment, poverty, fear, hospital appointments, and broken hearts—where they sometimes weep and comfort each other, but more often make jokes, so pitch black they can only be laughed at by a fellow hag.

In your coven, you attend to your busy, vital Hag Work: drawing up the lists of idiots to curse and heroes to bless; forming your battle plans and schedules. Scheming the downfall of asshats, and the uprising of the righteous. You do this in a place where non-hags can't hear you, because Hag Club takes a lifetime to join. And it is here where you launch into the comic routines that leave your ribs bruised from laughing the next morning: the bellyache of pain that only comes from other hags being truthful about their lives. The husbands sneezing, the hormones raging, the bosses perving, and the children being "a delightful challenge." This is where you realize there is a whole book full of truths about being middle aged that you have only ever heard spoken—and never read. I keep notes on what our conversations span, in a single night: socks, socialism, anal sex, first loves, what we would do in widowhood, whether to buy a fake fur gilet, how to get a pay raise, where the best trees are, kettling, communes, Botox, Sertraline, sexism in its many forms, the glory of Nora Ephron. This is where, one night, in our coven, we found out the origin of the word *witch*: *wych*, in Old English, means the thin, whippy branches that can be used to bind things—baskets, fences, boats—together. A witch is a binding thing. Without it, things fall apart. We are witches. "Worldcraft" is what they called it in the eighteenth century. The knowledge that comes only with age.

It's now 11 p.m., and we're lying out on the grass, under blankets, looking up at the stars.

"If you could travel back in time, and meet your younger self, what would you say to them?" I ask, as we drink tea from mugs. Oh! 11 p.m. tea is the best! "What are the things they need to know about getting older?"

We all pause for a moment, considering this.

"Always pee after sex—it prevents cystitis."

"And wipe *front to back*—God, I didn't know this until I was in my forties."

"Have a secret Running Away Fund, in a bank account no one—*no one*—knows about. You never know when you'll need it."

"Learn to drive in an automatic. Fuck it. You might as well. Who cares about gears?"

"Don't throw away the things that have always made you happy—drawing, music, dancing, animals, being outdoors—because they suddenly seem childish. They are the things that make being adult brilliant."

"Parenting has about fifteen stages, and you'll be shit at some of them and brilliant at others. No one is perfect at all of them. But they all only last a year or so, so just when you're feeling useless, a new phase will begin that you'll be awesome at."

"A teaspoon of Marmite in a baked potato will change your life."

"Your women friends will save your life over and over and over."

"You can never have too much toilet paper."

"Every woman will spend their life oscillating between thinking they're 'not enough' or that they're 'too much.' Neither thought can be, nor is, true."

"Oh God, yes, *this!*" I say, banging my fists on my knees. "I have lost count of the women I've met who worry that they are 'too much.' Do you know what women commonly do, when having their picture taken? It is an action that is so ripe with symbolism it *hurts*. They *stoop*. They crouch down. They apologize, simply for standing there: 'I'm a giantess!' or 'God—I look like Hagrid,' or 'Sorry—I'm Brienne of Tarth in these heels.' NO YOU AREN'T! YOU ARE A HUMAN BEING WITHIN A PERFECTLY NORMAL HEIGHT VECTOR! STAND TALL! Or they pull their stomachs in, bowing away from the camera, murmuring apologies for how 'fat' they are.

"Stand up! Don't apologize! Relax your stomach! TAKE UP YOUR SPACE. Take up your space, middle-aged women—take up your space. You spend all day saving the world; yet, you still feel you are physically too much. My God, hardworking women—you have earned your place. You have earned every inch. Straighten up, and take it! Oh, I wish I could shout this at every middle-aged woman I meet!"

Lauren starts laughing, then says: "'It gets so much fucking worse.' That's what I'd say. Then I'd wait for it to really sink in, and then say: 'but *then* it gets better than you could ever imagine.'"

We all nod. Yes, yes. These are all useful truths.

"What about you, Cat?" Nadia asks. "What would *you* say, if you could go back and talk to yourself?"

I ponder. "Well," I say, eventually. "I'd want to warn her, definitely—so it didn't all come as a shock. And I can't deny I'd want to wind her up just a *little* bit, because that would be funny, and she would appreciate my dark humor. But I think, mainly, I'd just want to tell her that I love her. She gave birth to me. I wouldn't be here if it wasn't for her. So, I think I'd just give her a hug. Oh! Imagine if women had time machines! It would change *everything*. I'm sure we'd make good use of them. I'm sure we'd say the right things and be of *comfort* to our younger selves. Because we are so fucking *wise* right now."

We all sigh. There is a long pause, whilst we all reflect on the last ten years of our lives: The middle age so many presume is dull, and uneventful, and bland, but which actually manifests like an epic Ring Quest, all conducted without leaving the house. Heroes, and demons, and sex, and work, and doubt, and despair, and hope—storms whirling onto and through the house, over and over, even as you still get the washing done, and try to end every day having said, to those who inspire it, the only thing, ultimately, ever worth saying: "I'm glad you're in my life. I love you."

The silence lasts almost three minutes, before I break it, eventually, saying: "But, even more than that, I wish we had some fags."

ACKNOWLEDGMENTS

Although I write all my books like chatty letters to all the women out there who I think *might* want to receive them—and read them going, "YES! JESUS! THIS IS ME! WHY HASN'T ANYONE ELSE SAID THIS!"—there are three women in particular I write them for: the world's best agent, Georgia Garrett; the world's best UK editor, Robyn Drury; and the world's best US editor, Jennifer Barth. I truly wish for every female writer to have a group of women so amazing to work with: you are my literary coven, and I will simply die if I can't work with you for the rest of my life. Indeed, thanks to all at HarperCollins US and Ebury UK for being, consistently, absolute *demons* to work with, in the best way possible. You've all got your shit *locked down*. Again, in the best way possible. I'm not suggesting you're constipated. I'm saying you're *great at business* despite how difficult business has been in 2020. I bow to your ability to make books during a pandemic. *Thank you.*

I want to thank my husband, Pete, for actually doing *more* than 50 percent of the heavy lifting in our relationship—I don't think I cooked a single Quorn nugget whilst writing this—despite the fact that Pete was writing his own book at the time, which is *astonishing*. I think I've probably really screwed you over in terms of "pulling my weight" housework-wise but will dispute that if you bring it up in a court of law. Let's never get divorced—the paperwork looks hor-

rendous, and I would be actively unhappy at having half your record collection. Also, thanks for all the great sex!

My daughters, obviously I adore you and would die for you, but I'm not going to thank you here as you never read a single thing I write, which is probably for the best, psychologically, but does mean you often ask me something which I actually answered very succinctly and, if I may say so, elegantly on page XXX of *Moranthology* (2012, $14.99 paperback). Thank you for both reading the specific bits about you—although under duress—and giving your approval; particularly My Girl for suggesting that I write about your hardest years in the first place. "I think it will help people," you said. I truly hope it does. You are both *incredible* young women.

My Janets: Lauren, Sali, and Nadia. Guys, I've literally broken off from talking to you on instant messenger to write this and will go back to talking to you on instant messenger the minute I've finished. Maaaaaaan, we've been through some dark shit. And yet, we were *constantly* amusing about it. I asked how much it would cost to print a picture of the Crazy Frog here and it was "quite spendy" so just imagine him, instead.

The men in my life, Hugo, Dorian, Garnold, and Niv: you are so not the bad guys I talk about in here. I adore you all. You are the best of times—a genuine party. Although, ask your wives about the stuff on the stairs. I bet they agree with me.

My editors at *The Times* are amazing—hello, Shaun!—but particular love and thanks to Nicola Jeal, who is a bona fide goddess of Fleet Street. You've both made me feel safe to write whatever I want—and *man*, I've pushed that—but you also given the wisest of advices in how to be better. I don't want to sound like a soppy wanker, but you have believed in me far more than I ever did, and having just *one* person who goes, "Don't be stupid—of *course* you could handle that," does actually rewire your brain. You have rewired my brain. You're like a very *brisk* brain surgeon. I would not be the writer I am without you. I think you made about 20 percent of me? The best bits. You are my Captain.

Er, I think that's it? I'd thank the dog, but it really is *very* stupid.

You can hold it upside down and it seems not to notice. I would also like to thank whoever it is that manufactured the vape that finally got me off the ciggies, Whistles for making comfortable jeans that don't camel-toe me, and Kargs Emmental & Pumpkin Seed Crackers, for being the delicious hand-sized slab of carbs my brain seems, unswervingly, to need at 3 p.m. No these aren't paid endorsements. I'm not a fucking Kardashian. I'm just a woman who likes nicotine, crackers, and a comfortable minge. But then, if you've read this book, you'll know that by now. THANK YOU for buying it. I love being Team Woman. Ladies-you're, literally, the best. xxxxx

ABOUT THE AUTHOR

CAITLIN MORAN'S debut book, *How to Be a Woman*, was an instant *New York Times* bestseller. Her first novel, *How to Build a Girl*, received widespread acclaim and was adapted into a major motion picture starring Beanie Feldstein and Emma Thompson. *People* called her follow-up novel, *How to Be Famous*, "hilarious. . . . Wonderfully original." She lives in London. You can follow Caitlin on Twitter @caitlinmoran.

ALSO BY CAITLIN MORAN

HOW TO BE A WOMAN

New York Times Bestseller

With humor, insight, and verve, *How to Be a Woman* lays bare the reasons why female rights and empowerment are essential issues not only for women today but also for society itself.

HOW TO BUILD A GIRL

Now a major motion picture starring Beanie Feldstein

Imagine *The Bell Jar* written by Rizzo from *Grease*. *How to Build a Girl* is a funny, poignant, and heartbreakingly evocative story of self-discovery and invention, as only Caitlin Moran could tell it.

HOW TO BE FAMOUS

For anyone who has been a girl or known one, who has admired fame or judged it, *How to Be Famous* is a big-hearted, hilarious tale of fame and fortune—and all that they entail.

MORANIFESTO

An engaging and mischievous rallying call for our times—covering everything from Hillary Clinton to UTIs.

MORANTHOLOGY

Ruminations on—and sometimes interviews with—subjects as varied as caffeine, Keith Richards, *Ghostbusters*, Twitter, transsexuals, the welfare state, royal weddings, Lady Gaga, and mortality, to name just a few.

HarperCollins*Publishers* | HARPER PERENNIAL
DISCOVER GREAT AUTHORS, EXCLUSIVE OFFERS, AND MORE AT HC.COM.